T H E

A V R O

A R R O W

D0783009

THE AVRO ARROW

For the Record

PALMIRO CAMPAGNA

DUNDURN
TORONTO

Cover image: Department of National Defence, PL-107099
Printer: Webcom, a division of Marquis Book Printing Inc.

Library and Archives Canada Cataloguing in Publication

Campagna, Palmiro, author
     The Avro Arrow : for the record / Palmiro Campagna.

Includes bibliographic references and index.
Issued in print and electronic formats.
ISBN 978-1-4597-4317-5 (softcover).--ISBN 978-1-4597-4318-2 (PDF).--
ISBN 978-1-4597-4319-9 (EPUB)

     1. Avro Arrow (Jet fighter plane). 2. Aircraft industry--Canada--
History. 3. Canada--Politics and government--1957-1963. I. Title.

TL685.3.C336 2019   338.4'762374640971   C2018-906397-1
                                                        C2018-906398-X

1   2   3   4   5   23   22   21   20   19

We acknowledge the support of the **Canada Council for the Arts**, which last year invested $153 million to bring the arts to Canadians throughout the country, and the **Ontario Arts Council** for our publishing program. We also acknowledge the financial support of the Government of Ontario, through the **Ontario Book Publishing Tax Credit** and **Ontario Creates**, and the **Government of Canada**.

Nous remercions le **Conseil des arts du Canada** de son soutien. L'an dernier, le Conseil a investi 153 millions de dollars pour mettre de l'art dans la vie des Canadiennes et des Canadiens de tout le pays.

Care has been taken to trace the ownership of copyright material used in this book. The author and the publisher welcome any information enabling them to rectify any references or credits in subsequent editions.

— *J. Kirk Howard, President*

The publisher is not responsible for websites or their content unless they are owned by the publisher.

Printed and bound in Canada.

VISIT US AT

dundurn.com | @dundurnpress | dundurnpress | dundurnpress

Dundurn
3 Church Street, Suite 500
Toronto, Ontario, Canada
M5E 1M2

For my wife, Jane, my parents, the late
Gilberto and Paolina, and brother Angelo

Contents

Preface

RECENTLY, THERE HAS BEEN a resurgence of interest in the Avro Arrow. This is partly because the Canadian government is in the midst of deciding which plane to buy to serve as the new fighter jet for the Royal Canadian Air Force. There are many who wish to see a homegrown product, a renewed Arrow developed. They argue that Canada could create a better and cheaper plane than anything that could be purchased elsewhere.

The Avro Arrow has also been in the news of late because of the renewed search for the one-eighth-scale test models of the plane that were launched into Lake Ontario in the 1950s, as part of the original test program to prove out the aerodynamics of the design. With this latest search for the models underway, the debate has resumed over the merits of the program and the reasons for its cancellation. Many of the same arguments and errors of fact are again being put forward.

Back in the day, the government stated that the decision to terminate the program was made because of the changing military threat Canada faced. It was claimed at the time that the threat from manned bombers was diminishing, while intercontinental ballistic missiles (ICBMs) were about to become the primary problem. The Arrow would have been useless against the latter. It was decided that rather than spend money on the Arrow to fight off a diminished manned-bomber threat, surface-to-air missiles, namely the U.S.-manufactured Bomarcs, would be deployed.

Some historians and journalists have argued that the Arrow was technically flawed (a position as it turned out that involved misidentification with another aircraft); others have claimed that it simply cost too much, partly because of cost-plus contracts[1] that Avro had negotiated with the government with increasing costs as the project progressed.

Confirming the facts has been difficult. To a significant degree, the atmosphere in which the debate about the Arrow has taken place has been clouded by emotion, and crucial information that would have helped to resolve the issues has not been available. It was once believed that all documents relating to the program had either been destroyed or had been classified, and that therefore there was little written proof of whether the aircraft really was good or bad, what the costs of the program were, or even who was ultimately responsible for the destruction of the plane, its parts, and the tools and plans used in its manufacture. Lack of certainty about the last point allowed the company and its president, Crawford Gordon Jr., to be maligned, as was the prime minister of the day, John Diefenbaker.

Indeed, commenting on the subject of documentation, Canadian historian Desmond Morton, in an interview printed in *Engineering Dimensions*, the journal published by the Professional Engineers of Ontario in 1988, noted the following:

> When I look at the story of the Arrow, which was only a quarter of a century ago, there's a great deal that's hidden. I'm denied access to what went on in Cabinet, in the Prime Minister's Office, in the Department of National Defence. What I'd like to see … would be access legislation being used to open up all the records related to the Arrow, including the decision to destroy the prototypes.

Fuelled by a desire to uncover what documents, if any, that had allegedly been destroyed as part of the termination of the Arrow program actually remained, and what documents still existed that had been intentionally sequestered, I sought to find as many of them as I could and have them all declassified if possible. My quest began in the late 1980s in the archives of Canada, the United States, and Britain. A number of these I referenced in my first two books on the subject, *Storms of Controversy: The Secret Avro Arrow Files Revealed* and *Requiem for a Giant: A.V. Roe Canada and the Avro Arrow*.

I have been asked how it was that I discovered so many of the documents. Simply: through a lot of hard work. When I initially requested the files on the Arrow in the early 1980s, archivists at Library and Archives Canada provided a small folder with very little information. To uncover more, I discovered that the trick was to search all of the finding aids provided. I subsequently requested, through the access-to-information procedure, records pertaining to North American continental air defence from 1946 to 1961, any files related to aircraft or aircraft equipment in that time period, and the records of the various departments involved in decisions about the Arrow program, not just those of National Defence. Once the records were declassified, it was necessary to wade through thousands of pages of documents, searching for anything related to the Arrow development and to the politics behind the decision to cancel.

Once a relevant document was found, it was possible to determine which other departments or individuals had received a copy and to then request additional information from their records. Not knowing where to look for things, or even what I was looking for, needless to say made the search extremely difficult. To ensure that I got as complete a picture as possible of the information and issues relating to the Arrow, it was essential that I look at everything available that might be even remotely connected to the program. This took years to do.

Today, one can call up online the thematic guide on the Avro Arrow on the Library and Archives Canada website and easily find the related government records and respective file numbers on the Arrow. Still, though, many records are not accessible online. For example, in the files for another development project from the 1950s, one related to the Arrow, the Velvet Glove development, there were 4,667 physical records to search through, just in case they might contain some additional information on the Arrow itself. These records were finally declassified and yielded what appears to be those allowing for the identification of the artifact pulled from Lake Ontario in August of 2018.

All classified records have to be reviewed in accordance with access-to-information legislation by the appropriate departments. Although many believe that there is a "thirty-year rule," by which documents are automatically declassified after thirty years, archivists maintain that there is no such rule per se. So, it is still necessary to file access requests for all records that one wishes to look at in order to have them reviewed. The archivists are not necessarily able to methodically go through all of the files to review them for possible release, because they either do not have the resources or the specific knowledge to make declassification decisions on the thousands upon thousands of records in the collections.

In order to make a determination whether something should still remain classified, regardless of the number of years that have passed since the creation of the document, knowledge of the subject area and of any applicable legislation is needed. Some of the documents on the Arrow took between one and two years for declassification because they contained information from countries other than Canada, and so had to be sent to those countries for their review. Other documents contained material relating to national security, and so that had to be severed by the appropriate authorities. In the end, as it is in all cases, it was application of the Access to Information Act, and of related legislation such as the Privacy Act, that determined what might or might not be declassified.

———

When one considers the impact of the Arrow story — the technical superiority of the plane, and the immense loss that resulted from the cancellation of the program (the effect on the company, the destruction of the plane, the loss of so many jobs, both at A.V. Roe Canada and at its suppliers, and, perhaps most significantly, the accompanying loss of so many talented engineers, who could have contributed so much more to Canada, i.e., the "brain drain") — one can begin to understand why interest in the Arrow has continued over the years and why emotions run so deep. If one looks at how the program has been maligned by some and then examines the actual records relating to the Arrow, which seem to demonstrate that, in fact, the plane was extraordinary, the result is frustration, if not anger.

Through the use of the documented record, I have sought to provide greater detail, clarification, and amplification of the facts relating to the key questions about the Arrow and its cancellation. Additional material is provided here, for the benefit of the reader, in hopes of finally putting to bed most if not all of the questions that are still the subject of controversy. The aim is also to introduce the story anew to those who are not familiar with the Arrow, but who may have heard of it in light of current events.

I

A Future Lost

DURING THE SECOND WORLD WAR, Britain looked to Canada for assistance in providing Lancaster bombers. The National Steel Car plant in Malton, Ontario, was chosen to manufacture those bombers, as it was already building aircraft parts. In November 1942, the federal government acquired the company, changing its name to Victory Aircraft Limited. The firm soon became renowned for building superior Lancasters. In 1943, Sir Roy Dobson, managing director of A.V. Roe, a division of Hawker Siddeley, located in Manchester, U.K., visited the company and was very impressed.

After the war, Sir Roy returned to Canada, and, working with Fred T. Smye, the director of aircraft production at Victory, and other Victory officials, established discussions with C.D. Howe, the Canadian minister of munitions and supply to acquire Victory on a rental-purchase plan, providing the management of Hawker Siddeley agreed. On December 1, 1945, the deal was finalized, and A.V. Roe Canada was established. Fred Smye was appointed assistant general manager and would become the administrative force behind A.V. Roe Canada's projects.

The creation of the company meant that Canada at last had the capacity to design and build its own aircraft, both for the commercial market and for the Royal Canadian Air Force (RCAF), freeing it from the necessity of relying on foreign sources.

In 1946, Turbo-Research Limited, another Crown Corporation, this one involved in engine research, was acquired by A.V. Roe to design and build engines. On December 2, 1954, A.V. Roe was split into the newly named Avro division, responsible for aircraft design and production, and Orenda, responsible for engine design and production. After much discussion with officials from Trans-Canada Airlines and C.D. Howe, A.V. Roe was given the go-ahead to embark on the C102 Jetliner design, a commercial, regional, passenger jet aircraft, a type of aircraft that didn't exist at the time. Likewise, after separate discussions with the RCAF and Howe, the CF-100, a military subsonic fighter, was given the green light. Both were begun in 1946. The Jetliner would fly in 1949 but would not be produced. At that time, it was said that the company had to focus on the CF-100 for the Korean War effort. The CF-100 though would not become operational until 1953, after that war was over.

In January 1952, the RCAF realized that the CF-100 would need to be replaced as it could soon be rendered obsolete as a defence tool for Canada by advances in Soviet aircraft design. Following deliberations between Canada, the United States, and Great Britain, and the examination of numerous studies of existing aircraft, a decision was made to design and develop a supersonic jet interceptor — the Avro Arrow. The plan was to design a plane able to prevent any attack from Soviet aircraft entering North American airspace from over the North Pole. It would need to have a speed and altitude capability not then available in any other military aircraft.

By the time the Avro Arrow program was cancelled on February 20, 1959, a date dubbed Black Friday by the media, A.V. Roe Canada Limited had become the third-largest company in Canada, behind the Canadian Pacific Railway and the Aluminum Company of Canada. Part of A.V. Roe's portfolio of companies included the Dominion Steel and Coal Corporation, along with numerous others, but its key subsidiaries remained Avro, its aircraft division, and Orenda, its engine division.

When the Arrow program was terminated, some twenty-five thousand employees lost their jobs; fourteen thousand of those had been working for Avro and Orenda, the rest were employed by the company's various other subsidiaries or by the subcontractors working on the program. On February 26, 1959, ten thousand employees packed into the Coliseum building at the Canadian National Exhibition grounds in Toronto in a massive protest against the cancellation, the government, and, in particular, the prime minister, John Diefenbaker. Many had signs indicating they had voted for the Conservatives once but would never do so again. In the end, the protests had no effect in getting the cancellation reversed. Diefenbaker would, however, go on to be defeated in the election of 1963.

The fallout from the cancellation was enormous and extended far beyond the obviously significant loss of twenty-five thousand jobs. The *Financial Post* of September 20, 1958, published a list of businesses across Canada that would lose contracts as a result of the termination. The article stated that one hundred thousand Canadians would be affected, along with many new industries, particularly in the area of electronics.

According to author and ex-Avro employee E.K. Shaw, 650 major subcontractors were working on various aspects of the program. Their orders for work in 1959 would total some $25 million. To quote from an internal memo that was sent to remaining employees some three months after the cancellation:

> No effort has been made to date to settle termination contracts with any of the hundreds of companies involved.... Many of them are owed from hundreds of thousands to millions of dollars for investments already made in plant equipment and tooling and for complete parts and equipment already supplied complete for the first 37 aircraft. Many of these firms are facing bankruptcy as a result. However, if these contract termination charges were to appear in the government's budget in the current year, it would become obvious at once to even the most thoughtless Canadian that we had not only lost a $300 million investment, but that it had also cost us as much to scrap it as it would have to complete it....[1]

Not only did the cancellation of the Arrow program have significant financial consequences for many companies, a *Globe and Mail* editorial in December 1958 observed the following:

> One of the virtues of the Arrow's development has been its contribution to Canada's industrial diversification. With the Arrow (and CF-100) expenditures, we have bought new skills, new techniques, new industrial processes and plants which otherwise would not exist, but which today range far beyond the needs of the Avro program in their service to Canada.[2]

With the demise of the Arrow, continued expansion into areas of advanced technology were lost. Many of the top employees left not just the company, but Canada. Writing in *Ideas in Exile*, historian J.J. Brown observed the following:

> [I]n economic terms alone, the decision [to cancel the Avro programs] was one that was to impair our standard of living for decades to come. This is not so much because of the money lost ... but chiefly because the Avro design team that it had gathered with so much difficulty from all over the world was, in 1958, considered the best aircraft team in North America. These men's ideas stimulated a ferment in nearly every other Canadian industry. This would have resulted in a host of new products and techniques. But with the cancellation of the Arrow, the team dispersed almost immediately.[3]

Indeed, twenty-five top engineers ended up at NASA working on John Glenn's space capsule and later gaining major positions in the Gemini and Apollo space programs. Jim Floyd returned to Britain to work for the Advanced Project Group at Hawker Siddeley Aviation. There, that group carried out the early feasibility studies with British Aircraft Corporation

(BAC), on what was being called the U.K. supersonic transport, or U.K. SST, before it was renamed the Concorde. Later, from 1965 to 1972, Floyd was a consultant with the British government on the operations and economics of the Concorde in an airline environment, including studies on the sonic boom. A few other employees ended up in various American and European firms, including McDonnell Douglas and Fokker International. But it was not like this for all.

Frank Harvey came to Canada in 1956 after serving as an apprentice with de Havilland in England. He started with Avro in October of 1956 in the repair and overhaul department working on the CF-100. From there, he moved to work on the Arrow, in the flight test department, until the axe fell on Black Friday. After losing his job in this high-technology sector, he went to work in delivery for Simpson's, a department store in downtown Toronto. From there, he moved to Thistletown, Ontario, to work at his dad's service station. In 1963, he returned to Toronto and obtained employment at de Havilland Canada, which by now had acquired the Avro plant.

Ian Mitchell joined Avro in 1957, after graduating as a mechanical engineer from McGill University in Montreal. He was interested in aviation and, in particular, with the work at Avro, but he also applied to Spartan Air Services in Ottawa and Genaire in St. Catharines. Avro offered him employment in the Arrow's ground support equipment design unit, and at a higher rate of pay than his other offers, so he moved to Toronto. The city had the added attraction of having an RCAF reserve unit, 400 squadron. He had been a member of the reserves in Montreal, and this was an opportunity to continue that involvement.

Mitchell enjoyed his brief period at Avro and was devastated by the cancellation. He found himself not just unemployed but rather disheartened with the state of aeronautical work in Canada — in his view, it was mostly tied to defence and, therefore, dependent on politics. As a young, single graduate, he knew he had options. He was also not so upset at being fired for any personal failing, because he had been fired in such excellent company, with some especially talented individuals. He did feel bad for many who had recently emigrated from other countries, most notably the United Kingdom. They had families, they had purchased homes, they had left careers back home, and, after a short period in Canada, they were now unemployed.

He considered his options, but took his time, noting that, for example, de Havilland, Canadair, and Trans-Canada Airlines were not hiring.

Mitchell briefly considered moving to the United States, but he wanted to remain in Canada, so he ended up applying to a consulting firm in Montreal with which he was familiar. The latter provided the mechanical, electrical, and other systems designs for new buildings. He was placed in the Toronto office, where he remained with 400 squadron. He later worked in the firm's Montreal and St. John's, Newfoundland, offices. In 1962 he left the company to complete a two year degree in hospital administration at the University of Toronto. Eventually, he retired after serving in the Public Service of Ontario, far removed from anything aviation-related.

Unfortunately, there are no statistics as to how many of the twenty-five thousand released employees got back into the workforce, in what areas, how long it took, how many had to move elsewhere, whether the new jobs were still in the high-technology sector, and what hardships were endured.

Some critics of the Arrow have stated that there was, in fact, no "brain drain," since, in their view, the plane was mostly designed and built by teams from Britain, so it was not a Canadian aircraft at all. James Floyd, the chief design engineer on the Arrow, noted, however, that while some individuals did come from the United Kingdom, most were recruited from Canadian universities like, for example, the brilliant Jim Chamberlin, chief aerodynamicist on the Arrow. Hailing from Kamloops, British Columbia, Jim was one of the twenty-five who went on to prominent positions in the United States' National Aeronautics and Space Administration (NASA) after the cancellation. James Floyd himself, though from Great Britain, became a Canadian citizen like many of the others who had immigrated to work on the program. It is clear, then, that the cancellation of the Arrow did result in a flight of technical talent.

The anger caused by this "brain drain" and the frustration regarding the potential for loss of developing technological industries in Canada help explain why the Arrow's legacy has endured as a subject of passionate interest over the years. Further contributing to the interest in the Arrow is the manner in which the program was cancelled. Many of the documents regarding the political and military discussions involved in the cancellation of the program were supposedly destroyed or remained classified secret and top secret; the company was told to immediately cease and desist all work; and, most significantly, no seemingly good explanation was offered at the time for the cancellation and the ultimate physical destruction of all completed aircraft, engines, tooling, and technical information. As a result, rumours spread that the aircraft was somehow technically flawed, that the company had been taking advantage of the taxpayer, and that the program in general was too expensive. All of these contributed in their own way to keeping the passion, and therefore the memory of the Arrow and the people who built and flew it, alive.

Say what you will about A.V. Roe Canada Ltd. itself, the fact remains that in an era in which high-profile military acquisitions have taken years just to get a contract in place and many more before deliveries start, this company took the Arrow from a scratch design in 1953 to first flight in 1958, a mere five years. This also at a time when supersonic jet aircraft development was still in its early stages.

Five Arrows flew by the end of 1958 and early 1959, achieving some 95 percent of the flight envelope. On its third flight, the Arrow went supersonic at Mach 1.1, at 40,000 feet. On only its seventh flight, using Pratt and Whitney J75 engines, not the more powerful Iroquois engines specifically developed for it, it achieved Mach 1.52 at 50,000 feet, while still accelerating and climbing, with excess thrust available.[4]

Arrows beginning with the sixth completed aircraft, Arrow 206, were designated the Mark II, as they would be fitted with the Iroquois. With the first five Mark I's flying, and the first Mark II, Arrow 206 being readied for taxi and subsequent flight trials, and with all the materials and tools in place for another thirty-one aircraft, all ready for assembly, the axe came down. The Arrow program was terminated without prior notice on Black Friday, February 20, 1959. Had the program been allowed to continue, deliveries would have started flowing well under the extended timeframes of today: not bad for a company that has been so maligned over the years.

This company also designed and developed, again starting from zero, including the initiation of the company itself, a world-class civilian regional jet, the Jetliner. Effectively on the drawing boards in 1946, designed for Trans-Canada Airlines (TCA), which later became Air Canada, the Jetliner took to the air on August 10, 1949, just three years after the start of development. The Jetliner story has been covered in previous works, but it must be noted here that the Jetliner was also a much maligned project. Although the plane is considered by some to have been a disastrous design, its design engineer, James C. Floyd, was awarded the prestigious Wright Brothers Medal, considered the Nobel Prize in aviation circles, by the Society of Automotive Engineers for excellence in design — the first non-American recipient.

The Jetliner was years ahead of any other intercity jet in the world. It flew almost flawlessly until it was ordered scrapped on December 10, 1956, some seven years after that first flight and just before the Boeing 707 would take to the skies as the first commercial North American jet.

Now, one point of clarification. The first commercial jet to take to the air anywhere was the British Comet, beating the Jetliner by a few weeks. The difference, though, is that the Comet was designed for transoceanic travel while the Jetliner, like some of the Bombardier jets of today, was an intercity or regional jet.

The Comet, unlike the Jetliner, suffered significant problems over time; indeed, it experienced several losses of aircraft killing all passengers on board. This resulted in the grounding of the fleet until the cause could be determined. Simply put, the problem was eventually traced to stress fractures initiating from the square corners of the aircraft's windows and propagating through the rest of the aircraft. The Jetliner, on the other hand, had been designed with circular windows precisely to avoid this type of issue. This and many other features of the Jetliner were heralded in *Aviation Week* magazine, which was later renamed *Aviation Week and Space Technology* (*Aviation Week* hereafter).

As with the Arrow, some have tried finding fault with the design of the Jetliner. For example, the plane had a straight-wing configuration, not swept-back wings. Critics claimed that this resulted in poor aerodynamic efficiency. In fact, the Jetliner wing configuration gave the aircraft added stability, enhancing the safety of the plane. Recall, it was 1949 and nothing like it had been seen before, with exception of some military jets. So, apprehension about the safety of commercial jets was extremely high and Avro sought to allay those fears. With its straight wings, the Jetliner was still far superior to any turboprop aircraft in terms of speed, interior noise, vibration, and overall passenger comfort.

When, during a flight test, a problem did occur with the landing gear, the aircraft was made to do a gentle belly-flop landing. There were no engine blades to break off when the plane landed, so there was nothing hitting the ground, spreading shrapnel across the airstrip. The plane simply slid to a stop, with minimal damage, proving the Jetliner was safer than turboprop aircraft.

At one point, the Jetliner was flown to Wright Patterson Air Force Base in the United States, where American test pilots were allowed to fly it as they would a military fighter. The results were so devastatingly good that in a secret letter from the Canadian Joint Staff in Washington, revealed for the first time in *Requiem for a Giant: A. V. Roe Canada and the Avro Arrow*, hereinafter referred to as *Requiem*, the following is stated: "It is now confirmed that the USAF wish to purchase 12 Jetliners ..."[5] This of course belies the comments made over the years that the Jetliner could not be sold to anyone. The USAF was prepared to use the Jetliner as a high-speed bombing trainer and possibly as a tanker for refuelling others.

The existence of this letter came as a complete surprise to Jim Floyd when discussed with him before publication in *Requiem* in 2003. It had been sent to the Department of National Defence. There is no paper trail to show where it went from there, but Floyd was certain that it was not sent to the company.

In 1952, it was decided the Jetliner could be used as a testbed for the Hughes MG2 fire control system that was to be fitted to the CF-100. The fire control system is what allows the aircraft to fire its weapons at a target. For this, the Jetliner was flown to the Hughes airfield in Culver City, California. There, it caught the attention of billionaire engineer Howard Hughes, himself. He held on to it for six months, flying down Avro's engineers and test pilots to assist with his evaluation of the plane. His intention was to study the plane and then, if he deemed it suitable, purchase it in quantity for his airline company, Trans World Airlines (TWA).

Hughes involved Convair, an American aircraft company, to develop a plan for production of the Jetliner in the United States. In his book, *The Avro Canada C102 Jetliner*, Jim Floyd notes that the Hughes report, produced in 1952, indicated that the first aircraft could be provided by 1954. When the plan was sent to officials in the U.S. government, though, they turned it down, because Convair, they said, had to focus on its military commitments. This was much the same line C.D. Howe used to stop all work on the Jetliner in Canada.

Those who built the Jetliner knew it was a great aircraft, as did all those who flew it, and those whose job it was to scrutinize the design, like the director of engineering and maintenance for Trans-Canada Airlines, Jas T. Bain. In a letter to the vice-president of operations, Bain stated:

> It was interesting to see the evidence of interest shown by most of the major airlines on this continent. In particular, Eastern Air Lines are serious enough in their discussion that the second prototype will be built with the double slotted flap which will meet Eastern's low landing speed requirement. A physical examination of the aircraft showed a quality of workmanship which I have never seen surpassed on a prototype aircraft nor indeed by many production aircraft. Taken by and large ... [the Jetliner] surpasses the quality achieved by Canadair in production of the North Star.[6]

This letter was never made public until published in *Requiem*.

With bona fide orders at hand, and even though Avro would have crushed its competition at the time, the Jetliner project was cancelled. The official government reason given for the termination was that Avro had to focus on developing and producing, again from scratch, a military fighter: the CF-100 Canuck. This fighter was to be made ready for the Korean War, and the Jetliner, it was claimed, was taking time and resources away from this effort.

The government official behind aircraft development at the time was C.D. Howe, the minister of munitions and supply. Howe was an expat American engineer. In 1946, Howe had pushed for the development of the North Star, the aircraft mentioned in the memo quoted above. The North Star was a piston-engined aircraft developed by Canadair, a company owned by the Canadian government. C.D. Howe had made special arrangements with the Douglas Corporation in the United States to allow Canadair to build the fuselage of this aircraft, since it was from the DC-4 design. He further managed to have British Merlin engines installed. The first North Star had been christened in 1946 by his wife.

As reported in *Requiem*, Trans-Canada Airlines was prepared to purchase ten North Stars, but was told by Howe to purchase twenty. Howe further told the Department of National Defence that they would purchase twenty-four. What they were to do with them, though, was not fully explained. Not long after production began in 1947, Howe authorized the sale of Canadair to the American Electric Boat Company, the forerunner to General Dynamics. This, he claimed, was to assist Canada in acquiring advanced American technology, a refrain that would be echoed years later in relation to the Arrow and the Bomarc missile.

By the early fifties, the North Star would have been in direct competition with the Jetliner, a competition the North Star would have lost, according to a government report prepared for Howe by the Department of Transport in June of 1950. This report, which looked at the cost-effectiveness of running the Jetliner versus the North Star between Toronto, Montreal, and New York, showed the Jetliner to be more than competitive. Also, since it would have cut the travel time of trips flown in propeller aircraft in half, the authors observed it would become extremely popular with the public.

C.D. Howe's reaction to the report has not been recorded but he did stop development of the Jetliner, allegedly to allow for focused development of the CF-100, which as noted, was supposedly needed to help fight the Korean War.

Did Howe have a stake in Canadair, the American Electric Boat Company, or both? Might this have swayed him in his decision on the jet? There is no record, but it's an interesting topic for speculation. Was he not aware of the USAF decision to purchase the Jetliner and of the interest from Howard Hughes and others? He must have been, but it would appear that none of it mattered. Howe made the decision that Avro should discontinue production of the Jetliner and focus on the CF-100, and that was that.

However, there appears to have been no real requirement for the CF-100 to join the battle in Korea — F-86 Sabre aircraft were already in use there and would remain the key fighter in the war. In addition, Canadian pilots who served did so under the auspices of the U.S. military, and, again, in Sabres. So, the explanation given for cancelling production of the Jetliner in favour of the CF-100, in order to make the latter available in time for the Korean War, is questionable. Whether the decision was valid at the time or whether there were ulterior motives is difficult to assess. Many records about this episode have disappeared, according to an archivist interviewed back in the early nineties.[7]

Officially, Avro was to focus on building the subsonic CF-100. This aircraft also went on the drawing boards in 1946 and first flew in 1950 — again, not bad by today's military acquisition standards. The design, though, was problematic because of structural issues, which delayed its development. One prototype crashed, killing the pilot, although subsequent investigation showed the crash was not due to the structural problems.

There were also communications breakdowns between the plant and the government, with accusations that Avro was not being forthright in its progress reports. Similar accusations were also made regarding the Arrow development program, though they were quickly resolved.

The CF-100's structural problems were eventually solved and operationally sound aircraft were delivered by 1953, seven years after initial start-up — quite an achievement when one looks at today's timelines for new aircraft, and on par with, if not better than, the aircraft production delivery times in other countries then — too late, though, for the Korean War.

In all, 692 CF-100s would be produced in Canada, with 53 sold to the Belgian Air Force. In addition, Orenda would produce 3,838 engines to power both the CF-100 and the Sabre.[8] It would be said that the CF-100 was the best all-weather fighter in its time: this from what, if one believed all the negative things from the critics, must have been one of the worst-managed companies in Canada.

With the CF-100 in the air, work began on the Arrow. The first Arrow took flight in March 1958 — again, just five years after the start of the program. Five Arrows would fly before the program was abruptly cancelled the following February. For years there was little hard coverage of what actually happened regarding the cancellation and the way in which the completed aircraft were reduced to scrap. Much of what did circulate was, as in the case of the Jetliner, based on stories and innuendo, supplied by both critics and supporters, and not on official records and documentation. This book is designed to look beyond the myths and examine the evidence to provide a clear and objective analysis of the Arrow, its merits and faults, a plain presentation of the facts relating to its creation and destruction, and a final settling of the question of who was responsible for the destruction of the Arrow prototypes and the attempted destruction of all material relating to the program.

2

Was the Arrow That Good?

AFTER ALL THE REVELATIONS over the years, one would think that there would no longer be any question regarding the technical merits of the Arrow. While most now agree that the Arrow was a superior aircraft, there are still some who claim that, in fact, the plane did not deserve the accolades that it has received. In making this claim, the detractors offer up ridiculous, long-disproven arguments.

Bill Sweetman was senior international defence editor for *Aviation Week* and author of more than thirty books on various aspects of aerospace and military technology. In 2015 he wrote an online piece titled "Broken Arrow,"[1] in which he revisited a 1957 article from *Aviation Week* that hailed the advanced features of the aircraft. The 1957 magazine featured an overhead view of the Arrow on rollout as its front cover. The article was titled "CF 105 Displays Advanced Engineering." Featuring additional photos, the article discussed in some detail the numerous advances embodied in the design. For example, it explained how the box-like fuselage, which some critics point to as aerodynamically problematic, was in fact carefully shaped for aerodynamic efficiency even though it did not appear to be at first glance.

The article also discussed measures that had been taken in the Arrow's design to reduce weight and labour in construction, such as using certain metallic bonding techniques instead of riveting, where appropriate. It discussed the development and utilization of the production tooling upon which all Arrows, including the first, would be built.

In the case of the Arrow, the preproduction aircraft performed better than expected. Redesigns, as shall be seen, were a result of changes in RCAF requirements as the aircraft was being developed, not because of flaws that became apparent when the preproduction aircraft were being test flown.

To ensure overall success, key aspects of the design were pretested. For example, a full-scale metal mockup was made to test out tooling and to train production crews. Test rigs were used to check out flying control systems, fuel systems, air conditioning, and crew escape systems. The Iroquois engine, the engine that Orenda developed specifically for use in the Arrow, was tested in the static test labs at Nobel, Ontario. For testing in flight, the Iroquois was mounted to the side of a B-47 aircraft on loan from the United States.

The weapons carriage on the Arrow was to be fully or semi-internal. The format depended on the type of weapon to be carried, whether the Sparrow missile, the Falcon, or some other. A separate weapons rig for testing the functioning of the weapons system was also developed.

Subsonic CF-100 aircraft were used during the testing of the Sparrow missile, along with other missiles. In one separate CF-100 ground test not related to the Arrow and with a missile other than Sparrow, the entire weapons package was lowered. Apparently, the testing of this experimental system with this aircraft led to confusion, causing some to think such a weapons pack would be lowered on the Arrow during supersonic flight. If that happened, it could act as a speed brake causing the aircraft to self-destruct. But this was not how the weapons pack on the Arrow would have performed — the missiles in the CF-105 would be lowered on their own launch rails.

Wind tunnels were used for testing flight aerodynamics. Aeroballistics tests, where very small-scale models are fired from high-calibre guns, were also used to collect early design data, but suffered from speed and range restrictions, and those models themselves could not be instrumented. Because of the limitations in these two test approaches, it was decided to build and launch one-eighth-scale free-flight, instrumented models. These were placed atop Nike rocket boosters, then launched from the test range at Point Petre, at the eastern end of Lake Ontario, to altitudes of 25,000 feet at speeds up to Mach 1.7. At that point, they would separate from the booster rocket and fly free until splashdown into Lake Ontario. In flight they would transmit data via telemetry. Nine models were launched into Lake Ontario, with another two being sent aloft from the test range at Wallops Island in the United States.

The result of all this work was production of a technologically advanced aircraft. In his article, Bill Sweetman noted,

> When *Aviation Week* reported on the fighter's rollout, in October 1957, the magazine called it "a serious contender for the top military aircraft of the next several years." High praise indeed, for a non-U.S. aircraft, given that the XB-58 supersonic bomber was in flight test and that new aircraft in the works included the A-5 Vigilante and the F-4 Phantom.... But the Arrow was extraordinary ... [the] CF-105 was a different kettle of fish entirely.... [It was] extraordinary, and more so, given that the industry that produced it was less than a decade old when the prototype contract was issued in March 1955.... The performance requirements meant that almost everything on the airplane had to be invented.[2]

Of particular interest is the last line, which states that almost everything had to be invented. It points to the fact that this was a research-and-development (R&D) undertaking from the ground up. It also clarifies that the Arrow was unlike anything available; if that were not the case, the company would not have had to invent anything. An understanding that it was an R&D program is critical in the later discussions regarding why cost-plus was the chosen method of contracting.

Now, in the same online article Sweetman asks, "Would it have worked?"[3] For the answer, he turns to the words of the late aviation guru and fellow of the Royal Aeronautical Society Bill Gunston, who was technical editor of *Flight* in the 1950s, a magazine that also carried an article hailing the engineering advances of the Arrow. Calling him a "shrewd reader of programs," he states that Gunston believed it would have worked. This was certainly being proven by the flight testing.

In his own book from 1976, Bill Gunston noted the following:

> In 1958, when the first CF-105 flew, it was by a wide margin the most advanced fighter in the world. In its airframe, avionics, weapons and — by no means least — flight performance it set standards which nothing else actually built in the West could rival until today's F-14 and F-15 (except for Kelly Johnson's Blackbird YF-12A, which is not so much a fighter as a research aircraft).[4]

These are extraordinary statements by an expert.

Bill Sweetman's online article referred to the American F-4 Phantom. Some have argued that this plane, which went into service in the early sixties, was far superior to the Arrow, yet Sweetman notes it was the Arrow that was extraordinary.

It must be remembered that the Arrow and the Phantom were designed for different purposes: the Arrow for interception of incoming high-altitude bombers but with a weapons bay that could be configured for other missions, including reconnaissance; and the Phantom was a multi-role fighter.

As good as it may have been, the Phantom suffered heavy casualties against the smaller and lighter Soviet MiG aircraft it encountered in the Vietnam War. It has been noted that the reason for this is that the Phantom was not very agile, and that its missiles were not very good against the more agile MiGs, which augmented their missiles with cannons for additional firepower.

As aircraft air-to-air missile technology improved, so, too, did the effectiveness of the Phantom. Later versions of Phantoms would be modified to improve agility, and the Phantom, too, was eventually equipped with onboard canons.[5] Of course, the Arrow would also have undergone modification, if that were deemed necessary for its interceptor role. Even as it was being built, Avro engineers were looking at upgraded versions. In the final analysis, though, comparing the two aircraft, which had different mission profiles and therefore different capabilities, is difficult at best.

It has been said the Arrow would have been a relic by the time it entered operation, dying, as it were, along with the need for its interceptor role. And yet, the American F-106 Delta Dart, a single-engine delta interceptor that was at one point in 1958 considered as a potential replacement for the Arrow, remained in service as America's front-line interceptor well into the mid-1980s. Had the Arrow gone into production, it, too, might have remained in service for an extended period.

As far as can be determined, the Arrow was the first production aircraft to be designed around the concept of a fully powered flight control system (known as fly-by-wire), from the start. This innovation was followed years later by other aircraft like the F-16 and F/A-18 Hornet. It is true that a test aircraft in the United States was fitted with a fly-by-wire system prior to the Arrow, but this was for test purposes only.

Pilot Jack Woodman, the only RCAF pilot to fly the Arrow, described the fly-by-wire system in normal mode, as follows:

> When the pilot exerted a force on the control column to move the elevators, a force transducer on the control column transmitted electrical signals to a series of servos, which converted electrical signals into mechanical movement by means of hydraulic pressure. The electrical output at the transducer was directly proportional to the force exerted at the grip. The control column would move as the force was exerted, as with a conventional system, but it was not moved directly by the pilot. Movement of the control column followed the positioning of the elevators. The response of the system was instantaneous, and it therefore appeared as if the control column were moved by the pilot.[6]

During the development, a team of British and American engineers visited the plant on separate occasions to review the program in detail. They studied every aspect of the development. Regarding fly-by-wire, the British team had this to say:

> Any aircraft of the performance of the CF 105 will require artificial stability and damping of some kind, while most firms are adopting the philosophy of designing the

aircraft to have the best possible inherent stability characteristics, and then bringing the aircraft to the required standard by the minimum of artificial means, this firm has taken the view that since artificial stability is required it should be exploited to the full. Their arguments include the saving of weight and better handling characteristics generally. The clear indication is that a high degree of reliability will be required from the system which may cause delays in development, *since it is in any case very advanced in concept.* We were however impressed with the thorough and realistic manner in which they are tackling the project. Their avowed objective is to obtain a system reliability equivalent to that demanded of the engines on a twin-engine aircraft.[7] (emphasis added)

Back in Canada, the National Aeronautical Establishment (NAE) believed failure of this system would cause the aircraft to break up in flight and was recommending against its use. For its part, the U.S. National Advisory Committee for Aeronautics (NACA, later NASA) noted this system was, in actuality, feasible.

The reader can refer to Appendix A in this book, written by ex-Avro engineer and NASA alumnus C. Fred Matthews, for a more detailed treatment of how fly-by-wire functioned in the Arrow. Of particular interest, Matthews notes that the Mercury capsule and later the Gemini series were designed with fly-by-wire control systems. Instrumental in those designs were ex-Avro engineers Jim Chamberlin and Richard R. Carley, working from the experience they had gained with the Arrow.

In addition to the normal mode described by Jack Woodman, the Arrow had an automatic mode wherein the aircraft could be manoeuvred by ground controllers. The body charged with developing this automatic flight control system (AFCS) and other flight controls was the aeronautical division of Minneapolis-Honeywell Regulator Company and Honeywell Controls in Toronto. According to John H. Baldwin, chief engineer, aeronautical division, of the Toronto plant, many of the flight control systems being developed were unique to the Arrow, with vacuum tubes in these systems being replaced with transistors and magnetic amplifiers for greater reliability and decreased size and weight.

While conventional aircraft used various sensors mounted throughout the airframe for calculating altitude, true air speed, altitude difference, Mach number, and so on, the Arrow had one central air data computer (CADC). It performed all the computations necessary. Centralizing these functions into one unit cut down on duplication of instruments, on complexity, and on weight.

A similar treatment was provided for the vertical heading and reference system (VHRS). Again, in conventional aircraft of the day, duplicate sets of gyros throughout the aircraft were used to derive some fifty independent signals for roll, pitch, and azimuth. The Arrow was fitted with one central gyro system via two centrally located repeaters. Signals from the CADC and VHRS would be provided to the AFCS, the radar, the navigation system, and other flight instruments.

Even the cockpit displays on the pilot's control panel were somewhat different than in other aircraft. Human factors engineers determined that circular displays could be confusing to the pilot, even though they were easy to manufacture. So, while fuel-quantity gauges and exhaust-gas temperature indicators already developed by Honeywell remained circular, the company designed a linear rectangular gauge for Mach indication and a square flight director/attitude indicator for blind or instrument flying. The rectangular displays, however, introduced many manufacturing problems not inherent in circular designs. Solutions required advances in integral lighting, hermetic sealing, and development of servo drives for linear scales, all issues effectively tackled by the engineers in Toronto.

Honeywell also designed what they termed a thermistor-level system and centre-of-gravity control system. These provided the pilot with information on the status of the fuel system. They also automatically controlled fuel transfer, to relieve the pilot from having to select different fuel tanks while in flight.

Baldwin notes that while much of the design of these instruments was being carried out in the United States, it was being effected there by Canadian engineers on loan. These engineers returned to the Toronto plant to form part of the eighty personnel working on Arrow projects.

Some have argued that the Arrow would have been difficult to maintain. Yet Honeywell was designing ground test equipment that, when connected to the aircraft, would quickly determine the condition of each subsystem and locate any faults that might require attention. This equipment consisted of portable units for quick daily inspections, and of additional equipment for more in-depth fault-finding if necessary. This method greatly decreased turnaround time, allowing the aircraft to be put back into service sooner. It also eliminated the need for self-checking equipment on board the aircraft, thereby saving on takeoff weight. All of this testing equipment was being designed in Toronto.[8]

Other advances embodied in the Arrow included increased pressure in the hydraulics systems (4,000 psi, far greater than other aircraft, which were at 3,000 psi). This higher pressure allowed for smaller piping and resulted overall in a reduction in weight but necessitated specialized development as noted by H. Ross Harris, a technical representative for Weatherhead, a Canadian subsidiary company, in *Canadian Aviation* of March 1958:

> [F]luid connections produced by the company for the Arrow are leading the way in the field of high pressure, high temperature hydraulic systems. No standard fittings were available for the 4,000 lb psi hydraulic system chosen for the Arrow. This meant that Weatherhead had to produce some entirely new fittings, and adapt others, working and testing to Avro's specifications. In addition to being necessary to cope with the increased stresses in an aircraft of the CF 105's potentiality, the high-pressure system also contributes to the compactness of the package.[9]

As for the engine, the original RCAF plan in 1953 was to secure an engine offshore and build it under license for use on the Arrow. The engine under consideration was the Rolls-Royce RB.106, then under development in Britain. Issues arose that delayed its development, and there were indications it would not actually go into production. As a result, the RCAF examined other engines, namely the Curtiss-Wright J67, the Pratt and Whitney J57 and J75, the de Havilland Gyron, and the Bristol

Olympus. Finally, the J75 was deemed closest to meeting the requirement, after the J67 also ran into difficulty.

As this analysis from the RCAF proceeded, Orenda had already begun developing the Iroquois engine as a follow-on to its successful Orenda series. It had invested $9 million of its own money in the development. The RCAF reviewed the design and concluded it was at a more advanced stage than any other engine, whether in the United Kingdom or the United States, and had the necessary output power. A prototype had already been tested, indicating the expected performance would be achieved.

The engine had been developed for supersonic flight, and engineers estimated that at least 20 percent of the engine was beyond the state of the art. This was partly due to the fact that the Iroquois was designed using titanium and titanium alloys. In addition, it had a two-compressor or twin-spool configuration, not just one heavier compressor, as other engines had. It also possessed a smaller combustion chamber. All these features made it at least eight hundred to a thousand pounds lighter than other engines then available for high power output.

While other manufacturers were attempting to use titanium blades on already existing steel supports within an engine, Orenda elected to use titanium in the Iroquois design from the outset; as a result, supporting structures could also be made lighter. For example, a steel supporting disc would have weighed forty-eight pounds, whereas the titanium equivalent weighed in at sixteen pounds. Likewise, steel blades would weigh twenty-nine pounds, compared to the titanium seventeen pounds. Not only did the use of titanium allow for a lighter design, working with titanium resulted in the development of new techniques in welding and machining, putting Orenda at the forefront of that technology as well. Additional high temperature alloys developed by the International Nickel Company (INCO) would be incorporated into the design.[10]

The RCAF noted that an acceptable means for comparing engines was to look at the thrust produced per pound of engine weight. Initially designated the PS13, the Iroquois was rated at 20,000 pounds thrust. This exceeded the ratings of the J75 and RB.106 by more than 50 percent. The RCAF decided this engine would likely be the only one available in time to provide the power necessary for the Arrow to achieve all of its performance requirements. Later numbers would quote 19,450 pounds dry thrust and 25,600 pounds with afterburner and a weight of 4,800 pounds. [11]

Given the engine's advanced state of design, the RCAF also noted that there was no advantage to procuring another engine offshore and building it under licence. Of particular note is the comment in a memo dated February 25, 1955, which stated, "The advantages of expending this money and effort in Canada rather than in another country places the PS13 engine in a very favourable light."[12] This is interesting, given that when the fate of the Arrow was being discussed years later one of the arguments put forward to defend the cancellation of the program was that it made better sense to purchase a complete aircraft offshore, an argument that completely ignored the advantage of keeping the development in Canada.

Orenda was praised for having a talented and competent design team as well as fine facilities. This combination, the RCAF said, would ensure Canada would be in a position to meet its requirements in engine design in peacetime and in war and would remain at the forefront of gas turbine or jet engine technology.

For all its advancements, there are those who have criticized the Iroquois development, suggesting there were major design flaws with the turbine blades and other components. In fact, in an October 7, 1958 memo from the RCAF that catalogued the mechanical problems with the blades and with other aspects of the design, it was stated that these issues were not uncommon in engine design and would be corrected. According to a follow-up memorandum dated October 21, 1958, just two weeks later, the corrections had been achieved. [13]

Finally, in recapping the design effort, the following is stated in a memo dated November 30, 1960:

> The engine history as tabled is a frank and factual resumé and, although many problems and errors are mentioned, it is RCAF technical opinion the engine had overcome the major mechanical difficulties. The aerodynamic config-uration as stated in the historical summary, was cleared by a 50 Hr PFRT [Preliminary Flight Rating Test] before the program terminated. [14]

Earlier criticism levelled at the design was based on stories and rumour, because the documentation detailing otherwise remained classified. Once declassified, it revealed both the problems and the solutions implemented.

Had the program not been cancelled, Arrow 206, once its Iroquois engines were installed, was scheduled to commence taxi trials, followed by flight trials. Since no Arrow flew with either the Iroquois engine or the Hughes fire control system — the electronic system for launching Falcon missiles during an attack — it has been said that "there never was an Arrow," in the sense that the designation "Arrow" should only be applied to a completed aircraft with proper engines and fire control. Indeed, this, *There Never Was an Arrow*, was even the title of E.K. Shaw's book.

To clarify, the nickname Arrow was given to the platform. There most definitely was an Arrow and five of them, the Mark I's, flew and flew very well between 1958 and early 1959. Of course, it is impossible to say for sure that there would not have been additional issues or problems as testing proceeded; but, as noted by a British team looking at Avro's track record, there would have been every probability of continued success rather than of failure.

In commenting on the overall progress of the entire program, Chief of the Air Staff Hugh Campbell would write to the minister of national defence on January 12, 1959:

> There are at present five Mark I aircraft. In flight their characteristics in both handling and performance are extremely reassuring. The aircraft has displayed no stability or handling problem so far and has flown at Mach 1.96 at 50,000 ft and has reached an altitude in test flying of 58,000 ft.... The Iroquois engine is proceeding satisfactorily in its development. Engines have been provided for installation for ground running in an Arrow 2 airframe in December 1958. This procedure is a preliminary to the installation of the engines which will be used in the actual flight testing.... Engineering assessments have indicated that the only difficulties to be expected in this installation [Hughes MA1 electronic system] will be those normally

associated with a fire control system which has been designed for another aircraft and is being adapted to a new one. The engineering appraisals which have been made have indicated that the airframe, engines, fire control and weapons make a compatible system and should give the CF 105 a good operational capability ...[15]

As for flight testing, pilot Jack Woodman noted that on his first flight the Arrow flew very well, but at some points the controls were sensitive and the Arrow was difficult to fly. At higher speeds, the transition from subsonic to supersonic speeds was smooth. On his second flight, after initial snags had been dealt with, he reported the handling of the aircraft was improved. On his 6th flight he reported additional improvements:

[A]pproximately 95 percent of the flight envelope was investigated.... I reported longitudinal control to be positive with good response, and breakout force and stick gradients to be very good. Lateral control was good, forces and gradients very good, and the erratic control in the rolling plane, encountered on the last flight, no longer there. Directionally, slip and skid was held to a minimum. At no time during the flight was there more than 1 (degree) of sideslip and the problem of turn coordination appears to be eliminated at this point.... To me, it appears obvious that excellent progress was being made in the development of the Arrow ... handling and performance characteristics of the Avro Arrow were shaping up very nicely. There were many problems still to be resolved at the time of cancellation, but from where I sat the Arrow was performing as predicted and was meeting all guarantees.[16]

The Arrow was not tested at the required Mach 1.5, 2 G turn at 50,000 feet as flight testing centred on other parameters first. In a memo dated January 17, 1958, the RCAF stated that a sustained factor of 2 G was no longer as critical as originally thought in 1952 and that the Astra and Sparrow missiles were adding considerable weight and drag, making this requirement unrealistic. Instead, it was believed that a load factor of 1.5 G would suffice.[17]

For their part, Avro calculated that the Mark II aircraft with Iroquois could be expected to reach 1.62 G at altitude and Mach 2 while other aircraft of the day were in the 1.3 G category, at significantly lower altitudes. There are those who argue the Arrow achieved a low G turn at a low altitude and was therefore substandard in some way. The fact is the Mach 1.5, 2 G turn and higher speed runs were not planned as part of the initial test program of the first five aircraft. Jan Zurakowski explains:

> [W]e had a high priority on testing the actual systems. Our engines at the time were not typical production engines. We were using the American engines, so we didn't spend much time investigating this engine at high altitudes. We knew the actual production engines would be the Iroquois, more powerful, on which we could do full investigation. What we were trying to do on the first five aircraft flying with the Pratt and Whitney engines was to get all basic information.[18]

It's clear that these tests show not the limitations of the aircraft but rather a desire by the design team to implement a methodical progression of proper testing, to ensure the operability and safety of a highly sophisticated and complex system upon which many lives would depend.

The real concern in the RCAF memo was more in the ferry range being possibly reduced to 1,254 nautical miles. An early company brochure had showed 1,279 nautical miles would be achieved, while Fred Smye, president and general manager, Avro Aircraft, indicated a 1,500 nautical mile ferry mission was expected.

Values of range and radius of action were as required by the RCAF. On this latter note, some, like the minister of national defence at the time, George R. Pearkes, would confuse range and radius of action. The radius of action was between three hundred and five hundred nautical miles (roughly 345 to 575 miles) depending on the type of mission being flown. Pearkes would incorrectly state this was the range, and critics would use this to incorrectly say the Arrow could not fly more than a few hundred miles. The RCAF asked if the radius for a Mark IIA version could be extended. Analytical results showed that enough fuel could indeed be worked in to the present configuration to extend the radius to 600 or 650 nautical miles, assuming a typical subsonic mission with supersonic combat.

Even though 95 percent of the flight envelope had been tested, only a portion of the first phase of testing was completed. In all, eight phases of testing were proposed and would include testing by both the contractor and the RCAF. While the first phases included exploring the flight envelope, flights were conducted to test systems, optimize damper and flying control systems, investigate stability, and check structural integrity. Additional phases would include Iroquois engine development, armament testing, further performance and handling with the Iroquois, all-weather operation, intensive flying with the RCAF, as well as weapons evaluation and operational suitability. As noted in *Storms*, twenty aircraft would be used for flight testing with the twenty-first aircraft becoming the final production standard. Aircraft from the first twenty would also be upgraded to the standard accordingly. The use of multiple aircraft for test purposes was not uncommon in the industry — it shortened the length of time to production, as much of the testing could proceed in parallel. Up to this early point in the test program, the RCAF stated that performance was better than estimated.[19]

In his flight testing experience, Pilot Jan Zurakowski reached a speed of Mach 1.52 on his seventh flight, at 50,000 feet while in a climb, with excess thrust available; this, with the lower-powered J75 engines. The highest speed he would fly would be to Mach 1.86 (indicated) at 50,000 feet while still accelerating, according to a flight progress report for the period between June 7, 1958, and November 3, 1958.[20] When asked a question at his talk to the Toronto Chapter of the Canadian Aviation Historical Society (CAHS) on March 1, 1978, he said the maximum speed he achieved was Mach 1.89, slightly above that officially recorded. He was also asked if the aircraft had ever been rolled. He indicated that it was, on many occasions. He stated that rolling manoeuvrability was very fast, particularly at higher speeds. Turning manoeuvrability, he said, was based more on the strength of the aircraft and on the ability of the pilot to withstand the G forces.[21]

C. Fred Matthews laughs as he recounts an interesting anecdote related to Zura's test flights. Fred had sought the assistance of a tracking station to follow and monitor some of the flights. He was in touch via an intercom system with those at the station. In one particular instance he notes that they left their intercom open, perhaps inadvertently. At one point he heard one of the individuals exclaim, "Look at that son of a bitch go!"

Pilot Spud Potocki found numerous snags or problems with the Arrow but, he "never doubted it was a thoroughbred."[22] In his testing of the Arrow, he told this author, he achieved a highest speed of Mach 1.98. Hugh Campbell stated in a memo to the minister of national defence, dated January 12, 1959, that the Arrow had been flown to Mach 1.96 at 50,000 feet and had reached altitudes during flight tests of 58,000 feet.[23] Years later, in the 1980s, when asked about the discrepancy between the two Mach numbers, Potocki stated the correct figure was Mach 1.98. The difference, he said, was simply that between what he was reading on his instruments in the cockpit and what ground crew were monitoring.

At the CAHS talk mentioned earlier, when asked what was the highest speed achieved by the Arrow, Jan Zurakowski responded: "The maximum speed any of the test aircraft achieved was Mach 1.98, flown by Spud Potocki.... We must bear in mind that this was not the maximum possible. We were still progressing slowly, recording every step we took, but there was no correct test for speed, as we did not have any priority in reaching maximum speed."[24]

This said, in his book, *Flight Test: The Avro Arrow and a Career in Aeronautical Engineering*, author David Waechter indicates the maximum speed achieved was Mach 1.9 in level flight and Mach 1.95 in a slight dive with engines at full and not in a climb, as had been reported by the pilots and newspapers of the day. His sources are the written Avro test reports from his father, Ralph Waechter, whose work at Avro included Machmeter calibration and aircraft performance analysis. It is unfortunate the material from Mr. Waechter was not available sooner. Both Spud and Jan could have been asked to reconcile their reports of speed achieved with what is now written in the Waechter book, especially since no absolutely correct test for speed had yet been developed when the Arrows flew.

Bryan Erb was one of the twenty-five who went to NASA. He had worked on the thermodynamics of the Arrow. He and his colleagues believed they had a world-beater and that there was no way it would be cancelled. He recalls naively believing that once Avro built the best aircraft, the RCAF and others would eventually buy it.

Owen Maynard, who also ended up at NASA, also knew the Arrow was leading-edge. He credits the absolute dedication and attention to detail of everyone from upper management to middle management to lower management, and especially to the personal attention to detail by the technicians, for establishing the quality required.

Had the Arrow flown with the more powerful Iroquois, speeds of Mach 2 and beyond would have been probable, and a speed record would likely have been attempted relatively soon, as part of the speed capability trials, as noted by Avro officials in the newspapers immediately after Spud's speed run. In *Storms*, an RCAF memo was quoted as indicating only a speed of Mach 1.9 might be achieved. This was a calculated value based on certain parameters and as testing had already shown, calculated performance figures were usually quite conservative, given that the Mark I had already achieved Mach 1.9 and 1.95, as described above, with the lower-powered test engines.

According to Jim Floyd, Mach 2.5, while not requested by the RCAF, was being considered for a Mark III version of the Arrow. The Mark III would have had a variable inlet ramp, and development of equipment to withstand the higher temperatures that would ensue. Radius of action would be on the order of 420 nautical miles for a supersonic mission or 500 subsonic with supersonic combat. Combat altitudes would be on the order of 68,000 feet. The ultimate Arrow would add ramjet assist, external fuel pods, and the like, as described in *Storms*. Limitations to speed would have been due mainly to high temperatures on the aircraft's body as a result from frictional heating.

Many have asked how the Arrow's skin could have withstood the higher temperatures from the heat of friction. It was able to do so because the structure consisted not only of steel but also magnesium, titanium, and Inconel X, all high-temperature resistant materials.[25] Inconel X was the chosen material for the experimental, rocket-powered, Mach 7, X-15. It is an alloy of nickel, chromium, and other metals. The Arrow engineers used the materials as necessary and knew that to push the envelope of the aircraft beyond the Mach 2 region, a renewed analysis of the structure and application of these materials would be required, along with any necessary modifications.

Given all of the above, it is clear that the Arrow was indeed a highly advanced aircraft. In discussing the superiority of the Arrow with shareholders, Crawford Gordon quoted from the prime minister's statement of September 23, 1958, in which the prime minister said:

> [T]he Arrow aircraft and the Iroquois engine appear now to be likely to be better than any alternative expected to be ready by 1961.... The Arrow supersonic plane has already thrilled us with its performance, its promise, and its proof of ability in design and technology ...[26]

So, the Arrow was highly advanced. It represented the state of the art in aeronautical technology in engine, airframe, and flight control design. As a consequence of what the Arrow team was doing, A.V. Roe Canada was able to attract some of the best aeronautical minds in the world, all of whom were anxious to participate in pushing the envelope further. Yet, as noted earlier, because the documentation regarding the Arrow's construction and test flight results were kept secret for so many years, critics of the program have had an easy task arguing that the program was cancelled because of a flawed design. Indeed, some have stated that there must have been little if anything of value in the design and test results since, after termination, almost everything about the program was ordered physically destroyed.

Desmond Morton, mentioned earlier as decrying the lack of information available, was one of those who wrote, back in the early eighties, that the Arrow had "crippling design flaws" and a design that even first-year engineering students would know was flawed. He cited unnamed sources as the authorities for his remarks, but admitted that he had no access to the documented record. (In the end, it turned out that the information he had been given was likely based on a prototype of the CF-100, not the Arrow, and he graciously took note of this.) He wrote about the flaws, he claimed, in order to draw out others who might have additional information. Of course, the engineers who felt disparaged by his article did write to complain and set the record straight, but they did not have the documented records either and could be accused of bias.

It has been said the Arrow was some twenty years or more ahead of its time. That is, the Arrow embodied some features that did not appear in other production aircraft over that length of time. For example, fly-by-wire finally found its way into the American F-16, designated the first fly-by-wire aircraft, which did not go into service until the mid-seventies. This system was used later still in the F-18. A 4,000 psi hydraulic system also took years to materialize in other production aircraft, but eventually did.

Does this mean one could take the Arrow of 1959 and pit it against aircraft of today? No, it simply means that, had the Arrow gone into production, it would have had these advantages and Avro would have had a considerable head start, allowing for modification and improvement of the Arrow design to be done as needed in the ensuing years.

The Arrow was not the mythical plane that some have come to believe it was, nor was it the flawed failure others would suggest. The Arrow was simply a highly sophisticated aircraft, extremely advanced for its time. Whatever flaws it had were minor and would have been corrected once it was in service, and it would no doubt have been improved when new materials, miniaturized components, and advanced design processes became available. And if the Arrow program had retained support, A.V. Roe Canada would have been able to build on the knowledge learned from developing that plane and go on to perhaps produce further, even more advanced aircraft designs, as well as, possibly, products in other areas of high technology.

Unfortunately, none of that was to be. With the cancellation of the Arrow, Canada lost a very great chance to be at the cutting edge of military aeronautical and technological design — as it had lost being at the forefront of commercial jet aircraft design with the termination of the Jetliner before it.

3

Why Was the Arrow Program Terminated?

WHY THE ARROW PROGRAM was terminated remains controversial. Some have cited the cost of the program. Others have claimed that with the appearance of ICBMs and the diminished threat from manned bombers, there was less of a need for interceptors like the Arrow. Still others have suggested that the cancellation of the Arrow program was the product of American influence. At the time of the cancellation, the first two arguments were certainly put forward by many. The last argument has been advanced mostly in the decades since. In the end, it's possible to argue that all three played roles in the decision to cancel, although the nature of the role each played is not necessarily what those who argue for it believe it to be. And, to some degree, all three are interconnected. I will try to disentangle them here.

———

There are those who believe that if the Liberals had remained in power instead of losing the election to Diefenbaker's Conservatives in 1957, they, too, would have cancelled the program. In this regard, the notes of the Liberal Party leader, Lester B. Pearson, make for interesting reading. Writing just after the cancellation, Pearson indicates that the decision to undertake the CF-105 was, in his words, "a wise one." He notes that the

ICBM threat had not yet been envisioned, and so, to meet the threat of long-range bombers, aircraft would be required. The costs of the Arrow were expected to be between $1.5 million and $2 million each, based on acquisition of some six hundred aircraft. Given these factors, he says, the decision was justified from a military point of view.

There was also an economic justification for the development of the Arrow. Given that it was to be in service for years to come, it would create employment opportunities and provide a skilled labour force. He then indicates that, even at the time he was writing (1959), there was no disagreement about the initial decision to build the Arrow. He quotes Diefenbaker:

> I am not condemning the Liberal government for what it did in laying the foundation of the CF-105. It did so on the basis of the information that it had at that time. It had no realization, nor did mankind anywhere in the free world, of the vast potentialities of nuclear weapons.[1]

Pearson then goes on to say that the total expenditures were within the government's financial capacity for the program. He also recognizes that, by 1957, even though costs were increasing, there had been no reason for a revision of the plan as set out in 1953.

In 1957, though, the situation did begin changing, with the launch of Sputnik. As the nature of the threat changed, the requirement for piloted aircraft, it was felt, would be significantly reduced. As a result, Pearson acknowledges, the cost per aircraft would have therefore increased, since fewer Arrows might be required, and the Arrow's costs would be on top of those needed for new and different equipment to counter the new threat. He indicates that, under these circumstances, the Liberals would have undertaken a review of the program. So, the problem was not that the cost of the Arrow was so great that something less expensive had to be found to replace it; the problem was with the advent of new threats, which it was not designed to counter, fewer, if any, planes would be necessary. These new threats took priority, and so the number of Arrows required would diminish, resulting in a higher cost per aircraft.

Along with Pearson's remarks, comments from Liberal minister of munitions and supply C.D. Howe are also available. He had been concerned about the program from its inception, and is often quoted as saying that the program was of such magnitude that it gave him the shudders.

In January of 1959, Pearson wrote to Howe asking for his views on the Arrow situation. Howe replied on January 22. In the letter Howe states that the Arrow project costs were out of control and that therefore the project should be terminated. He advised Pearson to take this stand against the Conservatives, who seemed to be hesitant about taking the decision. The Conservatives had stated they would reappraise the situation in March of 1959. Howe felt, however, that any delay would result in yet more unnecessary expenditures. He states:

> You will recall that when the matter [the Arrow] was last discussed by our Defence Committee in 1957, it was decided to continue the project for the time being, and have a complete review of the matter in September 1957. I had then recommended that the project be terminated due to runaway costs, but there were obvious reasons then why the decision should be deferred until autumn. I think you have been right in being completely non-committal as to the decision to continue or terminate, which is obviously one for the government of the day....[2]

If the costs were out of control in 1957, as Howe suggests, and the Liberal party was agreed on termination (as has been noted by others), why would it have been necessary to go ahead with a complete review in September? Would this not have allowed the Conservatives, if they had not won the election in 1957, to make the same argument against the Liberals — that by delaying the decision, the cost to Canadians was increasing unnecessarily — that he was now proposing Pearson make against them?

And what were the obvious reasons for continuing? Political? Was it the fear that if they did cancel sooner than later they might lose that election? But should this have been a concern if the financial situation he described was that clear cut? Would not Canadians have understood and perhaps even lauded the Liberals for making the right decision? After all, this was the thinking the Conservatives would later discuss to justify their decision on the matter.

And why, if the Liberal party was planning to terminate, was Pearson non-committal, especially if, as Howe believed, the finances spoke for themselves? It is difficult to determine the truth at this point. What can be deduced is that, given the party's plan to review the Arrow program and the non-committal stance of Pearson, it is unlikely that the Liberals *were* committed to cancelling the Arrow program before such a review might take place.

So, what can be said of the argument that the bomber threat diminished with the development of ICBMs, and as a consequence the need for interceptors like the Arrow also declined? Certainly, by 1958 news media outlets in Canada were claiming the Arrow was obsolete as a result of this.

As early as 1955, at the February 11 meeting of the Chiefs of Staff Committee, Chief of the General Staff Lieutenant General Guy Simonds had expressed a very similar view:

> The Chief of the General Staff stated that he considered that the proposed program [Arrow] was wrong in principle. *The development of guided missiles was proceeding so rapidly that manned aircraft would probably be obsolete before many years.* Before the CF-105 could be made operational its usefulness could be outstripped by events and there would be *no return for the very large investment* ...[3] (emphasis added)

The general went on to say that any development money would be better spent on weapons that could be used against what he believed was this new and more dangerous threat. He believed that if piloted aircraft were needed at all, even if they did not satisfy the full specifications of the Arrow, it would be better to purchase them from the United States. He believed not that the Arrow development was in and of itself problematic, but rather that it would be better to direct funds into ways he considered to be more appropriate for the future security of the country.

Responding to Simonds, the chief of the air staff, Air Marshal Roy Slemon, pointed out that the current threat was still the piloted bomber, and so he recommended continuing the Arrow program. However, he, too, stated that if at some future point missiles like Bomarcs became available it would be prudent to stop or modify the Arrow program. So the issue was the threat and how best to defend against it, not that costs of the Arrow were out of control, as Howe believed.

By October 1957 Canada was under a Conservative government, and the 273rd Air Council met in Ottawa to address the question of whether to continue with the Arrow program or not. It was noted by the vice-chief of the air staff that, in his talks with high-ranking officers in the USAF, the Americans believed that in the period from 1961 to 1970 North America would have to defend against both manned bombers and ICBMs. They further believed Russia might have a supersonic bomber by 1965 and possibly a nuclear-powered one later. They were of the opinion that attacking aircraft should be stopped as far out as possible, by aircraft possibly equipped with nuclear weapons, with shorter-range surface-to-air missiles (Bomarc) being used to handle any enemy aircraft still getting through.

The Americans saw missiles, with their limited range of 250 miles, as a complement to long-range interceptors, which they were endorsing:

> The Americans intend, therefore, to proceed with the development of the F108, a supersonic long-range interceptor. They regard the Arrow as a long-range interceptor, partly because of its radius [of action] and partly because of the geographical location of bases from which it might operate.[4]

This comment is significant because it makes clear that the Americans considered the Arrow a long-range aircraft because of its radius of action and location. This directly challenges later claims the Arrow's range was very limited.

At this same meeting, the Air Member Technical Services (AMTS) stated that:

In commenting on the USAF proposal to counter the threat of the super-sonic bomber (1965-1970) with Bomarc and the F108, AMTS pointed out that the Arrow would not only fill the gap from 1962 to 1965, but also, if its potential were exploited, might be given the capability to deal with super-sonic bombers through added range and speed ...[5]

In fact, the AMTS would later put forward a memo to the chief of the air staff in May of 1958 that suggested that he make a proposal to the USAF, through the minister, offering the Arrow for consideration. It was noted that the Mark IIA Arrows could have a radius of action of 500 nautical miles (nm) with a Mach 1.5 session at 55,000 feet, suitable for the long-range fighter role in 1962, and that it would be followed by a Mark III version in 1964, with a proposed 420 nm radius and a Mach 2.5 encounter at 65,000 feet. As this was only a suggestion, it seems to have gone nowhere, although plans at Avro were in the discussion stages for more advanced aircraft.[6]

The American concept called for an in-depth defensive posture: long-range aircraft backed by missiles like the Bomarc and possibly short range aircraft and anti-ICBM missiles, all controlled by a sophisticated electronic environment like the American Semi-Automatic Ground Environment or SAGE system.

At the 273rd Air Council meeting, the AMTS further stated that the American views confirmed his own. He "believed the RCAF should adopt a programme to embrace the Arrow, Bomarc and improved radar coverage. The VCAS [Vice-Chief of the Air Staff] agreed that a family of weapons would provide the best defence, *but expressed doubt that the national economy could provide a variety of expensive weapons.*"[7] (emphasis added)

This latter comment is crucial for understanding the true nature of the situation. The problem was not the cost of the Arrow alone but the combined cost of Arrow, Bomarc, SAGE, additional gap-filler radar, and research against the ICBM.

The Air Member Personnel (AMP) expressed similar sentiments as the VCAS. Specifically:

The AMP questioned the value to be received from building an expensive aircraft which he said, would be in service only two or three years before the American long-range F108 would come into operational use. He pointed out that Bomarc would be available about the same time as the Arrow, and he recommended that the RCAF concentrate on improving its ground environment and building missile bases. *He thought the cost of both Bomarc and the Arrow was prohibitive.*[8] (emphasis added)

The AMP was of the belief that the role of the Arrow was over, given the onset of the Americans' yet-to-be-developed F-108, and that the focus should be on building missile bases, even though the Bomarc was still developmental and had not yet proven itself.

To reiterate, the discussion was not a question of affordability of the Arrow but where best to invest the country's money for weapons. In the view of some, the answer was simple: the Bomarc. As for interceptors, the AMP had written that he was willing to accept American aircraft. Canada could either purchase these, or it could allow the Americans to defend Canada with its own planes and crews. To keep both the Arrow and the Bomarc was, in his view, going to be cost-prohibitive. If one or the other had to be let go, it had to be the Arrow.

In the end, the government agreed to continue with the Arrow for another twelve months.

Although the government had agreed to continue development, doubts persisted about the future of the program. On January 23, 1958, in the House of Commons, a question was asked about the fate of the Arrow. The minister of national defence, George Pearkes, provided the following response:

Mr. Speaker, some years ago research work was started to develop a supersonic interceptor capable of intercepting manned bombers which might be expected in about 5 years' time from now. Development work has proceeded on a year to year basis. Last fall the government authorized a further year's development of that aircraft which has now become known as the CF-105. The *future* of that aircraft *will depend entirely on the nature of the threat*. The matter is constantly under examination, and *as long as the threat exists development and production of the CF-105 will proceed*.[9] (emphasis added)

At this point in 1958, the government had a reasonable understanding of the costs of the program. Yet Pearkes was clear in stating that the future of the Arrow depended completely on the nature of the threat. His comment was prophetic.

By April, the army was expressing concern that Bomarc bases were being placed in areas already defended by aircraft and that this was being done simply to fill a gap in U.S. defences. Continuing along these lines, it was stated, would leave other parts of Canada exposed. In addressing these concerns, Air Commodore W.W. Bean stated in a memo to the chief of plans on April 25, 1958 that:

Insofar as filling a gap in U.S. defences at the expense of providing protection to other areas of Canada is concerned, this statement is also partly true. Bomarcs would partially fill a gap in U.S. defences and justifiably so as a Canadian contribution to the protection of the deterrent force. In addition, however, these bases provide protection for the most critical Canadian target areas. Further, many of the other areas of Canada which are presumably being neglected by the RCAF would, under the terms of NORAD, actually be protected by adjacent U.S. interceptors (both manned and unmanned).[10]

So, Air Commodore Bean was admitting the Bomarcs would fill in gaps for the American defences and that adjacent American aircraft would defend the rest of Canada. He went on to add that the cost of Bomarcs would not impact future programs. Unfortunately, the Bomarc's acceptance was impacting the Arrow.

The idea that the combination of all systems of air defence might be too much for Canada to handle was reiterated by the minister of national defence in his top secret brief to the Americans. The brief is dated July 8, 1958, and was first revealed in *Storms*. In it, Pearkes explained that by virtue of geographical location, Canada was compelled to spend nearly half of the defence budget on air defence requirements, and he complained that, despite close cooperation between the two countries, the United States had never accepted a Canadian aircraft nor had there been any success at a joint development.

He added that two major problems existed: developing a defence against the ICBM; and defending against the manned-bomber threat. Addressing the former, he stated:

> We feel very strongly that this development of defence against ballistic missiles in North America should be a joint effort and we are concerned lest we spend too much on rounding out the defence against the manned bomber and not have funds available to participate in the development and production against the ballistic missile.[11]

So, Pearkes was concerned about not having funds to spend on ballistic missile defence if the money was being spent on defence against the piloted bomber.

He further stated, "NORAD has also recommended the introduction of the Bomarc missile into the Ottawa-North Bay area to supplement the piloted interceptor, to round out the U.S. Bomarc chain, and to push the defences 250 miles further north."[12]

He noted that Bomarc was a NORAD (or rather, an American) requirement, and said that all these expenses coming now would add 25 to 30 percent to Canada's defence budget. He was seeking assistance or some arrangement from the United States in paying for all these requirements.

He inquired about some form of cost-sharing and wondered if the United States would consider equipping USAF squadrons at Harmon AFB (in Newfoundland) and at Goose Bay with the Arrow. The hope was that if the Americans bought into the Arrow, then allowances could be made for all of the required defences. The response he received was negative.

This was not the first time some sort of deal with the Americans had been discussed. As first reported in *Storms*, on January 30, 1958, then

Canadian ambassador to Washington, Mr. Norman Robertson, was the luncheon guest of James H. Douglas, secretary of the air force, along with Lieutenant General D.L. Putt, deputy chief of staff, research and development; Major General H.M. Estes, assistant chief of staff for air defence systems; and Dudley C. Sharp, assistant secretary (materiel), Department of the Air Force.

The discussion centred on the high costs of programs and the decisions required with respect to the types and quantities of new types of equipment. On the question of the Arrow development, Ambassador Robertson said: "The CF-105 ... was related to the evaluation of the manned-bomber threat, the rate of development of newer and superseding weapons, and indeed whether it makes sense for us to commit such a major portion of our resources and money to a weapons system which could become virtually obsolescent by the time it is operational."[13]

If he was trying to sell the airplane to the Americans, advising that it might be obsolete in short order seems an odd way to go about it. What is also interesting is that he echoes the refrain that continuation of the program depended on the threat and development of newer weapons, not on affordability per se. What was important was the connection between cost and the utility of the product.

Mr. Douglas stated categorically that there was no place in the USAF inventory for the CF-105, and that the USAF was going ahead with the F-108, which it felt would be more advanced and capable than the Arrow. His personal view, though, was that in the context of continental defence, the USAF could purchase the Arrow in squadron strength, have it operate from Canadian bases, but be piloted and maintained by the RCAF. The Canadian ambassador suggested Canada wished to be a contributor to defence and not a beneficiary, stating there would be political problems with this arrangement, noting that Canada would not accept aid from the United States or any other country.

For his part, General Putt asked whether a plan could be established through NORAD that would call for more CF-105 squadrons then currently envisaged by Canada, with the difference being funded by the USAF. As an alternative, he mentioned that some eight Strategic Air Command (SAC) refuelling bases were being planned for installation in Canada and that perhaps a swap could be arranged: purchase of CF-105s in exchange for work done in Canada in readying the refuelling bases.

This discussion, as well as the fact the USAF assisted in the development of the Arrow, through the use of its wind tunnels and the B-47 used to test the Iroquois, has been pointed to as proof the United States wished to help Canada in continuing the Arrow program rather than trying to see it terminated. But, this was the view of some USAF staff, not that of the United States government as a whole. Douglas was definite in pointedly stating there was no place in the USAF inventory for the Arrow, and subsequent meetings with other bureaucrats would echo this sentiment.

The point of view of the air staff in Washington regarding this meeting was as follows:

> There is no doubt in my mind that this meeting with the Secretary served a very good purpose. Mr Douglas seemed very well briefed on both USAF and RCAF problems and I have been informed by some of the people concerned that a good deal of homework was involved. *While I do not consider that the suggestions put forward would have any particular merit in themselves*, they do indicate a genuine concern for our position and a disposition to help in some way.... Staff echelons recognize the CF 105 as potentially a very fine weapons system.[14] (emphasis added)

General Putt's ideas for a swap never materialized. Again, while some officers and airmen wanted the Arrow, at the bureaucratic levels the situation was different. For example, on other occasions, such as at the Paris conference with U.S. Secretary of Defence Neil McElroy, the Canadians would be told that the United States would not purchase the Arrow.

Discussing this, ex-Avro employee and NASA alumnus C. Fred Matthews recounts how one individual who wanted to get the Arrow into the United States for evaluation was allegedly advised by an aircraft manufacturer that if he pursued this idea, once he retired from the USAF he would never get a job in the aircraft industry. The lobby was strong enough that, in one government document, it was noted that even if Canada, via

Canadair, were given a small contract for the Bomarc, "considerable political repercussions can be expected...."[15]

So, in discussing American interest, it is necessary to differentiate the wants and needs of officers and airmen, the secretary of the air force, the American government, and American industry. Not all shared the same viewpoint with respect to the Arrow. On the Canadian side, Pearson indicates he felt that more overtures should have been made to sell the aircraft, and that these should have been escalated to the prime ministerial/presidential levels at the earliest opportunity after the Conservatives took office, but that had not happened.

On August 19, 1958, the chairman of the Chiefs of Staff prepared a comprehensive report titled "Report on the Development of the CF-105 Aircraft and Associated Weapon System 1952–1958." In addition to summarizing all the studies and reports that had preceded this one, several observations were made that clearly show the direction the thinking on the Arrow was heading:

> [I]n 1956 there was some evidence that the Russians were developing ballistic missiles.... These observations were followed by a statement from Mr. Khrushchev that the manned bomber was obsolete and the Soviet Union was in possession of long-range missiles ... there was no further evidence to show that the Soviet Union was in fact developing supersonic jet bombers or increasing inventory of long-range bombers. The advent of Sputnik in 1957 [the very day of the Arrow rollout] confirmed the assumption that the USSR had made considerable progress in the technical fields of production of missiles and *it became obvious that the future main threat to North America may come from ballistic missiles in the period 1960–1967.* The arrival of Sputnik gave great impetus to the U.S. missile development and production programmes and some programmes, such as Bomarc, were now speeded up ... and the manned bomber will be a subordinate threat which is expected to decrease in importance after 1962–63.[16] (emphasis added)

The Arrow would have been operational in the period from 1960 to 1967, but the Arrow was not designed to take down ballistic missiles. It would have provided excellent defence against long-range bombers, even if that threat was diminishing, but it had to compete against the U.S.-backed Bomarc missile system, whose development was being accelerated. All of these factors together would render the Arrow obsolete as a defensive weapon system. A perceived shift in the military threat facing North America and the politics of defence spending doomed the Arrow. The aircraft was not technologically inferior.

A further observation is made in the report:

> [T]he early requirement in 1953 was for nineteen squadrons, a total of between 500 and 600 aircraft. This has now been reduced to nine squadrons and consideration has been given in the last few months to reducing the requirement to about 100 aircraft if the Bomarc missile is introduced.... [17]

The original requirement for nineteen squadrons included planes for the auxiliary reserve forces, but it had since been decided not to provide the Arrow to them, given its complexity, over subsonic fighters. This decision, too, resulted in a decrease in the number of aircraft required. Also, given that the Arrow was more capable than the CF-100, it had been decided that yet fewer of the CF-105 would be needed. Now, though, consideration was being given to reducing the number further still, this time to one hundred aircraft. The reason, according to the report, would be the introduction of the Bomarc missile, not the cost of the Arrow.

However, as the report adds, this reduction to one hundred would raise the cost of the aircraft and would make the program hardly economical, given the perception that the threat from long-range bombers had diminished. At no time does the report say the Arrow was unaffordable or that costs were out of control. The issue of cost was always linked to the diminished threat and the introduction of missiles to deal with that threat as the best means of spending defence funds.

As for the belief that there was a diminishing bomber threat, the question is, where was this intelligence assessment coming from? The report states that there was evidence the Soviets were developing missiles. In fact, in the late 1950s the American Central Intelligence Agency (CIA) began touting the possibility that a missile gap was developing. The CIA website describes it as follows:

> The Missile Gap was in essence a growing perception in the West, especially in the United States, that the Soviet Union was quickly developing an intercontinental range ballistic missile (ICBM) capability earlier, in greater numbers, and with far more capability than that of the United States. The perceived missile gap that ensued was based on a comparison between U.S. ICBM strength as then programmed, and reasonable, although erroneous estimates of prospective Soviet ICBM strength that were generally accepted.[18]

Notwithstanding that it is now known the intelligence estimates were indeed erroneous, at the time, they were accepted by the Canadian military.

On March 12, 1957, the CIA issued one of many reports regarding Soviet missile capability. It is titled "Soviet Capabilities and Probable Programs in the Guided Missile Field" and covers the period through to 1966. It is stamped top secret and provides details of Soviet capabilities, possible launch sites, types of missiles, and so on. Of note are these paragraphs:

> 1. We estimate that the Soviet guided missile program is extensive and enjoys a very high priority.... 2. We believe that the USSR has the native scientific resources and capabilities to develop during this period advanced types of guided missile systems, in all categories for which it has military requirements. We estimate that the USSR has the industrial base and related industrial experience to series produce the missile systems it will develop during this period. However, in view of competing demands, the limited availability of electronic equipment will seriously restrict the extent and variety of Soviet guided missile production until about 1958. Thereafter, expanding

electronics production will probably make this restriction much less severe…. We believe that the USSR has the capability of orbiting, in 1957, a satellite vehicle …[19]

The last sentence quoted is prophetic, for on October 4, 1957, the Soviet Union did launch a satellite, Sputnik. This was the same day as the Arrow rollout. This event would overtake the rollout in terms of importance and would give credence to the CIA analysis and the idea that there was a missile gap. It is likely some of the details from this or other analysis were shared with the Canadian military, giving rise to the issues regarding Soviet missiles raised in the report of the chairman Chiefs of Staff of August 19, 1958.

Guy Simonds was of the same opinion. He went public with his thinking on the subject. As noted by pilot Jan Zurakowski in an article for the *Journal of the Canadian Aviation Historical Society* years later, on September 24, 1958, the *Toronto Telegram* reported the following statement from Simonds: "The day of the airplane is finished as a defence mechanism. It has been replaced by the missile as the primary mechanism … the last of the fighters. The Arrow is just that — the last of its line and kind."[20]

Simonds was still of the opinion that missiles would supplant the interceptor, rendering the latter obsolete, and so missiles were the way to go.

Following the chief of staff report, a memorandum to the Cabinet Defence Committee meeting of August 28, 1958, was prepared by the minister of national defence. On the question of the Arrow he stated that:

> The Chiefs of Staff have grave doubts as to whether a limited number of aircraft of this extremely high cost *would provide defence returns commensurate with the expenditures in view of the changing threat* and the possibility that an aircraft of comparable performance can be obtained from United States production at a much less cost and in the same time period, 1961–1962.[21] (emphasis added)

Again, the comment shows that the government's main concern was ensuring that any money spent would be for the appropriate defensive weapon against the main threat, which was now perceived to be the missile.

This nuance is critical — the Arrow was cancelled on military grounds, and not on cost per se. On February 5, 1959, the Chiefs of Staff reiterated the recommendation in a memo to the Cabinet Defence Committee.

There has never been an argument that costs were not high, but the main issue involved the return on investment against a diminishing threat, not affordability. Certainly, the comments made by Minister Pearkes in the House of Commons on January 23, 1958, indicate that he thought that the future of the Arrow program depended on the military threat, and that since the threat of bombers was declining the utility of the Arrow was declining, as well. This same message was delivered by Ambassador Robertson to American representatives, when he questioned the wisdom of spending money on a system that would be obsolete as it became operational, as noted earlier.

Recommendations in the minister's report were also made to install Bomarcs and additional radar, investigate cost-sharing and alternative aircraft with the Americans, and abandon the Arrow. The minister noted further that the SAGE system had to be introduced whether or not the government proceeded with the Arrow. This was because SAGE was a requirement for Bomarc, and both were in the NORAD defence plan, which he believed Canada was obliged to adopt.

At the Cabinet Defence Committee meeting of August 28, 1958, various factors were discussed regarding the impact of continuing or abandoning the Arrow program. These included the potential layoff of twenty-five thousand employees and the extremely adverse effect on the economy of that, the possibility these workers might be absorbed in other areas, and the fact that the Arrow would be useless against missiles. Discontinuing, though, would mean the RCAF would be completely dependent on the United States for equipment.

In all of this discussion one paragraph stands out:

> If the CF-105 were not abandoned, it would mean an increase in the defence budget of $400 million a year for several years. Even without this the deficit in 1959–60 would be as much as in the current year. If it were at all responsible, the government would have no alternative but to increase taxes should the 105 be put into production. Adding it to

the present overall rate of deficit would mean the wrecking
of Canada's credit and the stimulation of inflation.[22]

It is not clear from the Cabinet Defence Committee notes of this meeting who actually made the comment above. It must be kept in context: the cost of the Arrow's production would be on top of the cost for Bomarc/ SAGE, additional radar installations, and research against the ICBM. The defence minister noted in his brief to the Americans that all this equipment coming now would add 25 to 30 percent to Canada's defence budget.

For all its concern, Cabinet deferred taking any decision. It has been said the Conservative government was simply waiting for a majority government before deciding to cancel the Arrow because of its cost, and yet if the number and depth of recorded deliberations on the subject is any indication, this could not be further from the truth.

On September 3, 1958, the Arrow subject was again addressed by Cabinet. The idea that the Arrow would be obsolete was again raised. It was noted that the Conservative Party had always maintained Canada should meet its needs by developing its own equipment, and so to cancel the Arrow, even though it was expensive and might be obsolete, would be difficult to explain. As for the Chiefs of Staff, it was stated that each service had its own reason for keeping or abandoning the program, but the chairman was of the view that Bomarc would represent the best defence for the money available against the changing threat.

Regarding this latter point, the minister of national defence tabled new figures obtained from Avro. They showed how the cost per aircraft would decrease markedly through installation of the Hughes/Falcon fire control and weapon system instead of the Astra/Sparrow system then in development. His only comment about the decrease was that the figures should be treated with reserve.

The minister of finance did not address cost or an economic breakdown or a recession at this meeting. He addressed representations made by Avro that upwards of twenty-five thousand people could lose their jobs and move to other countries, that Avro was primarily owned by Canadians, and that the RCAF had made a mistake in opting for the Astra/Sparrow combination instead of going with the Hughes/Falcon weapons system. His retort to Avro was that if the American weapons system was good enough, why wasn't a complete American aircraft? The ignorance behind the question is astonishing. The Arrow program had been established by the RCAF, not Avro, in response to the undeniable fact at the time that no other aircraft was then available that met or exceeded the Arrow's specifications. The minister's question, if asked at all, should have been directed to the RCAF.

What exactly, though, was the perspective of the minister of finance? If the Arrow was going to cause an increase in taxes, stimulate inflation, or destroy Canada's credit rating, as had been previously suggested in Cabinet, surely it would be a simple matter of economics to shut down the program immediately.

At the September 7, 1958, meeting of the Cabinet, the minister of finance, Donald Fleming, finally had his say:

> The prime minister opened the further discussion of the proposal of the minister of national defence to cancel the CF-105 programme. The serious problem still requiring consideration was the effect on employment and the general economic situation. *The minister of finance said that in considering matters of defence he naturally put the safety of the country ahead of finance. When it had been recommended a year ago that the CF-105 be continued, he supported the recommendation. Now, however, the military view was that the programme should be cancelled. In these circumstances, he did not see how the government could decide not to discontinue it.* The arguments for continuing were that Canadian military requirements should be found in Canada, that cancelling the programme would throw upwards of 25,000 men out of work with serious effects on the economy, and that national prestige should be taken into account. But in this case the cost per aircraft was twice as much as the cost of a comparable unit which could be obtained in the U.S., and *more important, the military authorities had now decided that the aircraft was not necessary* ... in cancelling now it could be said that the government

had considered all aspects of a project started by the previous administration and had come to the conclusion that the best course was to abandon it. Finally one had to keep in mind that by going ahead, and thereby adding approximately $400 million a year for four years to the defence appropriation, air defence would assume a disproportionate share in the defence budget. This was nearly the value of a year's wheat crop. A good deal of northern development could be undertaken for much less. In short, cancelling the programme would be of much greater help to the economy than continuing it.[23] (emphasis added)

These comments from the finance minister are most telling. Noticeably absent is any mention of increasing taxes, stimulating inflation, or destroying the credit rating of Canada, as had been suggested at the meeting in August. Strange how what seemed so important at that meeting was missing in the comments of the minister of finance less than a month later.

He did raise the issue of the $400 million, but states only that air defence would have a disproportionate share of the budget, not that the program was unaffordable. His comments that the amount would be similar to the value of a year's wheat crop and such are simply indicators of what else could be done with such an expense and is no different from what else could be done with any defence spending. And as for spending $400 million a year for four more years, it will be seen this number would reduce significantly in the ensuing months.

Of crucial import at this stage, though, is the finance minister's opening comment that he put security ahead of finance and that he had supported the program a year before. The fact is, a year previously, in 1957, the costs of the Arrow program, while they had increased somewhat, were not out of control. So, what of significance had changed?

The minister said he supported the program in the past but now the more important reason for cancelling was that the military did not find it necessary. This was the military view, not the financial view! The fact that he added the words "more important" in his statement above clearly indicates that the issue was not financial in nature but military, and the military view was focused on Bomarcs and anti-missile development, not aircraft. Yes, the Arrow was costing more than buying American aircraft, as the latter had already been developed. But, according to the RCAF, American aircraft were not comparable in capability and now there was an overall shift in importance toward missile defence.

What follows next in the discussion at this same meeting is also very telling. After the finance minister's address, the discussion continued with the following observations:

> In the forthcoming winter, unemployment would be higher than it was last year. Cancelling now, apart from the effect on the employees concerned, *might well be the one psychological factor which would result in a break in the economy* and lead to a drastic down-turn from which recovery would be extremely difficult. The programme should be allowed to continue over the winter and a decision taken then as to its future ... *while cancellation might be sound in theory, it might result in a recession.*[24] (emphasis added)

It was felt that a break in the economy and a drastic downturn could result from the cancellation of the Arrow, not because of financial factors but because of psychological ones. A recession might also ensue from cancellation, not from the spending of $400 million. This is quite the opposite of the comments made in August. Some have argued that a recession was already underway in Canada and that continuing the Arrow would exacerbate it, but that was not the stated view of the minister of finance at the September meeting.

In terms of the health of the Canadian economy, a NATO cosmic-top-secret memo dated December 6, 1958, made the following observations:

> Defence expenditures, as a percentage of the gross national product, dropped from a peak of 9% in 1953 to 6% in 1957. Allowing for price increases, the national product rose by about 13% while the real value of defence

expenditures declined by about 20% from 1953 to 1957. The Canadian economy appears able to carry the current defence effort without undue strain. There are indications that a resumption of economic expansion has just begun, following a period of moderate recession, but manufacturing capacity remains under-utilized. Prices generally have ceased to rise, and there is no shortage of skilled or unskilled manpower. With extensive natural resources and relatively high living standards, a rise in the level of defence expenditures throughout the period in order to meet military requirements ... is well within the capacity of the economy.[25]

The memo acknowledges a mild recession had occurred but the economy was seemingly back on the upswing. On the whole, the memo notes that it was expected the economy could handle upcoming military expenditures. It did, though, add the qualification that detailed spending forecasts were not available and the decision concerning the Canadian contribution to defence in North America had yet to be taken. Still, these observations from NATO would have been made on the basis of information supplied if not actually written by members of the Canadian delegation, who would have known of the financial situation and ongoing issues with the Canadian defence program.

If finances were truly the issue, why then did the minister of national defence order the acquisition of the Hughes/Falcon missile system for installation in the Arrow? Surely work could have continued on other aspects of the program until a decision to cancel was made. Oddly, this was not the case. On November 5, he had written to the minister of the Department of Defence Production (DDP), to put in place contracts for Avro to begin re-engineering the aircraft for acceptance of the Hughes/Falcon fire control and missile system:

There are sufficient funds in the 1958–59 Department of National Defence appropriation to cover these requirements [re-engineer and acquire the two systems with spares and test equipment]. Would you, therefore, arrange the necessary contractual coverage to permit this work to proceed at an early date. It is intended to proceed immediately to re-engineer and prototype the new system into one Arrow aircraft and simultaneously design and fabricate the armament pack for the Falcon and Genie missiles.... I have attached Contract Demand 462043, Amendment number 10, for the re-engineering and prototyping phase and Contract Demand 862021 for the procurement of two Hughes electronic systems, support spares and test equipment...[26]

In reply, on November 12, Raymond O'Hurley, minister of defence production, stated:

Avro Aircraft Limited has been advised to commence work in accordance with contract Demand 462043, Amendment Number 10. In addition, Treasury Board will be requested to authorize placement of a contract with the United States government for the supply of two MA-1 electronics systems, spares and test equipment as described in your Contract Demand 862021.[27]

So, according to the minister, there were enough funds to cover this extra expense, which also means there must have been enough funds to complete whatever would be required to the end of the fiscal year, which was March 1959. Additional appropriations would have been required in subsequent years to complete the development and procure aircraft in quantity. One can also surmise from the foregoing that from the company's perspective, since contracts for further work were still forthcoming, that cancellation of the program for now was not an issue.

Suddenly, though, everything changed. It was noted by Cabinet that the Americans were now prepared to consider cost-sharing for the Bomarc, and, therefore, on economic and military grounds, the decision to cancel would be seen as "good housekeeping" by the Canadian public and there was still the option to purchase American F-106 aircraft. With a prospect for cost-sharing in the Bomarc program increasingly likely, the fate of the Arrow was most definitely sealed. Still, the decision was again deferred. No one questioned the need or true relevancy of Bomarc, though.

It is clear that, based on the historical record, the overriding theme in determining the fate of the Arrow was the changing threat and how best to spend any money to deal with that threat, especially in light of NORAD requirements for missiles, SAGE, and additional radar. Yet these requirements were never questioned. Instead, what was a successful program to that point, the Arrow, was destroyed.

At the time, *Aviation Week* of March 2, 1959, reported the following:

> [The] government's position was that the Arrow decision had been made *primarily on military grounds* but that Canada also was seeking the *best defense bargain* it could find when it decided to rely almost exclusively upon the Boeing Bomarc interceptor missile for aerial defense. Prime Minister John Diefenbaker said: "I say with all of the seriousness that I can put at my command that the production of obsolete weapons as a make-work program is an unjustifiable expense of public funds." … Prime Minister Diefenbaker told the House of Commons that the primary reason behind the government's action was the belief that "events had overtaken the Arrow" and that it was now obsolete. He conceded that development of the aircraft was a significant technical achievement but offered no hope that the government could utilize the facilities of the Avro and Orenda companies in the immediate future.[28] (emphasis added)

The statement by the prime minister is consistent with the deliberations of the Cabinet Defence Committee (CDC) but is startling, especially in view of the fact that by acquisition of the Bomarc Canada was supporting a make-work program in the United States, propping up Boeing, the designer and manufacturer of Bomarc. The same article goes on to say that that A.V. Roe had put forward six proposals for continued work at Avro and Orenda, with no response from the government, whereas the latter had stated that no serious proposals had been forthcoming. Pearson also commented on the lack of response from the government on the proposals put forward by Avro, in his notes on the subject.

The Arrow came to be seen as problematic, not because of out-of-control costs, as has been alleged over the years since its cancellation, but rather, as is very clear from these statements, because it was considered obsolete as a weapon system, overtaken by events. There was no mention of breaking the economy, recession, and the like. There is mention, though, that the government was looking for a bargain, or "best bang for the buck." There was no mention that the Arrow was inherently unaffordable.

On the entire subject there is also the perspective from the American side about what the Canadian government was thinking. The following note from the Eisenhower Library, dated March 3, 1959, points this out:

> The present strong interest of Canada in production sharing is the result of the decision made by the Canadian government in September [1958] to curtail drastically the CF 105 supersonic interceptor aircraft program, and to introduce into the Canadian air defense system the U.S. produced BOMARC missile and SAGE control equipment. *This decision recognized the rapid strides being made in missiles by both the U.S. and Russia and the high cost of the CF 105 in relation to its potential contribution to North American defense ...*[29] (emphasis added)

The last sentence explains the issue: the cost of the Arrow was considered high, considering what it was believed it would contribute to the defence of North America, which, in the view of the Canadian military, was now very little. This small comment on cost is actually quite important. If it were not for the perceived changing of the threat, Arrow production would have continued, as Pearkes noted in Parliament back in January 1958.

Given that the threat was perceived to have changed, the question must be asked: Why should the government spend anything on an aircraft? The answer is easy: It shouldn't. The problem was, the threat had not changed.

That it had was simply the Canadian perception, one based on intelligence from the United States, most likely the CIA intelligence estimates on Soviet missile capability.

In his article "Is the RCAF Obsolete," featuring the famous photos of the destruction of the Arrows, Frank Lowe, associate editor of *Weekend Magazine*, noted regarding the cancellation, "Pearkes told me that the decision was non-political, merely something *based on U.S. intelligence reports ...*"[30] (emphasis added)

———————

The Arrow discussion carried on well after cancellation. In notes prepared in the United States for President Eisenhower, for his upcoming meeting on June 3, 1960, the following is stated:

> Prime Minister Diefenbaker would be interested in learning what the ultimate decision of the United States may be regarding the BOMARC B missile program. In Canada the BOMARC problem originated from a decision in February 1959 not to go into production of the CF-105, a supersonic jet interceptor designed and developed in Canada at a cost of over $400 million. *In lieu of the CF-105 Canada announced a decision developed by the military establishments of the two countries whereby the USAF would underwrite about two-thirds of the costs of an improved continental air defence system in Canada, which would include 2 BOMARC squadrons, 1 Sage fire control center, and improved radar....* On April 29, the House Appropriations Committee eliminated funding for BOMARC production and the House approved that action on May 6.... Downgrading of BOMARC has become a domestic political football in Canada. *The Opposition claims that a weapon is being retained in Canada which the United States is abandoning and that decisions on defense matters involving Canada are being made in*

Washington without sufficient consultation ... the prime minister is likely to be interested in (1) our assessment of the duration of the manned-bomber threat ... *on April 1 his Defence Minister indicated privately to Defense Secretary Gates that Canada would probably abandon interceptors unless the United States regards their retention as really important* and that Canada was strongly inclined further to reduce defense expenditures ...[31] (emphasis added)

In this document, it is clear that the decisions of the Canadian government and military regarding the fate of the Arrow were based on intelligence from the United States regarding the nature of the threat, and promised implementation of Bomarc, for which the United States had agreed to pay about two-thirds of the cost.

Further supporting the contention that termination was based on the changing military threat and not affordability of the Arrow are the "Top Secret minutes of the Canada–United States Ministerial Committee on Joint Defence," which met in Montebello, July 12 and 13, 1960, just after the meeting between Diefenbaker and Eisenhower. The following is noted on the Arrow termination:

Mr. Green [Howard Green, Canadian secretary of state for external affairs] stated they [the Canadians] *were told two years ago that the manned bomber was on its way out and that is why they cancelled the Arrow.* Now they have to go back and say that both are still needed. Mr. Fleming [Donald M. Fleming, Canadian minister of finance] referred to the fact that they tried to interest the Americans in buying the Arrow at the Paris Conference but had been turned down flat by Mr. McElroy. *Mr. Pearkes said we did not cancel the CF 105 because there was no bomber threat but because there was a lesser threat and we got the Bomarc in lieu of more airplanes to look after this. Now he said perhaps the expectation of two years ago that the bomber threat was lessening has not been fulfilled.* At the same time he said we expected Bomarcs to cover the whole country. These had been reduced, and therefore some more protection to the western part must be made in those areas which were to be protected by Bomarc. It wasn't fair, he said, for Canada to fill this western gap which had been created by the Americans all by themselves.[32] (emphasis added)

In the above exchange it is clear the Arrow was cancelled on the basis of incorrect intelligence data received from the United States and not on the basis of cost per se.

The missile gap had been promoted in hopes of accelerating missile developments in the United States and in the mistaken belief the Soviets were leading in this area. It would not be the first time nor the last that intelligence data would be used to further an American cause, as those familiar with the war on Iraq and Saddam Hussein in March 2003 will attest. The latter, it was assured, was in possession of or was about to obtain weapons of mass destruction. This proved not to be true, of course, and the negative impact of the decision to attack Iraq is still being felt today.

For those who believe the decision to cancel was the correct one and the decision to go with Bomarc was also correct, here was the minister of national defence, George Pearkes, admitting that the expectations that the bomber threat was diminishing were incorrect and noting that installations of Bomarc bases were being curtailed. All in all, Pearkes's comments appear to be an admission of a massive error in judgment.

It could be argued, of course, that the scaling back of the Bomarc program was something that Pearkes should not be held accountable for. Still, the decision to commit to the program while it was still under test was not a prudent one, especially since with the Arrow Canada had an alternative that was much further along in the development process.

The decision to scale back the Bomarc program was made for a number of reasons, not the least of which was the realization that the whole Bomarc concept was flawed. As noted in *Requiem*, the bases themselves were huge targets for enemy aircraft, given that they were fixed, above-ground installations.

With the scaling back of the Bomarc program, Pearkes realized that there was no defence for Canada in the West. This is odd, since in 1967 he confided to his biographer that he did have an alternative plan for the defence of Canada. The details were first made known in *Requiem* and are in part reiterated here as they are germane to the discussion.

> Pearkes: I took chances. We were defenceless against the high-power bomber where we had the old CF-100. It couldn't compete with the modern Russian bombers. We had no supersonic fighter but the Americans emphasized the fact that they had lots of them. Now ... one thing I had to face was, if you scrap the Arrow you've got nothing. What will you do? Will you buy American aircraft to fill this gap? ... Or, say, here, you can rely on American aircraft, not having bought them, but putting your pride in your pocket and saying, here, we will give facilities [to] American fighter squadrons to come and be stationed in Canada, so that they can get the advantage there, or, if not actually stationed in there, when the situation deteriorates they can move forward and operate from Canadian airfields.... And I had the assurance that the Americans at this time had lots of fighters. That was when I was talking to [the] Undersecretary of Defense. I flew out from Washington to Colorado Springs the first time I went to see NORAD. On that aircraft he told me, "We have got lots of fighters." [Pearkes pounds the table with each word, for emphasis] We were sitting together like this talking. He said to me, and we can't quote this [his voice goes soft here], "If I was you I wouldn't put all that money into that aircraft. If you don't want to buy aircraft from us you may rest assured that we have got lots of them [emphasis in voice here] which we can use to help in the defence of the North American continent if a crisis comes." *That's what convinced me more than anything else.* So I said, let us make full arrangements for these American fighter squadrons to come in, to practice from our airfields. Let them store equipment and aircraft if they want

to, at places such as Cold Lake and various other points all across Canada, and they came there and then carried out training exercises, moving a squadron up at short notice to one of these airfields. Now, that was how I filled in this defenceless gap during those times. He [name of another author that is not clear on the tapes] doesn't bring that out and I don't know how he would have known about that ...[33] (emphasis added)

The arrangement of which Pearkes speaks was not known to anyone else at the time, as it was obviously not well advertised. By allowing American fighters to handle the defence of Canada, Pearkes was able to close the protection gap between the cancellation of the Arrow and installation of Bomarcs. He put Canadian pride in his pocket and made his decision to cancel the Arrow and allow U.S. fighters into the country to train and to handle the interim air defence posture for Canada.

If he had known of the musings from General Putt earlier about the USAF wanting to purchase Arrows and then give them back to Canada, would he have gone for that deal? It would have been better than being completely under the American wing. But the same thing was stated earlier by Air Commodore W.W. Bean, when he remarked that parts of Canada would be left undefended by the introduction of Bomarc and so would in fact need to be defended by adjacent American interceptors.

It is not known why Pearkes didn't want his biographer to quote the part in which he described being told by the U.S. undersecretary of defence not to put so much money into the aircraft since the United States had lots of them. What was he afraid of? It's impossible to believe that that statement could be more damaging than his admission that he put Canadian pride in his pocket and made the deal with the United States in the first place.

In the end, a deal was struck, but it seems that the promises made quickly evaporated. Looking back with hindsight, some questions come to mind: Where were those adjacent American interceptors that were to handle the undefended parts of Canada? And had the United States reneged on the deal once the Arrow was fully out of the picture and the only thing left was to purchase American aircraft after all? Pearkes was not asked these questions.

The issue of U.S. missile capability was, however, broached in Cabinet. Records of July 15, 1960, note that

> *The U.S. were now re-emphasizing the bomber* because in their own experience missiles had not developed to the extent expected and presumably the U.S.S.R was running into similar problems in its missile programme. In fact it was said in Montebello that only 5 U.S. I.C.B.M.s were operational. This was *quite a different figure from that which the prime minister had been given in Washington in June.*[34] (emphasis added)

Until that point, the received wisdom was that the bomber threat was diminishing, missiles were just beyond the horizon, and a missile gap had been created; and yet, a scant four to five months after termination of the Arrow, the situation was completely reversed. If nothing else, this scenario illustrates the extreme importance in getting intelligence estimates as right as can be, and in trying to obtain information from more than one source. It is clear the prime minister himself had been given poor information, and it seems bizarre that the United States did not know how many operational ICBMs they themselves had. If that was the case, how could they know what the Soviets had?

At this same meeting, a question was raised regarding whether the defence of North America was to be assumed by the United States in the absence of Canadian interceptors. This was the exact scenario that the minister of national defence had in mind. However, he failed to raise it at this meeting.

What was noted at the meeting was that the CF-100 was gradually being retired because of its age, and that by 1962 there would be none left in service. According to the Cabinet notes:

> The CF-100 was incapable of policing Canadian skies against intrusions from aircraft similar to the U-2. The F101B would fulfil this policing role.... Without them there would be no Canadian surveillance of Canadian air

space … it was made clear that acquiring F101Bs would require a great deal of explanation in Canada. This would be most difficult if not impossible to do successfully.[35]

Policing the skies against intruders like the U-2 was exactly what the Arrow was designed to do, given its speed and altitude capability.

As noted by Group Captain E.H. Evans, in a memo dated December 4, 1958, in wartime, over and above defending against bombers, the Arrow would also be able to target reconnaissance aircraft. In peacetime, the Arrow would expose any violations of airspace and take the necessary countermeasures. In addition, the interceptor would bring to bear human judgment regarding countermeasures. Implied in the latter statement is the recognition that, since aircraft are piloted by humans, human judgment could be used to protect against accidently downing an aircraft that had, for example, merely strayed off course. This was not a role that could be fulfilled by a missile that, once launched, could not be called back if a mistake had been made.

Minister Pearkes appears to have had no interest in any of this, of course. Indeed, he revealed his feelings about aircraft, telling the Americans, as noted above, that he would abandon aircraft in defence entirely, unless the United States felt their retention was important.

But what did his chief of the air staff think about the need for manned aircraft? In the records of the Cabinet Defence Committee meeting of February 5, 1959, just prior to cancellation, the following note appears: "In reply to a question whether interceptors would be needed, as well as Bomarc, the chief of the air staff said it was his opinion that they would be. He was thinking in terms of 100 to 115 aircraft, which would provide the necessary fighters for back up. Where they would be obtained was the big question, if the development of the Arrow were discontinued."[36]

And, would any aircraft do? In discussing the role of the interceptor, Group Captain Evans noted the following: "An alternative supersonic two-place all-weather interceptor that generally meets the operational requirement [is] defined in OCH 1/1-63. This aircraft would have to be equal to or superior to the Arrow Weapons System."[37]

So, while Campbell maintained aircraft were necessary, there were no other aircraft equal to or superior to the Arrow at that time. The opinion of

Hugh Campbell, chief of the air staff, was completely ignored. But, Pearkes had been willing to listen to the Americans on the need for missiles and forego aircraft altogether until, of course, the American perspective changed.

Almost a full year after the cancellation of the Arrow, on February 6, 1960, Diefenbaker spoke to Cabinet. The official notes for the meeting are extremely interesting:

> The prime minister said that a committee of the ministers who were members of the Cabinet Defence Committee plus Messrs. Churchill, Harkness, Nowlan, and Maclean should meet to consider the proposal [to obtain F-101Bs] and make recommendations. If the committee reported that security demanded the acquisition of these aircraft, then that would have to be the decision. To purchase them, however, would cause great difficulties. It would place him and the minister of national defence in impossible positions. On the other hand, failure to re-equip would be bad for the moral[e] of the R.C.A.F. He thought the public had been convinced of the wisdom of the government's decision to cancel the Arrow. To obtain other aircraft now in the face of statements that the threat of the manned bomber was diminishing and that the day of the interceptor would soon be over would be most embarrassing unless a reasonable explanation could be given.... *He had been against cancelling the Arrow but had been persuaded otherwise....* During the brief discussion it was said that, even though a logical, reasoned case might be made for obtaining the F101B's, such a decision could not be explained to the public. The repercussions of telling CINCNORAD that Canada was not prepared to re-equip the CF-100 squadrons would not be too great.[38] (emphasis added)

In this statement, it is readily apparent that cost of the Arrow was not the driving factor in the cancellation. If it were, it would have been only too easy for the prime minister to release some figures along with the statements from 1958 that continuing would have caused a potential increase in taxes, a recession, and a hit to Canada's credit rating. Canadians would likely have understood. But he knew this was not the case.

He actually says he was against cancelling the Arrow but had been persuaded otherwise. Why would he need persuasion if the cost of the Arrow was the driving factor behind cancellation? What form of persuasion got him to go along with termination — an incorrect estimate of Soviet and American ICBM capability?

He knew now that a grave mistake had been made, so much so that it would be impossible to explain to the public why Canada was now purchasing American aircraft even though they would presumably be less expensive than the Arrow. Instead, he and Cabinet were prepared to take a reprimand from the commander in chief of NORAD (CINCNORAD) for not re-equipping the air squadrons, rather than face the Canadian public on the issue.

In his memoir, *One Canada*, Diefenbaker acknowledges it was the military factors that pushed the final decision to cancel:

> There is no doubt that from a construction standpoint the Avro Arrow was an impressive aircraft, superior to any other known contemporary all-weather fighter — something all Canadians could be proud of as their product. The Orenda Iroquois engine boasted the highest thrust, the lowest specific weight, the greatest mass flow and the greatest growth potential of all known engines under development. I said at the time it was a tribute to the high standards of technological achievement and development of the Canadian aircraft industry.... *However, the issue was decided finally by the inability of the Chiefs of Staff to report any new military developments that would justify the Arrow's production....* Our decision to introduce the Bomarc did not work out well. To begin with *the Bomarc was very soon proven to be virtually obsolete, even before it was set up.* Further, no information was given us that the United States would abandon, or had abandoned, its plans

to manufacture a conventional warhead for the missile.... Had I had even an inkling of what was to come, there would have been no announcement, on 23 September 1958, of our decision to introduce the Bomarc, because no such decision would have been taken.[39] (emphasis added)

He believed the Arrow would be obsolete, having been overtaken by events; that it had become a make-work project as a result. He had been advised of the increasing missile capabilities of the Soviets, only to be told afterwards that the estimates had been incorrect. He recognized and praised the superiority of the Arrow, and finally admitted it was the Bomarc that was obsolete before its time. And he states that had he known the United States was not going to provide a conventional warhead for the Bomarc, he never would have accepted it. That he did not know this is somewhat surprising. Even leaving that aside, if he had not accepted Bomarc, would the Arrow then have had a chance? It would seem so, given that no other aircraft were suitable, according to the RCAF at the time.

In May of 1960, the minister of national defence reported on his proposal to discuss the acquisition of aircraft from the United States. The Cabinet Committee noted that CINCNORAD had recommended replacing the nine CF-100 squadrons with six supersonic squadrons equipped with nuclear weapons. The committee was unanimous in agreeing this was not the time for this. It was stated that Canada's defence in 1962 would be no different than if the Arrow had not been cancelled. Then the following is noted: "Interceptors in North America were primarily for the defence of the U.S. Strategic Air Command. Sixty-six aircraft [the number of Voodoos eventually procured] would be of very little defensive value to Canadian cities."[40]

The observation here is clear: the few aircraft to be purchased were primarily for the defence of the U.S. Strategic Air Command and had little value for the defence of Canada.

Recall that a similar statement had been made by Commodore Bean about the Bomarcs' being introduced to Canada for the protection of the U.S. deterrent force. Recall, too, that Group Captain Evans had gone to some length on the role of the interceptor. The Arrow was definitely for the defence of Canadian cities across the country, and had it not been for the

Bomarc, the numbers that would have been acquired would not have been reduced to the degree they were, making the overall cost per aircraft much less than what was being discussed at the time.

So, why suddenly would the Voodoo, in reduced numbers, now be good enough as a replacement for the Arrow, especially since the Chiefs of Staff Committee meeting of February 11, 1955, deemed the Voodoo unsuitable?

The answer lies in a secret letter from Minster of National Defence Douglas Harkness to his colleague Secretary of State for External Affairs Howard Green, dated December 19, 1961. He admits in the letter that the number of F-101s to be acquired was based on availability and that they were short of the operational requirement, which as we know had been for at least one hundred Arrows.

Harkness goes on to say the smaller numbers were justifiable only to a small extent, because of the decreased bomber threat. The real reason, he says, for the reduced numbers, "stems from the equipping of these various weapons [Bomarcs and the F-101B] with nuclear armament. Without such armament the combined strength of the United States and Canadian air defence forces would be woefully inadequate, resulting in an obvious serious gap in our deterrent posture."[41]

So, in reality, the F-101s, like the Bomarc, would be effective only with nuclear payloads, given their shortcomings and smaller numbers, not because they were less expensive and "just as good as" the Arrow.

In the same letter, he mentions that a nuclear warhead was indeed required, to totally destroy any nuclear weapons being carried by the enemy so they would not detonate on the ground if the aircraft crashed without being completely incinerated in flight. Going further, he minimizes the risk of nuclear fallout from nuclear explosions in the sky, but fails to acknowledge the devastation that might arise from the immediate blast and thermal effects.

As noted in *Requiem*, discussions were underway regarding having the Arrow carry nuclear armament in the form of the Genie missile, the same weapon carried by the Voodoo, but, at the time of cancellation, focus was on the Falcon. Still, nuclear capability for the Arrow was feasible.

It is clear that the reason for cancellation was not due to financial concerns per se but, rather, was due to the belief that no expense, let alone a high one, could be justified on a system expected to be obsolete almost before it was implemented. While the costs of the Arrow program were high, there was not an issue of affordability. It was simply stated by Pearkes that the combined effect of all the equipment required by NORAD for air defence would increase the Canadian defence budget by 25 to 30 percent. According to the NATO document cited earlier, however, the real value of defence expenditures had actually declined by about 20 percent from 1953 to 1957.

Little discussed was the cost of the Bomarc system that Canada, according to Pearkes, felt obliged to purchase as part of the NORAD agreement. It was noted that by sharing the costs of an American system (Bomarc) with the United States, the expense to Canada would be less than if it were to develop a comparable system of its own. The difficulty in this argument is that the lion's share of Bomarc development would remain in the United States, while Canadian contractors would be afforded minimal contracts in return.

Defence production sharing arrangements would be established, but the much-touted benefits of lessening the cost of equipment and opening the doors for reciprocal work did not materialize to the extent expected. While more Canadian dollars were going over the border, fewer American dollars were coming in. In addition, advanced technological development in Canada diminished in favour of building already designed piece parts. As noted in a Cabinet paper for the U.S. president, regarding production sharing:

> [T]he Canadians expressed dissatisfaction with progress to date, on the basis that the short term objective of filling the gap created by the CF 105 terminations has not and probably will not be fully satisfied. The Canadians have been hoping for a few large items which would satisfy national pride and be significant enough to prove to the public that production sharing will work.... It is generally agreed that production sharing must be made to work. This can only be done, however, if the Administration expresses the clear intention of getting results and is prepared to face up to the inevitable political repercussions.[42]

In fact, the production sharing arrangements did not live up to the expectations. As E.K. Shaw points out, in respect to Bomarc, for example, Canadian firms got to produce wing sections and the like, but nothing like the sophisticated electronic components and advanced technology commonplace in the Arrow development. In *Storms*, documents are produced that show the sharing arrangements did not benefit Canada. They also show that the United States believed that Canada did not have the expertise for more sophisticated work. This was true, of course, because some of that expertise was lost with the demise of the Arrow and the subsequent drain of talent out of Canada.

And what of the Bomarc missile, which Diefenbaker admitted was a mistake?

The Bomarc was a surface-to-air missile developed by Boeing as a weapon against incoming bombers. It required a nuclear warhead to be effective, as well as a sophisticated automatic ground control system, SAGE, to target its attack. The Bomarc was susceptible to various electronic countermeasures and its bases were open targets. It was an unproven system that suffered numerous failures in test trials. Still, the RCAF felt that the Bomarc could counter the manned-bomber threat through to 1967, according to the paper prepared by the Chiefs of Staff Committee on April 23, 1958.

An article published in the *Economist* on February 5, 1959, notes that the Canadian military was simply following the dictates of American defence policy regarding the Bomarc. It states:

> Canadian officers' recommendations to the government are invariably along the lines of USAF doctrine.... If Canada did not happen to lie along the northern border of the United States, no one — not even the air force chiefs — would suggest installing the complicated system of ground-to- air missiles (Bomarcs) and semi-automatic ground environment (built around U.S.-developed computers) which NORAD calls for. Even now many Canadians question how much useful defence Canadian cities will get from the planned system — or whether they need it.[43]

The author of this article was bang on. The RCAF was clearly taking the USAF lead on all matters of Canadian defence, including the requirement for Bomarc. In "Glued to the Ground: Sees RCAF Like Wingless Kiwi," an article published in the *Toronto Star* of November 11, 1958, retired Major General W.H.S. Macklin, former adjutant-general of the Canadian army, is quoted as saying, "The RCAF is preparing to give up air warfare and get right down to earth to fire untested, obsolescent U.S. antiaircraft missiles. It will soon wield no more air power than a flock of common barnyard hens."

In the United States, the matter of Bomarc was discussed at length in the House of Representatives as the American government pondered why Canada still wanted it. While the USAF maintained the Bomarc would be effective and was necessary, several members of the House expressed great doubts about this. Typical of some of the American comments are those from the meeting of March 24, 1960:

> The Committee would be willing to appropriate the full budget estimate and more if it had full confidence in the proposed BOMARC missile — if it had the assurance that the system would actually work.... Insofar as the moment is concerned, other than General White's statement that he has high hopes and reason for high hopes for the success of BOMARC, *there is no proof before this committee that BOMARC has ever proved that it will work* to any great degree ... so you scale back but keep enough on order to maintain appearance of defence and bail out Boeing....[44] (emphasis added)

What is ironic is that it was the Canadian orders for Bomarcs that helped bail out Boeing. Boeing is the same company that in 2017 attacked the Canadian company Bombardier, claiming the latter received unfair government subsidies, which allowed it to sell its commercial aircraft at less than cost in the U.S. market. Duties of 300 percent were levied against Bombardier as a result of the Boeing complaints. Luckily, these were overturned by the U.S. International Trade Commission in Washington. Perhaps Canada should have reminded Boeing of its own bailout back in the fifties.

In the end, Bomarc bases were not placed in the western part of the United States, which meant Canada had to augment protection there. Also, all Bomarc bases began being phased out by the USAF by 1964, not two years after the two Canadian bases had become operational. By 1972 the two Canadian Bomarc bases were closed out, too.

———————

In the final analysis, the Arrow was cancelled because the piloted-bomber threat was seen as diminishing in face of the new threat from missiles. The Bomarc, it was erroneously believed, could handle the diminishing bomber threat; further, it was claimed to be less expensive. As a result, the Arrow was deemed obsolete as a defensive weapon system and therefore useless, and it was decided that there was no justification for spending any more money on it at all. Absent from the decision though, was any notion that the cost of the Arrow alone, in the absence of these other factors, would have been a reason for termination.

4

What Did the Arrow Program Cost?

THERE IS NO DENYING costs were high and rising as the program progressed, but toward the end they were actually decreasing. What factors account for this? How much was spent and how much was lost because of the cancellation?

Over the years, per-aircraft costs cited have ranged from $3.5 million, to over $12 million, down to just over $7 million. The question is why? The answer lies in whether one is talking flyaway cost that is, the cost without development included, or total cost, with development included. Following is an examination of the costs involved and the reasons they increased and then decreased toward the end of the program.

———

In 1953, the RCAF asked Avro to develop a new, all-weather, supersonic interceptor. After examining Avro's proposal and wind tunnel tests had demonstrated the feasibility of the design, the federal government on December 2, 1953, awarded the company a contract for the production of two prototype airframes. The amount was for $26.925 million, spread to 1958, and it included $4 million for engines and fire control systems from either the United States or the United Kingdom. The order for two was based on what had been required to develop subsonic aircraft like the CF-100. It turned out, though, that a supersonic design would require more aircraft upfront, for test purposes, before going into production.

By 1955, there were indications that the Soviet Union had produced a long-range jet bomber capable of delivering nuclear weapons. This development would give rise to the alleged 'bomber gap.' According to the CIA's website, "A serious overestimation of Soviet heavy bomber production and a corollary overestimation of refueling tankers from 1955 through 1957 led to a public outcry over an alleged 'bomber gap' to Soviet advantage, imperiling U.S. superiority and security."[1] It was believed the Soviets had advanced in the number of bombers capable of an attack against North America.

The immediate impact on the Arrow program was acknowledgement that two prototype aircraft would not be enough to prove out the capability and move into production in time to defend against this threat. Therefore, in 1955, in order to accelerate development, the RCAF decided to increase the number of prototypes for testing to eleven aircraft, while at the same time placing an order for twenty-nine preproduction aircraft, giving a total of forty. This of course would require more funding, not because of runaway costs in the development, but because the number of aircraft required had increased.

There were also issues regarding which engines should be employed to power the aircraft. This, too, had an impact on costs, as each selection required modifications to the Arrow. Writes Jim Floyd:

> When the programme finally got under way, and the engines scheduled for the project fell by the wayside one by one, we had to re-design our fuselage three or four times, and while the aircraft had been designed from the outset with flexibility to make re-engineering as simple as possible, it appeared to us that every engine manufacturer had gone out of his way to make things different! Some engines had three-point mounts, some four, and pressure ratios differed, which meant an almost complete re-design of the air conditioning system, since this is dependent on the engine for its prime inputs.[2]

Much has been made of the fact that in addition to the airframe, Avro also took on development of the engine, and the argument is that this increase in development was too much.

Now, the initial engine selected by the RCAF to power the aircraft was the Rolls-Royce RB.106. This engine was in development in Britain. As time passed, it became clear this engine development was not going to succeed in time for use on the Arrow. As a result, a different engine was chosen, the American Curtiss-Wright J67. As Floyd points out, all the work that had been completed regarding the RB.106 had to be, effectively, discarded. This meant lost time in the overall program and therefore increasing costs.

The Curtiss-Wright J67 was also a paper product. It, too, ran into difficulty and did not materialize. This led to selection of the Pratt & Whitney J75 and another redesign. The RCAF finally decided that the J75 was underpowered, but, since it was a more proven design, J75s should power the first five aircraft, to ensure a measure of safety in testing the airframe in flight.

In February 1955, the RCAF finally decided production aircraft would use the Iroquois, an engine being developed by Orenda, on which the company had already spent $9 million. It was deemed to be in a more advanced stage of development and, unlike the others, was proving itself in static tests. This decision, however, meant more redesign yet again. If the initial decision had been to go with the Iroquois from the outset, redesign would have been minimal, the costs would not have increased to the same degree, and time for redesign would not have been lost. Perhaps, first flights might have occurred much earlier, as well.

On March 3, 1955, a sum of $191 million was approved for forty aircraft and an additional $70 million was approved for production of fourteen engines, along with production tooling. Total commitment became $261 million, to be spread into 1960. All costs were to be met from defence estimates that had been contemplated to cover the next several years.

Now, in 1954, the RCAF had examined potential weapon systems for use on the CF-100. The most effective was deemed to be the Sparrow 2 air-to-air guided missile then under development for the U.S. Navy. When approval was given to arm four CF-100 Mark VI squadrons with this weapon, it was also decided this would be the best missile for use with the Arrow.

A point of context is required here. Canada had under development an air-to-air missile, the Velvet Glove. The purpose of the Glove program was not so much to produce a missile for use on aircraft but rather to give Canadian scientists and engineers an opportunity to obtain insight into missile technology. If fully developed, the missile might be used on the subsonic CF-100 and Sabre aircraft, as it was being designed for subsonic use. While there had been mention of use on the supersonic Arrow, this was never really the intended purpose, and any attempt to use it with the Arrow would have involved considerably more research and development. The Glove program was eventually stopped, and the RCAF turned to the Sparrow for use on future versions of the CF-100 and the Arrow. More on the Glove will appear later.

Unfortunately, the U.S. Navy elected to abandon Sparrow 2, leaving the RCAF to continue its development alone. Also, by September of 1955, Avro reassessed program costs and noted that an additional $59 million would be required. This was due to increasing labour and raw material rates and additional engineering costs, which had not been foreseen, in relation to the Iroquois engine.

As a result, a special panel was convened to review the entire project. The panel consisted of the chief of the air staff, the deputy minister of national defence, the chairman of the Defence Research Board and the deputy minister of defence production. Representation also came from the Cabinet Secretariat, the departments of Finance and External Affairs, and a representative of the president of the National Research Council.

The panel concluded the design was technically feasible and superior to existing aircraft and that this was required in light of the Soviet threat. Three possibilities were identified: (a) improve the high-altitude capability of the CF-100 and provide it with air-to-air missiles while abandoning the Arrow; (b) improve the CF-100 as in (a) and replace the Arrow with the American F-102B; and (c) improve the CF-100, proceed with the Arrow, but introduce the Bomarc missile as soon as possible into the defence plan.

The cost of completing the Arrow was shown as approximately $300 million at a production cost of $2.6 million each. There was also a call for $308 million for CF-100 and Sparrow missile improvements as well as $210 million for the Bomarc and $128 million for bases. It was also noted that, while the F-102B was less expensive, the Arrow provided more defence for the dollar.

The study results were discussed at the 584th Chiefs of Staff Committee meeting of November 1, 1955. The RCAF recommended approval of nine additional fighter squadrons and more air bases, and approval in principle of twenty-six heavy radar and 123 gap-filler radar stations. It was further recommended to open negotiations with the United States on cost-sharing. The Cabinet Defence Committee was briefed November 17, 1955, and assistance from the United States was sought. The latter urged Canada to continue the Arrow development as there was nothing comparable in the American inventory.

The Cabinet Defence Committee was briefed again December 7, 1955. After additional analysis, it was decided to reduce the number of aircraft to eleven, to cost roughly $170.4 million spread over three fiscal years, to modify 137 CF-100s at a cost of $12.4 million spread over four fiscal years, and to procure the Sparrow for the CF-100, at an approximate cost of $65 million to be spread over five fiscal years. This, it was noted, would fit in the defence budget along with other economies to be made.

The Arrow program was also stretched out over an additional year, which, according to the same report, not only would set the program back by that long, but would also lead to some increase in costs because of overhead. Still, this was the option selected. The Chiefs of Staff had considered alternatives to the Arrow that were deemed less expensive, but after every analysis the program was allowed to go forward under the proviso of continued scrutiny.

In 1956, the RCAF finally decided on a fire control system for the Sparrow. A contract was given to RCA for development of what was called Astra. This selection, like that of the engine, also led to re-engineering as the Arrow design had started with the Hughes/Falcon system in mind. RCA had little experience in developing fire control systems and costs there would soon increase.

Two additional meetings of the Cabinet Defence Committee were held, on April 19 and June 13, 1956. Discussions centred on the number of fighter squadrons required. Air Defence planners called for eighteen squadrons and bases across Canada. The Chiefs of Staff argued for fifteen squadrons and bases, some of which would be Bomarc sites. It was also agreed to reduce the numbers of auxiliary fighter squadrons of the reserve force, which also meant a reduction in reserve aircraft from some 500–600 to 150–100. Reductions in numbers were also due to the increased capability of the Arrow and the introduction of Bomarc.

In what is believed to be the last meeting of the Chiefs of Staff in February 1957, while still under a Liberal government, the following was captured regarding cost escalations:

> The Chiefs of Staff reported to the Government that, while the technical development of the aircraft was continuing satisfactorily, the programme had been slipping in time and increasing in cost.... Increased costs were due to the following:
>
> a. The integrated electronic system [Astra] has required more electrical power and more cooling than planned, involving considerable redesign of aircraft details. Some costs of the development of the electronic system were originally to have been borne by USAF contracts, but these have been altered recently by the USAF, thereby throwing increased cost on the RCAF.
> b. Adjustments to design of the aircraft for these two engines [J75 and Iroquois] has consumed more time and cost than estimated.
> c. Progress on the PS 13 engine [Iroquois] development has been so satisfactory that it will shift into a phase of higher expenditure sooner than expected.
> d. The CF-100 Aircraft production rate has been stretched out at the factory, which throws more overhead on the CF 105.
> e. Substantial increases have occurred in wage rates and costs of materials.... On 7 February 1957 the Government approved the continuation of the development programme, limited to 8 aircraft, at a cost of $216 million.[3]

Costs were increasing for known and valid reasons. According to the meeting, an approximate $46 million was the stated amount. The breakout was $19.8 million for the airframe, $20.5 million for engines, and $6 million more for Astra.

The changes in engines coupled with the move to the Astra all contributed to increases in design costs. These increases were direct results of RCAF decisions that impacted the design, not of runaway costs from mismanagement by the company. Again, had the RCAF stuck with the Hughes/Falcon weapon system, the design changes and lost time that resulted would not have ensued.

The costs of materials and wage rates were also increasing. This was true of all programs being worked on. Of interest though is that work on the Iroquois was progressing better than expected and so was entering a phase of higher expenditure sooner. This was actually a good thing in terms of time and savings in the longer term, but gave the illusion of cost increases in the short term. So rising cost, at least in this instance, was related to efficient work.

In the face of the report from the Chiefs of Staff, on February 7, 1957, the 113th Cabinet Defence Committee meeting approved continuation of the program with the proviso of another review later in the fall. The number of initial aircraft to be produced, however, was reduced from eleven to eight for a cost of approximately $216 million. The expansion to fifteen bases with additional radar was also deferred as it did not appear that the United States was going to assist. The proposal finally agreed to would create an additional delay in the Arrow program. The program continued throughout the summer. But by the fall of 1957, the Liberal government had fallen and the Progressive Conservatives were in power.

On October 29, 1957, the new Progressive Conservative government under John Diefenbaker agreed that development of the Arrow would continue for another twelve months, with an order to purchase twenty-nine preproduction aircraft at a cost of $172 million for the fiscal year 1958–59, bringing the total number of aircraft to thirty-seven, including the previous eight. Cost was not to exceed $216 million, with the total cost of the program estimated at $646 million. The figure of $646 could now be arrived at because the RCAF had finally decided on all the systems required.

This continuation was a Progressive Conservative decision, since now it was the party in power, and recall that the new minister of finance, Donald Fleming, was in support.

Development of Astra, though, soon became problematic. The cost of the Astra was going to jump from a 1957 estimate of $72 million to $208 million by August 1958. If anything was out of control, it was this. As mentioned previously, the contractor, RCA, had no prior experience in developing fire control systems and so its initial predicted costs were inaccurate. This was not a fault of A.V. Roe, as they had nothing to do with this aspect of the program. Thankfully, Astra would eventually be terminated in September 1958 and succeeded by the Hughes/Falcon fire control and weapon combination. While this switch would eventually mean considerable cost reductions, it again required some additional re-work by Avro.

The implications of the continual changes resulting in delay and cost increases were not lost on the company. Commenting on them in 1958, Jim Floyd observed:

> The R.C.A.F. naturally wanted the best and latest integrat-ed electronic system and weapon in the aircraft and finally chose these, after a considerable portion of the aircraft had been designed around an earlier system. This is, of course, normal to some extent in our business. However, since this is the major military project in Canada and involves almost all aircraft and associated industries, the whole programme is in the "shop window" so to speak, and every setback becomes almost a national calamity. This can be quite embarrassing from an engineering point of view, especially superimposed upon the added pressures of attempting to meet what was probably the most advanced contemporary interceptor requirement.[4]

Originally, only the aircraft was to have been designed and built in Canada, with engines, fire control, and weapons purchased from foreign companies. As discussed previously, the scope widened to include engine development when outside engines either ran into development delays and difficulties or were simply deemed inferior to the Iroquois.

Development of both the fire control and weapons systems added time and cost again. The company would be blamed, and the engineering and design staff were made to appear incapable of managing the program or the designs effectively.

On August 19, 1958, the chairman of the Chiefs of Staff prepared a report summarizing the costs to date and the various meetings held in which they had been discussed and approved. The report noted that cost of the airframe had increased by $48 million. It was due to a complete re-analysis of all aspects of the program as the result of defined statements of work. The report noted this was now a realistic estimate with no further increases anticipated except for inflationary costs or costs if an aircraft crashed or a slip in the schedule occurred.

One other point of interest is noted in this report of the chairman of the Chiefs of Staff. It says:

> Avro has been assigned responsibility for coordinating the work of all contractors associated with the programme to avoid duplication and ensure that no work is overlooked in the areas where two or more contractor[s] responsibilities meet. The coordinating function required considerable engineering effort and is responsible for a good part of the increase in the estimate for development. Coordination of contractors' statements of work brought to light some phases of work which had not been clearly defined and although the increased costs are not great individually the overall estimate is affected.[5]

That Avro was finally put in charge as the prime contractor for coordination of all contracts was a good thing, since they would be responsible if anything went amiss and, as noted, they could ensure there was no duplication of effort. As well, proper and final statements of work could be written.

In the report's final "General Remarks," it is stated that, while the program had been subject to rising costs, they were due to increasing technical complexity, especially as the project evolved into a complete weapon system. It was further stated that it was not until October 1957 that better estimates could be made. This was because prior to this, decisions regarding subsystems and equipment for the aircraft, each with its own impacts on the design and final totals, were still being made; recall the changing decisions on engines, weapons, and the fire control system.

The remarks go on to say that Canada was not alone in realizing the costs of developing modern weapon systems, and that all countries were having difficulties in estimating costs because of the rapid rate of technological progress, complexity, and compressed time schedules. In addition:

a. The state of the art of designing and developing a supersonic interceptor has continually been refined. Every advantage had to be taken of new concepts of design. As new information became available, design changes had to be made.

b. New materials and techniques were introduced, i.e. titanium and area rule [area rule is the shaping of the fuselage for aerodynamic efficiency].

c. Each selection and subsequent design change in one sub-system invariably affected most of the other sub-systems. For example, the airframe was selected in 1953, the engine in 1954, the electronic system and the missile in 1956.

d. The biggest single change in concept was the ordering of 40 development and preproduction aircraft. This came about as a result of confidence in the "feasibility" of the programme. It of course considerably increases costs initially, but will save time and money in future, in quantity production.[6]

Absent was any mention that the program was unaffordable, that costs were completely out of control, that there was poor management on the part of Avro, or that the latter was taking advantage of its cost-plus contracts. That is because it was simply not the case.

At the 121st meeting of the Cabinet Defence Committee (CDC), on August 21, 1958, the program was reviewed again and several alternatives were considered, including other aircraft and Bomarc missiles. This was also the time when real concern about threats shifted from piloted bombers to missiles, as shall be seen.

The alternative aircraft being considered now was the U.S. F-106C (the Delta Dart), basically a modified F-102B (Delta Dagger). The committee was looking at one hundred of these, at a flyaway cost of $2.8 million exclusive of sales tax, or $5.59 million with weapons, support, and Arrow cancellation charges, but without sunk costs of the Arrow development factored in. This was matched against the Arrow's flyaway cost at the time estimated at $5 million per aircraft or $12.615 million with weapons, support, and cost of completion of development. In his memorandum to Cabinet dated August 22, 1958, wherein these costs were tabled, the minister of national defence noted that the cost to complete the development and preproduction would be $862 million, of which $476 million had been committed.[7]

Apart from cost, the key difference between the two planes was the fact that the F-106C was a single-engine aircraft, which did not satisfy the RCAF's requirements, according to the RCAF themselves. It was less expensive because it was being produced in quantity in the United States and the latter had already absorbed the costs of development. If Canada purchased this aircraft over the Arrow, however, the money spent would go to the United States and not remain in this country.

On this latter point, there was at least one article, among a growing negative press, that argued in favour of the Arrow. Noting that the cost of defence is high but must be kept within reason, *Canadian Aviation* made the following observations regarding cost:

> [T]here is good reason to doubt if cutting down on total appropriation (at a sacrifice in defense efficiency), and diverting a major portion of funds available to procure equipment from sources of supply outside the country, represents any real saving as far as national economy is concerned.... Of the total amount spent ... such as that being carried out on the CF-105, surveys show that

45 cents of every dollar goes in salaries to the prime contractor's working force; 35 cents goes for materials and
to sub-contractors for components and parts; and the
remaining 20 cents covers plant overheads, operating
expenses, profits and payments to shareholders, and corporation taxes. Of the amount which goes to subcontractors and for materials, an estimated 50 cents in the
dollar is paid out in further salaries. Of the over-all
amount spent, an estimated 25 percent finds its way back
to the federal treasury in taxes.[8]

The article made the point that money spent would remain in Canada
and not be lost to a foreign economy, and that if the project were cancelled,
the already sunk cost would have been an investment wasted. This was essentially similar to part of the RCAF argument in selecting the Iroquois as
a home-grown product, with the added bonus of having the company and
talent in-house and available for future programs. The article also surmised
that the best course of action would be to have both aircraft and Bomarcs,
regardless of the combined cost, but that this outcome would be unlikely.

The article recognized the continued need for aircraft and then made
this prophetic statement:

Going to the U.S. sources for our aircraft needs after
abandoning our own extremely advanced project would
be bitter crow, and something less than sound economy
… an arrangement under which the bulk of the spending
goes to sources of supply outside the country will be in-
finitely more costly to our over-all economic well-being.[9]

Yet, going outside the country is exactly what was done when the
Bomarc was acquired over the Arrow.

And what was the projected cost of possibly going to the United States?
The total expense for an F-106/Bomarc combination was given by the
Cabinet Defence Committee as $967.5 million (though the numbers in
the documents actually add up to $968.1 million), including $169 million

in cancellation charges, $145 million for the Arrow, and $15.1 million for the Sparrow program. The number does not appear to have included the $236.1 million sunk costs expended to March 1958, allocated as $221 million for the aircraft and $15.1 million for Sparrow. If included, this would bring the total for the F-106/Bomarc combination to $1.2 billion. This was before the deal for cost-sharing on the Bomarcs was made with the United States.

The Arrow/Bomarc alternative with the Sparrow missile, on the other hand, was estimated as $1,669.7 million plus $236.1 million in sunk costs, but without cost-sharing, while Bomarc/SAGE costs alone were pegged at $663.5 million, including cancellation charges for Arrow/Sparrow but without the $236.1 million in sunk costs.[10]

In his top-secret brief of July of 1958 to the Americans, Minister Pearkes noted:

> [T]he development of this aircraft to date has cost $250 million, and its development will be continued for the next two or three years, to cost about $530 million, making a total of $780 million. Our requirements for this aircraft will be relatively small, somewhere around 100, and therefore the individual cost of the aircraft will be about $5 million, plus the cost of development ... *we could perhaps make provision for it in our succeeding defence budgets*; but in order that aircraft of this type and the type to be used by the United States can operate in Canadian airspace we will be required to introduce a semi-automatic ground environment into Canada. The introduction of SAGE in Canada will cost in the neighbourhood of $107 million. Further improvements are required in the radar and other associated communications which will also bring greater expense within the next few years. NORAD has also recommended the introduction of the Bomarc missile into the Ottawa-North Bay area to supplement the manned interceptor, to round out the U.S. Bomarc chain, and to push the defences 250 miles further north. This development will be a further commitment of some $164 million.

> All these commitments coming at this particular time, between 1960 and 1963, will tend to increase our defence budget by as much as 25 to 30%.[11] (emphasis added)

Arrow costs had increased but the reasons were well known. By July 1958, as has been discussed above, even though the minister of national defence noted that the Arrow program could be continued, the need for Bomarc/SAGE, additional radar, and defence against ICBMs would add significantly to the budget. So, the issue for Pearkes was not the cost of the Arrow program alone but the added expenses of all the other requirements, which would increase the defence budget by some 25 to 30 percent. The real issue, though, was whether those extra requirements were indeed essential for Canada. Time would prove that the Bomarc certainly was not.

Perhaps sensing concern over rising costs, Pratt & Whitney Canada submitted a proposal in early September to provide an upgraded J75 engine, to be used in lieu of the Iroquois. The contention was that great savings in development could be had. The RCAF, though, still regarded even the modified J75 as inferior to the Iroquois.

Based on information from Pratt & Whitney, as well as Avro, the Department of Defence Production reviewed the proposal anyway and undertook a brief cost-differential analysis. They provided the results in a memo dated September 10, 1958.

The analysis showed that $31 million would be involved in termination costs of the Iroquois and another $37 million would be required in modifications yet again, to the Arrow airframe, along with a one-year delay in schedule. In the end, direct savings would amount only to $22 million. Needless to say, the proposal was rejected in favour of continuing with the Iroquois.

Writing on October 21, 1958, directly to the minister of national defence, Fred Smye, president of Avro Aircraft, provided a final price on the Arrow itself:

> [I]t is now estimated that we can produce and deliver 100 operational aircraft, complete in all respects including the Iroquois engine and the [Hughes] MA1 fire control system, for approximately $3,500,000 each.... In order to

substantiate the validity of this estimate, and on the basis that it would make a substantial contribution to the government's deliberations concerning the Arrow programme, it was stated that the Company would be prepared to enter into a fixed-price type of contract on the basis of $3,750,000. For a complete, operational aircraft, including the Iroquois engine and the MA1 fire control system, excluding only GFE [Government Furnished Equipment].[12]

By January 12, 1959, according to Chief of the Air Staff Hugh Campbell, with the cancellation of Astra/Sparrow and adoption of the Hughes/Falcon combination, the date of entry into squadron service of the Arrow was being advanced from a projected spring of 1961 to September 1960. As suggested earlier, had the program remained with the Iroquois and Hughes/Falcon from the outset, perhaps this savings in time of some seven months could have had the Arrow introduced much earlier than even the September 1960 time frame.

Campbell also stated costs were decreasing significantly and that the revised program would reduce the yearly spending rate from the original 1959–60 forecast of $385 million and a peak of $447 million to a 1959 forecast of $162 million and a peak of $245 million (not the $400 million discussed in Cabinet back in August and September 1958.) He cited the cost per aircraft, based on ninety-two aircraft with the cost of completing the program included, at $7.02 million. This was exclusive of sunk costs and at a flyaway price of $3.75 million per aircraft including taxes, versus the original $5 million per aircraft.[13]

The flyaway cost per aircraft had dropped from $5 million to $3.5 million or, as per Campbell's memo, to $3.75 million with taxes included. This was comparable to the less-sophisticated $2.8-million F-106.

On this issue of decreasing costs, an article in the British *Royal Airforce Flying Review* in Britain, prepared just prior to its publication in February 1959, noted the following:

[T]wo new factors are raising confidence in the Canadian aircraft industry that the government will reverse its

apparent plan to change over entirely to missiles for
Canada's air defence. The first of these factors is that of
cost. Revised cost estimates for the Arrow, in the light of
the replacement of the Astra electronic system and Sparrow
missiles by a Hughes fire control system and Falcon missiles … with other economies will result in a cost from this
point on of £1,392,800 per aircraft, against £3,428,800
per aircraft previously quoted on the basis of one hundred
machines. The second factor is that of performance.[14]

In Britain, costs of the Arrow program were acknowledged as decreasing and that this, together with the excellent performance of the existing
aircraft, described in the latter part of the article, would likely be enough
to allow the program to continue. These factors though were not enough
to save the program, though, because cost was not the immediate threat
to the Arrow.

So, what was the final cost? In *Requiem*, a document titled "Pre-
termination Activity" was revealed. Written after the fact as a result of au-
dits, this document showed the monies expended to termination and what
would have been required to complete the entire program including production. The figures vary somewhat from what the government initially
reported, because of more refined auditing.

It showed that by February 1959, five Mark I aircraft with J75 engines
and thirty-two Mark II aircraft with Iroquois engines had been ordered
from Avro. In addition, twenty prototype Iroquois engines and eighty-seven
preproduction engines were on order from Orenda Engines Ltd.

Up until February 20, 1959, $318.6 million had been spent on the
entire program, including engines and fire control. This money had paid
for development, including redesign, tooling, production, and support,
and had been spread roughly over a five-year time period, not as one huge
chunk in one year.

Of no less import but often forgotten, this $318.6 million had paid for
the salaries of the twenty-five thousand employees engaged in the program
and who in turn had paid taxes back into Canada and who had spent that
salary on goods and services in Canada, including housing.

The report notes that an additional $257.8 million would have been required to complete all of the development work while producing the thirty-seven aircraft ordered, bringing the total with $318.6 million in sunk costs to $576.4 million. This was significantly less than the figure of $862 million tabled by the minister on August 28, 1958. Also, this would have paid for the continued employment of the twenty-five thousand people affected the day the Arrow was cancelled.

Now, the figures are broken down further. The cost of completing the airframe to February 20, 1959, had been $67.7 million. The remaining cost to complete development was shown as $24.9 million, an amount that must have been already on hand, given that some $41 million was returned after cancellation. The total then from start to finish for the airframe was $92.6 million. This amount would have been significantly less had it not been for all the redesigns and resultant time delays.

On the engine side, the breakdown shows $55.4 million spent with an additional $53 million remaining for a total of $108 million. The engine had not been tested in the Arrow or in any aircraft save for the limited testing on the B-47, so much additional flight testing would be required to ensure reliability.

The bulk of the remaining $257.8 million expense lay in production and support at $136.5 million with an additional $43.4 million to finish the tooling and for the Hughes system installation and also with additional flight work with the J75 engines.

On December 2, 1953, the RCAF had commissioned Avro to build two prototype aircraft at a cost of $26.925 million. It is not clear if this also included the establishment of a production line and everything associated with that. It most certainly did not include the cost of redesigns, support, increases in material costs, and increases in labour rates.

After the two prototypes, additional aircraft were expected to cost some $2 million on the basis of producing nearly six hundred aircraft. At cancellation, the aircraft were going to cost $3.5 million, assuming that there would be an order for 120 aircraft. The next one hundred would have dropped in price to $2.6 million, according to Fred Smye, and further drops could have been expected after that. One would have thought that if costs had indeed spiraled out of control, the cost differential between the original $2 million and $3.5 million should have been appreciably greater. Weapons and support would have added to the cost, as they do with any aircraft purchased.

Now, records from 1960 show that the Department of National Defence actually returned $262 million to the government in unspent funds. One might assume this money came from the cancellation of the Avro Arrow. This was not the case. As Pearkes explained to the House, the Arrow cancellation accounted for about $41 million. That left another $221 million in unspent monies. This was not, as they say, "new" money, but the result of unspent appropriations from the previous year.

Some of the $221 million had resulted from savings in salaries within the department and some from other contracts that were to have been negotiated but for various reasons had not been. This is not unlike the situation even today. Money is allocated in the new fiscal year in March, but actual allowable expenditures may not be known until months later. Depending on the type and size of contract and how negotiations and internal processes are proceeding, there may not be enough time to actually get a contract in place and have goods delivered in time to spend the money by the end of the fiscal year.

Over and above these stated reasons, Navy projects created a large under-expenditure from what had been estimated at the time. Likewise, Army expenditures were lower than expected and, aside from the Arrow, the RCAF had a further $24 million in under-expenditures.

Of interest is the exchange that occurred in the House of Commons Special Committee on Defence Expenditures on May 3, 1960, and reported in *Requiem*. The expenditures for fiscal year 1958–59 were under review. The exchange took place between minister of national defence George Pearkes and Paul Hellyer, defence critic in the opposition shadow cabinet of Lester B. Pearson.

As noted above, Pearkes had just stated that in 1958–59, the Department of National Defence underspent its funding to the tune of $262 million.

> Mr. Hellyer: Mr. Chairman, I have two or three short general questions before we proceed … Mr. Minister, on March 31, 1959, were your army, navy and air force as well equipped as you would like to have seen them?

The Chairman: Before you answer that Mr. Minister, I would like to say that this is one of those all embracing questions that is going to start an argument —

Mr. Hellyer: Mr. Chairman, I think it is a fair question, and one he [the Minister of National Defence], can answer, because when he spent $262 million less than was authorized by parliament, we should know whether this was due to improper estimating or incompetent management. Something obviously is very wrong, and I think the minister should tell us whether he thought at that time he had the equipment necessary for his armed forces, or whether he did not....

Mr. Chambers: I think the member should have listened to the explanations given for the difference between the expenditures and the estimates.

Mr. Hellyer: I did — and I think these were made up by a public relations man, whose orders were to make it as dull and uninteresting as possible, and rationalize everything that has happened.[15]

So, on the one hand the Arrow program needed another $257.8 million to complete all of the development and production of thirty-seven aircraft. On the other, this record from 1960 shows that $262 million was returned by the Department of National Defence, to the government coffers. If there had been an appropriate mechanism in place perhaps this money could have been redirected to the Arrow program. It would not have involved any new appropriations and would certainly not have bankrupted the economy. Indeed twenty-five thousand people would have remained employed.

Had the program continued, the pre-termination report goes on to explain, eighty-three additional aircraft would have been purchased. These eighty-three aircraft were not going to cost $12 million each. They were not going to cost $8 million or $5 million. They were going to be sold by Avro on a fixed-price contract, not a cost-plus contract, for $3.5 million each. The report quotes $3.75 million. (It will be assumed this latter figure included sales tax, as per Campbell's memo noted earlier.)

Fred Smye has stated, in his own book on the subject, that if an additional one hundred aircraft had been produced, the price would have dropped to $2.6 million: $0.2 million less than the F-106 for a far superior aircraft. Would another country have purchased at that point? Belgium had, in the acquisition of the CF-100, so, one can only speculate.[16] And would there have been a need for more Arrows? Yes, if the Bomarc had not entered the picture, according to previous meetings and discussions.

In a memo dated March 28, 1958, the chief aeronautical engineer for the RCAF made a comparison of the costs of the Arrow with those of the USAF F-106, F-102, and F-101, in order to determine if these American aircraft were less expensive and whether there was justification in purchasing these instead of the Arrow:

> Previous attempts have been made to assemble, design and development costs for the USAF F106 in order that they might be compared with our Arrow programme. While the costs directly attributable to the various USAF orders for the F106 have been obtained it has been impossible to assemble true costs of the F106 design and development phase.... There are other major areas of this nature which preclude the desired comparison, the most important of which are the fact that U.S. contractors enjoy the use of certain government facilities without cost and that the J75 has several applications whereas the more advanced Iroquois is still in the development stage.... Arrow costs compare favourably with the somewhat less sophisticated aircraft in the United States. It has been interesting to learn that RCAF fly-away costs for the CF-100 from production were less than for the comparable F89 Scorpion. Similarly, quantity production of the F86 and T33 was undertaken in Canada at a lower per aircraft cost than from U.S. production. Quantity production of an aircraft as complex as the Arrow can be undertaken in Canada at a cost comparable to that for production of a like aircraft in the United States.[17]

Unfortunately, the chief aeronautical engineer did not have access to the development costs of the F-106 and noted that since the F-106 was a derivative of the F-102, some costs from that program should be included. Also, U.S. manufacturers were enjoying the use of test facilities at no cost, giving them an advantage in cost savings.

The F-102 had begun service in 1951. Because of numerous complications including issues of engine performance and initial prototype fuselage design, which had not been aerodynamically shaped in accordance with the area rule, a false criticism levelled against the Arrow, the program suffered numerous delays. By 1956, after many modifications and improvements, the aircraft was re-designated the F-106. As the redesigned F-106, it continued to run into numerous difficulties, not the least of which was engine performance. Delays in production because of the difficulties led to a reduction in the numbers ordered, from an initial thousand, down to 260. The Cook-Craige plan, which was supposed to help speed up production by going straight to pre-production by bypassing the hand-built prototype stage, to save time and money, and which was effective on the Arrow, was no help, because of these numerous problems in development. This meant a redesign of production tooling in addition to redesign of the aircraft.[18]

The F-101 Voodoo was ordered by the USAF as an interim replacement for the F-106 program, which was almost terminated because of all the difficulties. Some thirty-five F-106 aircraft were used for flight test development. This serves to illustrate how far the original two Arrow prototypes that had been ordered would have been from being enough to satisfy their test program, and why more Arrows were ordered. It also illustrates the complexity of developing supersonic aircraft.

As a side note, the production F-106 incorporated a notch in the wing, similar to that on the Arrow, which had been designed with this feature from the start. Deliveries of the F-106 finally began in 1959, five years after the initial target date. From that point forward modifications continued, eventually turning the F-106 into America's front-line interceptor well into the 1980s.[19]

This digression to the F-106 is here to indicate how, even though its flyaway cost was $2.8 million, given all the issues, redesigns, and cut backs on orders, the development costs of the F-106 were likely very high and, given the schedule delays, could have been on a par with or, more likely, greater than those of the Arrow development. As stated earlier, when the RCAF did their cost comparison, the Arrow costs compared favourably with those of other aircraft being developed at the time.

The F-106 discussion is also included here to illustrate the fact that Avro did know what they were doing in developing a more sophisticated aircraft, as they were solving their problems through ongoing, rigorous testing on the ground. Flight testing proved that this approach had reduced the problems still to be encountered, to minor ones.

At a flyaway of $3.5 million, or $3.75 million inclusive of sales tax, the more-advanced Arrow was a bargain. The final total cost of the Arrow program, including all development, as discussed in the pre-termination report, was going to be $1,111.2 million, including missiles and support. As noted, $257.8 million would have completed the development and bought thirty-seven aircraft, after which eighty-three more could have been purchased for $3.75 million each.

Support would add an additional $181 million and a stock of Falcon missiles would add $42.6 million. The bulk of the money spent would remain in Canada, along with the twenty-five thousand jobs and maintenance of the industry. The expenditure would be phased over several years.

The Bomarc/F-106 combination was going to cost $967.5 million according to the documents (but if one totals the line items in the document the addition actually comes to $968.1 million not $967.5 million) before cost-sharing and without the $318.6 million in sunk costs factored in. Adding the sunk costs would put the cost of the alternative combination at $1,286.1 million (or $1,286.7 million if adding to the $968.1 million), a cost more than the Arrow program. In this latter case, the money would have gone offshore.

Regarding the question of cost, Prime Minister John Diefenbaker states in his memoirs:

> It came before the Cabinet Defence Committee on 21 August and before Cabinet on 28 August. My colleagues and I took particular note of that part of the air defence review which read, "*Finally the cost of the CF 105 programme as a whole is now of such magnitude that the Chiefs of Staff*

feel that to meet the modest requirements of manned aircraft presently considered advisable, it would be more economical to secure a fully developed interceptor of comparable performance in the United Sates."[20] (emphasis added)

In this quotation, Diefenbaker does not say the Arrow was unaffordable. He does state, however, that the Chiefs of Staff had recommended that it would be more economical to secure another aircraft "of comparable performance," although, as noted by the RCAF, there were no aircraft of comparable performance. What is particularly remarkable about this reflection, however, is that the stated quote differs from what was in the memo to Cabinet.

The memo to Cabinet to which the prime minster presumably refers was discussed in the previous chapters but is restated here. The primary reason for considering alternatives was the changing threat from bombers to missiles. The second reason was the rapid advance in technology, most notably in ground-to-air missiles — Bomarc in particular. The third reason was the diminishing requirement for piloted interceptors, given the introduction of the Bomarc. This was also one of the reasons behind the reduction in numbers of Arrows. The last reason finally comes to the issue of cost and the quotation cited by the prime minister. The quote actually reads as follows:

As mentioned earlier, consideration has been given to reducing the requirement to five squadrons, requiring an overall number of 100 aircraft.... *The Chiefs of Staff have grave doubts as to whether a limited number of aircraft at this extremely high cost would provide defence returns commensurate with expenditures in view of the changing threat* and the possibility that an aircraft of comparable performance can be obtained from United States production at a much less cost in the same time period, 1961–1962.... *Therefore the Chiefs of Staff consider to meet this modest requirement for interceptor aircraft it would be more economical to procure a fully developed interceptor of comparable performance from United States sources.*[21] (emphasis added)

The reason for the discrepancy in the quotation from what is recorded in Diefenbaker's memoirs and what is actually written and available from the archives is not the issue here. The issue is the context. The Chiefs of Staff were discussing the cost of the Arrow in terms of whether or not the reduced numbers at high cost would justify the expense at all in terms of providing defence, in light of the changing threat and given that the Bomarc was going to take care of the diminished threat; not that the Arrow was unaffordable in and of itself.

In his memoirs Diefenbaker notes that the financial folks in the department calculated that the cost per aircraft would be on the order of $7.8 million, slightly more than the $7.02 million reported by the chief of the air staff, and this included missiles, support, and completed development, but exclusive of sunk costs. He then includes the following: "However, the issue was decided finally by the inability of the Chiefs of Staff to report any new military developments that would justify the Arrow's production."[22]

By inference, if the Chiefs of Staff and the minister of national defence had said they had it wrong and that the piloted-bomber threat was not diminishing, the Arrow would presumably have gone into production because there were no comparable aircraft, according to the RCAF.

For his part the prime minister does not mention the millions that were returned as unspent funds in March 1960 that would have paid for completion of the development. Given that $262 million was returned to the government, and at a fixed flyaway cost of $3.75 million and presumably less, without the burden of Bomarc the Arrow would have been produced and variants thereof might have been in use well into the sixties and possibly beyond, as was the case with the USAF F-106. It is certain the Iroquois engine would have found export sales as well, given pending orders from France that were cancelled when rumours arose that the entire program would be terminated.

From a post-termination report, the government spent approximately $29.4 million in termination charges to Avro and Orenda. This paid for existing inventory, severance pay, certain overhead for Avro, Orenda, and five subcontractors, as well as capital equipment for Avro, Orenda, and Lucas-Rotax. Termination costs for the Sparrow missile program were estimated at $3.6 million, after $17.5 million had already been expended on development. Some $15.1 million had been spent on the Astra development, with cancellation charges estimated at $28 million. It is not known if additional monies were paid out to the subcontractors that were allegedly on the verge of bankruptcy as a result of the cancellation.

In all, when one totals the known penalty charges and the $318.6 million spent, in terms of financials, Canada lost approximately $412.2 million and likely far more, which is similar to the loss of some $478 million in 1993, when the Liberal government under Jean Chrétien cancelled the replacement for the Sea King helicopter, the EH101.[23]

The purely financial loss related to the Arrow does not take into account the overall impact to Canada in terms of the economy, as well as the loss of the contributions of the brilliant and talented individuals who left for other countries and the high technology industry that was lost with them.

When the program was terminated, and some twenty-five thousand employees lost their jobs, some anger was directed at the company for releasing all those employees in a seeming act of vengeance or embarrassment to the government of the day. Prime Minister Diefenbaker criticized the company's actions, noting that "there was available millions of dollars until March 31 and that these dollars might have been used in order to alleviate the condition of these people who would be removed from their jobs in consequence of the cancellation of the CF-105 (p. 1306 of *Hansard*)."[24]

From government records, part of the reason for terminating the project in February rather than on March 31, was to recoup on the order of $50 million. So this money was not, in fact, available to the company as stated by Diefenbaker. As well, the decision taken in September of 1958 had been to conduct a review in March of 1959, not to cancel in February. More importantly, the wording of the notification received by the company at the time of cancellation was very clear: "You shall cease all work immediately."[25] In addition, all subcontracts were terminated as of the announcement. This left the company with no contract, no work, and therefore no choice. In the final analysis, only some $41 million was returned to the government coffers from the Arrow project.

As a separate issue and noted previously, an argument that has been put forward to account for the high cost of the Arrow was that the company had secured the much-sought-after cost-plus contracting approach. Cost-plus contracts mean that the company is paid for allowable expenses and receives a percentage profit margin on top of this. This puts all the risk on the government, and it is alleged that the company can artificially inflate and extend the work required in order to increase the amount of profit obtained. As shown above, this was not the reason for cost increases with the Arrow, though.

Cost-plus is still an issue today. In the first presidential debate in 2008 between Senator McCain and the future President Obama, Senator McCain stated:

> [W]e have to do away with cost-plus contracts. We now have defense systems that the costs are completely out of control. We tried to build a little ship called the Littoral Combat Ship that was supposed to cost $140 million, ended up costing $400 million, and we still haven't done it. So we need to have fixed-cost contracts.[26]

This being said, the following is offered for consideration. Cost-plus contracts remain in use. Why? This excerpt from the Center for Strategic and International Studies sheds some light:

> The government often has difficulty predicting the cost of large scale projects. Michael Sullivan, GAO's [General Accounting Office] director of acquisition and sourcing management, argues that contractors would simply not bid on high-risk endeavors, such as R&D [Research and Development] projects, if they were operated under fixed-priced contract structures.[27]

If there are problems with cost-plus they tend to lie with the governments, not the contractors. The article from the Center for Strategic Studies continues:

> [O]verruns often result from the government's failure to understand and define requirements adequately up-front. Moreover, requirements that are still changing can lead to

the expansion of cost-plus contracting beyond R&D into production.... Beyond requirements and cost realism, proper oversight and management and the application of reasonable incentive and award fee standards will contribute to controlling program costs.[28]

Given that A.V. Roe only came into existence in 1946, for the purpose of producing military aircraft that were to be state-of-the-art and cutting-edge, what, if anything other than a research and development effort followed by production, was this company all about? This fact was noted earlier by Bill Sweetman, when he said almost everything on the Arrow had to be invented. And so, cost-plus contracting was the logical choice.

Failure to adequately define requirements and program scope has been a constant source of difficulty in many large-scale defence projects and was a running theme in the case of the Arrow. As noted, the RCAF started with an airframe, then had to add the engine development when foreign engines failed to materialize, and then added the fire control and weapons system, with each having a major impact in terms of time and cost. None of these changes were due to bad management, or to abusing the cost-plus contracting approach, as far as can be determined.

Does this absolve Avro of any responsibility for the way the situation evolved? Perhaps not, but they are points that must be considered in the discussion. In fact, when one studies the Arrow one realizes almost immediately that government requirements as noted were fluctuating and there had been no realistic baseline at the outset, as this development was a complete first for Canada.

Military jet design was itself still somewhat in its infancy worldwide when the program began in 1953. Although there was complete general oversight, a dedicated project office in the RCAF was not established until years into the project, nor was Avro made the prime contractor until late in the program. All of these problem areas lay at the feet of the governments of the day, not in the fact that cost-plus was used as the instrument for contracting.

The solution to cost-plus, as many have argued and as McCain noted, would have been in the use of fixed-price contracts, wherein a given amount is not to be exceeded — and, if it is, the balance is carried by the contractor.

These contracts have their own risks, as noted above. Firstly, would there be any bidders? Then, how much more would a contractor have to add into the upfront cost estimate of the project to cover his increased risk? Then, once in place, how much more would be requested to accommodate late government-requested changes along the way?

As a side note, the "Report of the Auditor General to the House of Commons for the Fiscal Year Ended 31 March 1987" noted the following with respect to their analysis of Canadian National Defence projects:

> In our 1984 Report, we noted that projects managed by the department are often bound by fixed funding ceilings. But in many cases *they involve a high level of technological complexity and uncertainty because weapons systems are often still being designed and tested during the acquisition process.* In the case of the CF-18, we reported in 1984 that this resulted in the *identification of a large number of related highly desirable projects budgeted outside of the main project.* To help address this dilemma, we put forward three recommendations: uncertainties in the concept of operation should be minimized before a project begins; *alternatives to fixed ceiling funding should be considered for equipment that is still in the development stage*; and DND should ensure that all significant scope or cost changes are reported to Treasury Board.[29] (emphasis added)

And so the Office of the Auditor General, the federal government's watchdog on costing, recommended alternatives to fixed-ceiling or fixed-price, for projects still in development.

One interesting observation to the OAG's report is the technique used to get around the problem of fixed-ceiling or fixed-price; that of introducing projects budgeted outside of the main contract. In this scheme, the Iroquois engine development would have been a separate project. The end result would have been the same in terms of the overall cost of the end product, but perhaps would not have given the illusion of increasing costs in the airframe development.

Indeed, the Canadian military procurement landscape is littered with large-scale projects — whether fixed-price or not — that went off the rails in both time and money because of fluctuating requirements. The reader is referred to Kim Nossal's book *Charlie Foxtrot: Fixing Defence Procurement in Canada* for additional insight into this.[30]

In respect of the Arrow, twenty-five meetings were held between November 25, 1953, and July 15, 1958. These were a combination of Chiefs of Staff Committee meetings and Cabinet Defence Committee meetings. A number involved a detailed reappraisal of the Arrow program and discussion of the introduction of missiles into Canadian air defence. Costs of the Arrow were carefully assessed at these meetings, and each increase was tabled with reasons given. Decisions to cover the costs and continue or cancel were voted upon, and each time the program was given the go-ahead. At no time was the affordability of the program in question. What did begin being questioned by some was why so much was being spent on a system that was seemingly being overtaken by events and would therefore be considered obsolete shortly after becoming operational.

The Jetliner in California, after a flight with Howard Hughes. On the left is Don Rodgers, Avro chief test pilot, with Bill Wildfong, flight engineer, on the ladder, and Johnny Thorne, inspector, to the right.

The Aerospace Heritage Foundation of Canada

Souvenir from the Jetliner fiftieth anniversary reunion in Toronto. The photo is signed by the designers, pilots, and others who worked on it.

The Velvet Glove missile atop its quad booster in flight.

A one-eighth-scale test model of the Arrow ready for launch.

Avro Arrow assembly.

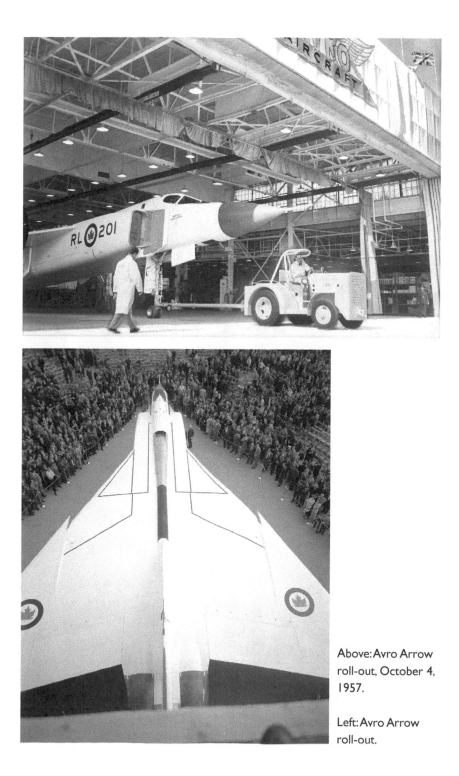

Above: Avro Arrow
roll-out, October 4,
1957.

Left: Avro Arrow
roll-out.

Avro Arrow roll-out.

Pilots hoping to fly the Arrow.

RCAF members inspecting the Arrow.

Arrow landing with drag chute deployed.

Congratulations for pilot Jan Zurakowski on a successful first flight, March 25, 1958. Front left are C. Fred Matthews, supervisor, experimental flight test engineering operations; Don Rogers, chief test pilot; Jan Zurakowski, chief experimental test pilot; Stan Brown, electrical engineer; and an unamed Arrow project office engineer. In back, Harry Belford, manufacturing manager; John Plant (with hat), Avro Aircraft general manager and former air vice-marshal; Fred Smye (wearing a hat), president of Avro; Frank Chalmers (head turned and wearing a hat), flight test engineer; Gord Essilman (with glasses), flight test engineer; and, far right, Peter Cope, experimental test pilot (only head is visible).

RCAF looking over RL 204.

The old and the new: the CF-100 and the Arrow.

A landing gear malfunction causes Arrow 201 to skid off the runway. The problem was quickly discovered and fixed.

Arrow 201 is back on its feet.

The end of the Arrow approaches.

What once was!

Fired after six years at Avro, worker Pat Gallacher purchased a model of the CF-105 in the plant hobby store and quipped, "Better get one of these in memory of the plane that will never see the air."

Dismissed workers leave Avro.

Dismissed workers leave Avro.

February 26, 1959. Ten thousand fired employees crowd into the Coliseum building at the Canadian National Exhibition in Toronto, in protest of the cancellation.

Two of the ten thousand representing the human side of the Arrow cancellation and the tragedy that ensued for many.

The poster in back refers to the memory of the R.B. Bennett Conservative government of the thirties, which was largely blamed for Canada's last Depression. Other posters offer the view that Canada could be cast as the fiftieth state of the United States.

The torch crews have not yet arrived.

As per memos on file, some Arrows were being kept pending news from Britain in the event the British might be interested.

The Arrows are finally destroyed.

Remnants of two great Canadian achievements, the Arrow and the Iroquois engine, housed at the Canadian Aviation and Space Museum in Ottawa.

Artist rendering of an Avro automobile being considered for development after cancellation of the Arrow. It was not pursued.

The Avrocar, a research vehicle designed by Avro's special projects group to investigate vertical takeoff and landing, proved unstable, never getting more than a few feet off the ground. Further funding from the USAF and U.S. Army, for additional work to overcome the problems, was not forthcoming, and the project was abandoned.

5

Who Ordered the
Blowtorching and
Why Was Everyone Fired?

IN 1988, WHEN INTERVIEWED about the Arrow, Canadian historian Professor Desmond Morton asked, "Who precisely ordered the destruction of the existing prototypes and why? It was an act of extraordinary vandalism and vengefulness and no one has formally taken responsibility for it ... it was a tragedy that the opportunity to perfect it was never achieved."[1]

This question continues to be posed today.

There are many who firmly believe that John Diefenbaker, the prime minister of Canada in 1959, was behind the affair. Some of these say that the lack of any evidence confirming this can be explained by the fact that it's likely that the memo or piece of paper ordering the destruction of everything related to the Arrow program was later incinerated. Others have maintained that the absence of any record can be explained by the possibility that the order was given via a nod or other unspoken sign. In his memoirs, Diefenbaker stated that while he took the ultimate decision to cancel the program he was incorrectly reviled for ordering the physical destruction of the aircraft, something of which he had no knowledge. Diefenbaker did not order the blowtorching and final destruction of the completed aircraft, tooling, drawings, and technical information.

Discounting that line of thought, some are convinced that Crawford Gordon, the president of A.V. Roe in 1959, ordered the destruction, in retaliation for the cancellation of the program. The problem with this theory is that the aircraft, tooling, and technical information did not belong to Mr. Gordon or the company. They belonged to the government. So any act of destruction on his part would have landed him in jail for destroying government property. Of course, this did not happen. He simply did not have the authority to issue such an order.

It is important to note that until the revelations made back in 1992 in *Storms*, no one had admitted knowing anything about who was behind the destruction. A television documentary in 1979 on the subject did not resolve this mystery, even though a significant number of the key players who had been connected to the program, both inside the government and within the RCAF, were interviewed. Although the makers of the documentary were unable to solve the mystery of the Arrow's destruction at the time, they stated that there was still hope that the answer would be revealed some day, noting that there were likely files squirrelled away in the archives that might hold the answers. Those files were revealed in *Storms*.

For the record, the following is an in-depth accounting of the sequence of events that led to the destruction of the existing aircraft and engines.

———

On Black Friday, February 20, 1959, the Arrow program, including the development of the Iroquois engines, was terminated. Once the decision was made, the problem of what to do with all the Arrow-related "stuff" arose. There was a huge amount of material and documentation associated with the program: tooling, jigs, mockups, aircraft, engines, drawings, technical data, and so on. One thing is very clear: torches were not sent in overnight. In fact, even though A.V. Roe's employees were let go the same afternoon, the materiel was left intact for some months as the RCAF and government bureaucrats pondered what they wanted to do with it.

Again, the final decision did not come from the Prime Minister's Office, as shall be seen. If it had come from the PMO, the time from the date of cancellation to the date of destruction would not have been so long.

So, what happened? Some background is in order.

Today, government-owned equipment such as trucks, boats, farm equipment, office equipment, and military hardware can be purchased through the government agency called GCSurplus. This is the arm of the federal government that disposes of government equipment that is no longer required, by putting it up for sale to whoever is interested, including the general public. Some excellent bargains can be had. In the 1950s, this group was known as Crown Assets Disposal Corporation (CADC), and this would be the group that would be charged with dealing with the Arrow and related equipment.

In early February 1959, perhaps in anticipation of cancellation at some future point, Group Captain H.R. Foottit, assistant for the Arrow Weapon System project, asked whether the Defence Research Board (DRB), the research arm of the government, could make any use of surplus Arrow aircraft should they become available as a result of future government actions. The DRB reply, dated February 10, explained a number of possibilities that could be explored wherein the National Aeronautical Establishment (NAE) might make use of the Arrow. It was noted, though: "It is not possible to be much more explicit about possible research projects within the NAE until a number of policy and practical engineering problems have been resolved."[2]

On February 20, 1959, Foottit's worst nightmare came true. In September of 1958 the government had terminated the Astra/Sparrow fire control and weapons system and said that the entire program would be reviewed in March 1959. Here, though, in February 1959, not March, was Cabinet jumping the gun, as it were, by agreeing to discontinue the complete development of the aircraft and engine, to be effective when the announcement was made on February 20. During the same announcement, Cabinet agreed that notice would be given that all contracts would be terminated immediately.

When the cancellation of the Arrow program was announced in Parliament by the prime minister, no order had yet been given to destroy anything related to the development. The directives that had been sent to the company through the Department of Defence Production (DDP) stated that all contracts and subcontracts were terminated, effective immediately, and that the company had to cease all work and terminate any outstanding subcontracts. It was the wording of these orders that led to the immediate firing of all employees, as there could be no further work without the cancelled contracts.

By March 4 the RCAF had formed a Termination Group, which was charged with reviewing all of the equipment at the company for any material still in use or that could be used by the RCAF. Headed by Group Captain Abe Lieff, this team had not been given any instructions about disposal of the aircraft, so everything for the time being remained intact.

On March 6, 1959, Group Captain Lieff wrote to the DDP, stating: "It is considered desirable that complete engineering data including drawings, process data, methods, procedures, etc. for the Arrow aircraft and Iroquois engine be retained by the respective companies for a limited period...."[3]

Lieff received a reply from the DDP on April 10, 1959, stating that the companies had been so advised; that is, to retain the information requested. DND would decide what to do with the material, but, as the contract administrators, DDP would implement the necessary actions.

On March 11, 1959, in replying to Foottit's letter from February, concerning use of any surplus aircraft by the DRB, the latter wrote stating that the conduct of any research with the aircraft and engines would involve considerable cost. Specifically, the cost of operation and maintenance of the aircraft would be considerable and work would have to be contracted back to A.V. Roe. The latter, though, had dismissed its employees after the announcement in February. The costs of utilizing the engines would also be high. Implied in the response was that, without more money, no real use of the engines or airframes could be made; and, indeed, no such funds were forthcoming.

In a memo dated March 13, 1959, Chief of the Air Staff Hugh Campbell wrote to Defence Minister George R. Pearkes and advised him of the definitive decision from the NAE; i.e., that it would not be practical to use the aircraft or engines for research. He further stated that the RCAF could not make use of the items, as they had not been completely flight-tested. Also, he remarked, spare parts would be in short supply — an odd statement, given that there were parts on hand to assemble at least twenty-nine others, if not more, not counting the eight he would specifically mention in his memo. There were questions, though: What would it cost to store the parts, where would that be done, and who would handle maintenance and repairs?

Campbell noted that, along with everything else, the five aircraft that had flown, and the three Mark II aircraft with their Iroquois engines and airframes that were in various stages of assembly, would have to be disposed of. He also noted that something would have to be done with the Hughes electronic system. He concluded:

> Since there is no practical use for the Arrow or its major components, the RCAF intends with your approval to (a) negotiate with the USAF for the return of the 19 J75 engines (original cost: $6.9M) and the 2 MA-1 electronic systems (original cost $1.7M); (b) make the necessary arrangements to dispose of the Arrow airframes and Iroquois engines.[4]

Minister Pearkes wrote back to Campbell on March 18, 1959, concurring, but adding that he wished to be informed of the method of disposal of the airframes and engines before final action was taken.

Now, if there had been a direct order from the prime minister, there would almost certainly have been no overtures to the DRB or NAE; and if any overtures were made before termination, they would have been quashed immediately. Also, the minister would not have been asking the chief of the air staff for his recommendation for disposal. And, of course, this paper trail would not exist if orders did come directly from the Prime Minister's Office. (It is noted here that, thankfully, none of this message traffic was destroyed — a fact that has allowed this particular question to be put to bed, hopefully once and for all.)

In replying to the minister's request of March 18, Campbell wrote back on March 26, 1959. This is the fateful memo, reproduced in *Storms*, that sealed the fate of the existing aircraft, engines, and so forth. In this memo, Campbell recommended that the Arrow and its engines be reduced to scrap. He noted that other disposal would involve sending the completed airframes and engines to the aforementioned Crown Assets Disposal

Corporation (CADC). The latter would have the power to sell them in their whole state, which, he said, could cause embarrassment, especially if they turned up in public view — even, possibly, as a roadside stand.

Pearkes forwarded the memo from Campbell to his deputy minister, Frank Miller, asking for his advice and comments. Why would he need his DM's comments if he already had Diefenbaker's order in hand or if Gordon had already ordered the destruction? Why would Campbell have recommended anything if the prime minister had already issued a directive? The answer, of course, is that he wouldn't have. At this point, the discussion did not involve Diefenbaker or anyone in the PMO. Despite all this, none of the people actually involved — Campbell, Pearkes, and Miller — ever acknowledged this exchange of memos, in which they themselves discussed and decided on the fate of everything Arrow. They seem to have been content to let Diefenbaker and Gordon be vilified for it.

A legitimate question is why these individuals were allowed to remain invisible, even denying publicly that they knew anything about the destruction. On this one can only speculate. Suffice to say that, back then, transparency and openness had not yet been embraced to the degree that they are today — and some might argue that there has been little embracing of them yet. So, those in government then were less likely to share any secrets. Also, there was no legislation compelling them to do so.

As for being used as a roadside stand, today, some military hardware is considered controlled goods, and not just anyone can purchase what is put up for sale. A similar situation likely existed then. In other words, even if CADC were to try to sell the aircraft in their whole state, the buyer would have been carefully scrutinized. This situation never arose, however. The RCAF and Hugh Campbell decided, instead, to get rid of the planes and the related material another way: destroy everything first, before turning it over to CADC.

On April 7 Hugh Campbell again wrote to his minister with a progress report on the termination proceedings. He explained the co-operation between the RCAF and the DDP. He noted the DDP had been told to dispose of new material and any work in process, along with the tooling. He also indicated arrangements had been made to return the B-47 the RCAF had obtained from the United States for the testing of the Iroquois engine. He also outlined the arrangements for the return of the Hughes MA-1 electronic control systems to the USAF. He ended with a request asking the minister for his approval in disposing of the completed airframes and engines, as per his recommendation of March 26. Campbell carbon-copied the deputy minister, Frank Miller, as he had in his previous correspondence.

Also on April 7, a memo from the aircraft branch of the DDP to its representatives in Avro outlined the disposition of all Arrow-related materiel as per Campbell's memo. Interestingly, this memo stated that the completed aircraft were expected to be returned to the DDP for "mutilation" prior to handover to the Crown Assets Disposal Corporation. It went on to say:

> [T]here is still a remote possibility that one or two aircraft may be required by DND, and therefore, the two best aircraft should be retained intact for the present.... Recognizable components and aircraft are to be mutilated to the extent that they cannot be assembled in the form of an aircraft.... Three Iroquois engines are to be retained pending possible requirements.... The balance of the engines and parts are to be mutilated to the extent that they cannot be assembled in the form of an engine and declared surplus to CADC.... One complete cockpit in the configuration established by the RCAF is to be made available to the Institute of Aviation Medicine.[5]

Several points here are worthy of note: The memo states that destruction should begin, even though the minister of national defence had not yet replied to Campbell in agreement with Campbell's recommendation to reduce everything to scrap. Also of interest is the notion that two aircraft be retained pending further instruction. The last statement is revealing as well: it explains why the cockpit of Arrow 206 remains to this day. It was not spirited out, as some have alleged, by employees in the darkness of night. It was deliberately sent to the Institute of Environmental Medicine, (later the Defence and Civil Institute of Environmental Medicine (DCIEM)) in Downsview. It was to be used as a pressure vessel for testing of flight suits and the like. It would eventually end up at the Canadian Aviation and Space Museum in Ottawa.

The procedure for the destruction of the Arrow is outlined in this memo. Had this memo been made available when it was written — or shortly thereafter — or if the individuals involved had spoken openly about it, there would have been no rumours of men stealing away the cockpit for posterity. There would have been no questions regarding who ordered the scrapping of the air frames and engines either, as a paper trail would have led back to the chief of the air staff and the minister of national defence. In hindsight, there was no reason to keep all of this information hidden from the public. All it did was foment the rumour mill and raise the anger level against the prime minister and Crawford Gordon.

On April 8, 1959, Minister Pearkes finally wrote back to Hugh Campbell. He stated his understanding of the proposal from his chief of the air staff that the aircraft would be reduced to scrap: "The aircraft, as a whole aircraft, will not be put up for disposal but will be reduced to scrap after all useful and creditable materiel has been removed. On the above understanding I agree to your proposal."[6]

On April 22, Gordon Hunter, assistant deputy minister of the DDP, wrote to Raymond O'Hurley. He advised the minister that five aircraft were still intact but that aircraft 6, 7, 8, 9, and 10, which were in partial stages of completion on the production line, had indeed been or were in the process of being reduced to scrap. Apparently, the day before, this minister had said no aircraft had yet been so reduced.

On April 24 Hugh Campbell again wrote to the minister. He noted the difference in wording between his memo of March 26 and Minister Pearkes' reply of April 8, namely that he had told the DDP that they "can reduce it to scrap," whereas the minister had replied that it "will be reduced to scrap."[7] He went on to state that a memo communicating the intent of the minister's direction was sent to DDP, and that agreement with them had been obtained on the method of disposal. He also stated: "However, we are informed that such action is being withheld in respect to 5 aircraft pending the outcome of the enquiries being made on behalf of the Royal Aeronautical Establishment, Farnborough, of which I understand you are aware."[8]

In using the words *will be reduced to scrap*, the documents reveal the minister of national defence, acting on Campbell's recommendation, effectively ordered the destruction of the Arrow. The prime minister himself later stated he was unaware of this decision, and there is no reason why he should have been alerted to it — the process used to get rid of the Arrow and the material related to it was the usual one employed when the department wished to dispose of its equipment.

The fact that Campbell was advised that five aircraft were being held intact pending information from the Royal Air Force (RAF) in Britain suggests a behind-the-scenes attempt at salvaging something from the program. The action to hold these planes seems to disprove the notion that there were orders from the prime minister to destroy everything. It also contradicts the direction by the DDP, given on April 7, to keep only two aircraft intact. In any event, the five Aircraft were not destroyed for the time being.

The memo quoted above has several signatures including that of the minister, noting that, yes, five aircraft were to be kept pending information from the United Kingdom. Not all the initials are legible, but every one of these individuals was aware of the decision to scrap and not one came forward over the years that followed, to explain that the order had come from the minister and was based on the recommendation of the chief of the air staff.

On April 27, a letter from Frank Miller was sent to the deputy minister of defence production. In it he reiterated the instructions from Campbell and Pearkes. He wrote: "It would be our understanding that in relinquishing DND interest to your department in the existing Arrow airframes and Iroquois engines now in their whole state, that ... the aircraft, as a whole aircraft, or airframe or engine will not be put up for disposal as such but will be reduced to scrap after all useful and creditable materiel has been removed...."[9]

He ended by asking for agreement on this and stating that the department could change its position pending a response from the RAF. This memo carries three signatures, that of Frank Miller, Air Vice-Marshal J.A. Easton, and Air Commodore M.B. Mackinnon. Every one of these individuals would likely have known where the orders to scrap were coming from, but said nothing over the years.

A response to Miller came on May 12, 1959, from Deputy Minister D.A. Golden of the DDP. He noted that he was in complete agreement with Miller's understanding as to the scrapping. He further advised that the five Arrows were still being held intact pending news of possible interest from Great Britain. The rest were all being destroyed. This letter also carried a number of other initials and signatures. It is possible that some of these individuals would not now have known from where the directives had originated.

For his part, Jim Floyd has stated:

> The first thing that I did was to get on to the RAE (Royal Aeronautical Establishment) in the U.K. to see if they'd be interested in taking some of these airplanes and they said of course provided we could back them up with parts. Well, we had 31 aircraft back through the plant in different stages of production, so we had plenty of parts. We'd even worked out a method of transportation over the northern route — and then the order to scrap came down.[10]

What had happened regarding the supposed interest from Britain? A telegram on file dated May 11, 1959, from the liaison staff in London states that there was a rumour afoot from Boscombe Down, the British military testing ground, that the Arrow program might be picked up over there. A reply dated May 12, 1959, though, reads as follows:

> The British have shown some interest in acquiring the Arrow aircraft which are capable of being flown. As we understand it they are not interested in continuing the development of the Arrow for its original purpose as a fighter aircraft but would like to have these aircraft as a flying test bed probably in connection with research required to produce a supersonic transport aircraft. This matter is not being handled by the RCAF but has been turned over for negotiation to DDP. I do not think the British interest is very strong and unless they can get the aircraft and engines for a very nominal price I doubt if they will proceed with the plan....[11]

What is ironic is that while the Arrow itself did not make it to Britain, Jim Floyd went on to consult on aspects of the successful British/French supersonic Concorde.

On May 15, 1959, roughly three months after termination, a message was sent from Mr. J.L. Bush of the DDP in Ottawa to Mr. C.A. Hore of the DDP in Malton:

> It has been confirmed that there is no requirement for any Arrow aircraft or Iroquois engines. It is therefore in order to proceed with reduction of the Mark one airframes and Iroquois engines to scrap as previously discussed.[12]

Now, it may be argued that these individuals were also not privy to all the preceding message traffic and may legitimately not have known from where the original directions came from. The others have no excuse.

Some five months after cancellation, a memo was placed on file at the Department of Defence Production. It is dated July 6, 1959, and is titled "CF-105 Termination Status." In part, it reads:

> Three of the five completed Mark I aircraft have been completely dismantled. The fourth and fifth will be finished about July 10th and 17th respectively. The partially completed Mark II aircraft has already been dismantled. All completed Iroquois engines together with spare parts and tooling will be retained for the time being and are being moved to the test cells at Malton for storage....[13]

So, it would not be until mid-July when all the aircraft were finally reduced to scrap. There is no indication that any could have survived the torches.

Author and journalist June Callwood, who was covering the Iroquois development, reported hearing an Iroquois being revved up one last time and thought perhaps one Arrow was being flown away for posterity. The truth is that no Arrow flew with the Iroquois, so whatever she may have heard, it was not an Arrow/Iroquois combination and not likely any of the Mark I's.

In May 1960, Orenda submitted proposals to the USAF regarding possible use of the Iroquois in the B-58C or in short takeoff and landing (STOL) aircraft. The Canadian Joint Staff in Washington followed up with a letter to the USAF on December 8, 1960. In that letter it was noted that a total of seven engines had been built and that the aerodynamic configuration had completed and cleared the fifty-hour preliminary flight rating test, or PFRT. Five complete engines were in storage, others were in various stages of being completed, one had been shipped to the United Kingdom to Bristol/Siddeley, seven no longer existed, and there were enough spare parts for twenty more. If the Americans were interested, the letter indicated, an engine could be made ready for test within two months or, if modifications were required, within eight months.[14]

A negative reply from the USAF was received on February 3, 1961. Essentially, it stated that the B-58C program was not going to continue, and that other engines were available for use in their short takeoff and landing (STOL) program. Overall, the need for additional engines was expected to decrease in the ensuing years.[15] As it turned out, one Iroquois engine made its way to the Canadian Aviation and Space Museum in Ottawa and at least one Iroquois engine was sent to the United Kingdom. The one tested on the B-47 is housed at the Canadian Warplane Heritage Museum in Hamilton, while another is said to be in the hands of a private collector in British Columbia. The rest were presumably destroyed.

Many have asked why Canada did not just continue with the development of the engine. David J. Caple had been administrative assistant to the vice-president, engineering at Orenda until 1957, when he became sales engineering manager, and he finally became the last vice-president and general manager before Orenda was acquired by Magellan Aerospace. He told this author that, because there was no customer base for the Iroquois, it would have been too costly for production. As shown above, the United States had declined it, and, according to Mr. Caple, the United Kingdom had its own engines in development. France, as noted previously, had terminated their interest when they believed the entire program was about to be cancelled and so had also turned to other engines for their aircraft. With no potential customers, the Iroquois could not be continued.

While everything was being destroyed, a curious decision was made at the Cabinet meeting of July 7, 1959. According to the July 6 "Termination Status" memo, two aircraft were not yet destroyed, though they were expected to be completely dismantled by July 17. The Cabinet decision of July 7 reads as follows: "The Cabinet agreed that now that the classified equipment on the surplus Arrow (CF 105) aircraft had been removed, there would be no objection to authorizing photographs of the aircraft itself for publication."[16]

It is not immediately evident which aircraft was "the surplus Arrow" being discussed. They were all mostly in scrap form, but at least someone must have thought it important enough for Cabinet to decide what to do with one of them. Perhaps it was Arrow 202. That was the aircraft being fitted with the classified Hughes equipment. As for photos, many have survived, including videos. No orders requesting these be destroyed have been found, though some of those who were in the plant swear these, too, were to have been scrapped.

Whatever the case, as the five Mark I's were being dismantled on the tarmac, an overhead photograph of the dismantling was taken by person(s) unknown. This photo showed all five aircraft looking straight down and a little from the back. It is a black-and-white photo only. Subsequently, photographer Herb Nott rented a small aircraft in late June and flew several circuits around the tarmac and snapped several full-colour photos of the destruction. Somewhere between the black-and-white photo and the Nott photos, Arrow 202 went missing. In *Storms*, it was stated that it had likely been returned to the hangar for removal of the Hughes electronic control system and dismantled there.[17]

That Arrow 202 was indeed being fitted with the Hughes System is corroborated by a memo written back on December 10, 1958. The memo, from Group Captain Foottit, opens by stating, "As you are aware, approval was granted recently by the minister of national defence for the installation of the MA-1 Aircraft Control and Weapon System in one Mark I Arrow aircraft. It is planned that the MA-1 system be modified ... to permit its accommodation in the Arrow 202 ..."[18]

At this point in 1959, most of the planes had been scrapped; however, reports and engines were still being held. On September 1, 1959, the Ministry of Supply in the United Kingdom requested a number of the reports. They felt the information could be of use in the development of their own TSR-2 aircraft and were planning to provide them to their contractor, Vickers-Armstrongs of Weybridge. Although the reports were classified, it was suggested the Ministry of Supply could use them at their own discretion. They were sent to the ministry through the Canadian Joint Staff in London.[19]

In Canada, a decision was made to destroy the records and reports on file. On January 21, 1960, Mr. Hore of the DDP advised Mr. J.C. Wilson, Arrow termination coordinator, of the following: "As the R.C.A.F. have now advised that there appears to be no purpose in retaining the engineering data on the Arrow aircraft, you are instructed to dispose of it in the same manner as you have disposed of other records, drawings, etc."[20] And so all technical information was presumably, finally destroyed, save for what made its way to the United Kingdom and what was spirited out by employees.

One might ask why at least one Arrow was not kept. As noted in *Storms*, there was concern from a security perspective. Air Vice-Marshal John Easton, effectively the last project manager of the Arrow, told this author that the RCAF did not want the Arrow, the most sophisticated aircraft in existence at the time, to remain sitting there in front of prying eyes. Recall, this was 1959 at the height of the Cold War. There was no way to maintain twenty-four-hour surveillance around it and there was no way it would be flown again. He also noted there were Soviet moles operating within Avro. As an interesting side note, author E.K. Shaw writes that a Soviet delegation of scientists and engineers were actually given a tour of the Avro facilities in October 1958, and remarked that the Arrow was an excellent aircraft. Perhaps they had inside information.

There are those who do not believe the stories that Soviet moles were in the Avro plant, ferreting technical information back to the Soviets. However, the truth of this state of affairs was revealed by journalist John Sawatsky in his investigations into the RCMP. He discovered the existence of a mole who was indeed providing information on the Arrow. His information was confirmed in 1998, when one Vasili Nikitich Mitrokhin co-authored the bestseller *The Sword and the Shield: The Mitrokhin Archives and the Secret History of the KGB* with Christopher Andrew, head of the Faculty of History at Cambridge University.

Mitrokhin had been the archivist for the KGB. He fled Russia with thousands of pages of documents, which he had transcribed and which formed the basis for the book. The documents exposed Soviet activities in North America. The Mitrokhin archives detailed the workings of one mole, codenamed "Lind," who was gaining information on the development of the Arrow and passing it to his KGB handler, codenamed "Gideon," who was later revealed to be Yevgeni Brik, also known as David Soboloff. Additional information behind this aspect in the Arrow's development and the Soviet moles was subsequently provided in 2016 with the publication of *Shattered Illusions: KGB Cold War Espionage in Canada*, by Donald G. Mahar, a forty-one-year veteran of the RCMP, the Canadian Security Intelligence Service (CSIS), and the Communications Security Establishment (CSE).

In 1992 CSIS learned from British intelligence that Brik was alive and wanted to return to Canada. He had become a double agent but had been betrayed back in 1955 by an RCMP officer in need of money. He had been summoned back to Russia as a result, and it was thought he had been executed for being a traitor. He had not. Mahar's involvement in 1992 was as part of the team to bring Brik safely back to Canada and conduct his debriefings.

Mahar explained to this author that, by 1953, Brik had become a KGB deep-cover "Illegals Resident." He was responsible for servicing agents that the Soviet embassy wished to keep at arm's length but who could provide intelligence on various things, including agriculture, politics, and, of course, military technology. The Arrow, he noted, would certainly have come under the intelligence interests of the Soviet Union via the KGB and GRU, the former being roughly equivalent to the CIA and the latter being the Russian military intelligence service. One of the agents, Brik, was responsible for was the agent codenamed Lind, the individual referred to by Mitrokhin.

Lind was an employee at Avro. He provided Brik with schematics, drawings, photographs, and technical reports on the Avro Arrow. Essentially, Brik and Lind would work to a schedule. Brik would travel from his home in Montreal to a predesignated dead-drop area in Toronto. There he would look for a signal from Lind that items had been deposited. Upon retrieving the items, he would leave his own signal to that effect. Signals could be anything — a newspaper placed a certain way and in a given spot, or a tin can left at the area, and so on. The use of such signals meant the agents would never have to meet.

Unknown to Lind and Moscow, though, by this time Brik had become a double agent, working on behalf of Canada for a fictional organization called the Canadian Security Agency (CSA). The CSA was, in fact, the RCMP. Brik's handler at the RCMP was counter-intelligence officer Charles Sweeny. Before passing the information obtained from Lind to Moscow, Brik would pass it to Sweeny, who would alter it in some important fashion. For example, photographs were somewhat obscured or doctored before being provided to Moscow.

As far as this author has been able to determine, Lind was the only operative actually within the Avro plant. To this day, his name has not been revealed, nor has his position within the company. Mitrokhin indicates he was an Irish-Canadian Communist.

What could the Soviets do with such information? In the Second World War, three American B-29 aircraft (the type of plane used to drop the atomic bomb) made forced landings in the Soviet Union. Rather than return the aircraft as allies normally would, the Soviets elected to keep them. They reverse-engineered them to develop their own bomber, the Tupolev Tu-4, an aircraft almost identical to the B-29. [21]

In the case of the Arrow, detailed plans and test results might serve a similar purpose, helping the Soviets to develop their own interceptor or even a reconnaissance aircraft. Besides defending against North American bombers, such an aircraft could have been used to thwart intrusions into Soviet airspace by aircraft, like the American spy plane, the U-2.

But were the Americans concerned that their U-2 missions could be compromised in such a manner by other aircraft? The answer is yes, even to the extent mock intercept trials were conducted. On March 31, 1959, the CIA prepared a document, then marked top secret, titled "Project Chalice." It details the importance of the U-2 overflights. The very first page carries the title "U-2 Vulnerability Tests." It details how the U-2 was flight-tested against American fighters, the F-102 and F-104, whose altitude capabilities were greater than those of Soviet aircraft. Neither fighter was able to successfully attack the U-2. However, at the time, a Soviet fighter with a higher altitude capability, not yet deemed operational, was in the process of being developed. The report concludes, "Successful intercept of the U-2 by the Soviet defensive fighters for the next few months is unlikely."[22] The U-2 would eventually be downed by a missile, something not predicted in 1959.

Aviation Week ran an article shortly after the cancellation indicating that technical information was also being destroyed because it might aid a potential enemy. So, security seems to have been of paramount concern. This is understandable, given the Cold War paranoia in effect at the time.

In the final analysis, the assertion by AVM Easton and the *Aviation Week* article that security concerns necessitated the destruction of the Arrow can be seen as logical, even if misguided. Here again, if full documentation had been made available early on, perhaps a full accounting of what happened could have been demanded. Those responsible could have been compelled to explain their actions. However, that never happened.

Another, less significant, rationale for the destruction was put forward by Hugh Campbell. In a memo, he noted that if the Arrow was disposed of in its whole state, it could be an embarrassment to the government. It might be that the government did not wish the plane, on which millions of dollars had been spent, to be available for display in a cheap and common way.

Perhaps an unofficial motive for destroying everything was to ensure no one would ever be able to understand just how good the Arrow was. In absence of information to the contrary, its destruction could be taken to mean the Arrow was simply not a good aircraft — as some have argued — and so its destruction was of no particular consequence. This, of course, is conjecture only.

———

Apart from the question of why it was decided that the destruction of the plane was necessary, there is the question of why it was decided to immediately fire all of the employees of A.V. Roe on the afternoon of the cancellation announcement. Crawford Gordon has been blamed for attempting to embarrass the government. Jim Floyd, vice-president of engineering at the time, recalled it this way:

> We were in a board meeting with John Plant (president
> of Avro Aircraft) trying to settle some very mundane
> union situation about seniority. Joe Morley (sales and
> service manager) came running down the corridor
> with a man from the DDP (Department of Defence
> Production) saying they'd heard on the radio that
> Diefenbaker had cancelled the Arrow.... We were told
> to close everything down and that nothing would be
> paid as from that day....[23]

Fred Smye has stated that he got the news by telephone from Gordon
Hunter, the deputy minister of the Department of Defence Production, at
10:10 a.m. After advising Smye that the prime minister was making a state-
ment in the House on the fate of the Arrow, he made the following remark:
"All work is to be stopped forthwith and no further costs are to be incurred.
No other work will be made available to the companies."[24]

This message was followed later in the day by telegrams ordering the
company to cease and desist immediately. Smye met with Gordon and other
senior staff of A.V. Roe, and after much discussion they concluded that
there was no alternative but to let everyone go save for some supervisory
staff and senior engineers. "I [Smye] relayed this conclusion to Mr. Hunter
at about 2:00 p.m. It was emphasized to him that this was not to be con-
strued as putting pressure on the government, and no other motive was
involved. It was simply, that no other course was open in light of the government's instructions … unless instructions to the contrary were received
by 4:00 p.m., notice would be given...."[25]

No further instructions were forthcoming from the government and so
notice was given. As Smye has stated, the company had no choice. Perhaps
Ottawa simply did not realize what a cease and desist order might entail.
Rather than owning up to their responsibility for the loss of jobs, they
allowed the company and Gordon to take the blame, stating that their
actions were taken to embarrass the government.

Regarding the staff, Floyd states the following: "My first thought was
to see if any of our other projects could be got into shape so I could keep
my 1,500 engineers. I'd been pleading for years to get another project going

at the same time as the Arrow, but Fred Smye, who was a most sincere man, felt we had a duty to do the best we could on that airplane."[26]

Smye notes that the company began receiving phone calls from other companies and NASA, to determine if employees would be available for hire. Of course they were, and soon many began leaving. Appendix B contains additional information on those who went to NASA.

Not all employees went elsewhere, however. While all employees were initially let go, Avro, in order to develop other products, began to rehire some of them. Of the approximately 14,000 employees dismissed when the Arrow was cancelled, 3,500 were brought back. Employment at Avro went from 8,800 to 2,000, while that at Orenda from 5,000 to 1,500, according to a post-termination audit.[27]

As for other projects, the minister did not understand that it would have taken some time to prepare to undertake a new development and that nothing could be started overnight. Discussions between Avro and the government had been held for production of a jet replacement for the turboprop Viscount, but this was to have gone into development after production of the Arrow. Still, Smye indicates a call was made to Gordon McGregor, president of Trans-Canada Airlines (TCA), to determine if he would entertain the suggestion to replace the Viscount. McGregor advised he had already had talks with British Aircraft Corporation for an aircraft and was going that route.

That Avro was to focus on the Arrow development, as noted by Floyd, is telling. Recall that in 1949, when Avro produced the world-leading civilian regional jet, the Jetliner, Avro had abruptly been told to scrap it, allegedly to focus on the military CF-100 for the Korean War effort. Understandably, Smye had been reluctant to entertain other major projects, like a new commercial jet, in parallel with the Arrow.

It is true that one small group, the special projects group at Avro, was working on a circular-wing aircraft: the Avrocar, or "flying saucer." This development was being funded jointly by the USAF and the U.S. Army. It was a research and development effort separate from Avro's other work. The prototype never got more than a few feet off the ground because of inherent instability, lack of power, and excess heating. The problems were being solved when the USAF discontinued funding. It is unlikely the saucer would have become viable, but interestingly, the general concept it used has now found its way into the development of the vertical-takeoff version of the American F-35.

As the Avrocar was being tested, Avro attempted to get into other markets. One area was aluminum boats. This proved not viable. Another area was automobiles. According to Fred Smye, Avro approached American Motors in Detroit. A prototype was even developed and was being tested. This, too, though, did not progress beyond an initial test vehicle as the entire effort was abandoned with a changeover in management at A.V. Roe. Also on tap was a gyroplane concept. It, too, did not progress at Avro, but was restarted by Avian Industries in Georgetown, Ontario. In July 1962, de Havilland Canada, now owned by Hawker Siddeley in Britain, took over the facilities of Avro, while the remaining companies were sold off or came under Hawker Siddeley Canada. In essence, what had been the third-largest corporation in the country, A.V. Roe Canada Limited, ceased to exist.

Although A.V. Roe was diversified, engaged in numerous other activities, such as mining, production of steel products, rails for train transport and so on, its key contract was the Arrow. It was the way the company had been established: to design and build homegrown military, not commercial, aircraft. This is not an excuse for how matters evolved, simply a fact when one looks at the documented record.

So, in the end, documents show it was the minister of national defence, acting on recommendations from the chief of the air staff, who ultimately ordered the physical destruction of the Arrow. The procedure followed was similar to that which would be followed today. While one might expect the prime minister to have been consulted, there was no compelling reason for that, since the Arrow was treated as just another piece of military hardware to be disposed of. Diefenbaker, rather than requesting a full accounting, just let the matter drop — ever after insisting he knew nothing about the decision to destroy.

Conclusion

THERE ARE THOSE WHO ARGUE the right decision was made in cancelling the Arrow. They are urged to consider the following:

NEED

In the 1950s, the Government of Canada entered into discussions regarding the needs of the country's military forces. It was the Cold War, and it was perceived that Soviet bombers presented a real threat to North America. Accordingly, it was decided that there was a need for an advanced interceptor to meet that threat. And so, a contract was given to A.V. Roe to develop an advanced interceptor for use by the Royal Canadian Air Force. The government, together with the RCAF, the Americans, and the British, appraised and reappraised the need and value of the aircraft numerous times after the initial decision to develop what became the Arrow; each time it was agreed that there was a requirement for an interceptor, and so the Arrow program was given the green light. From November 25, 1953, to July 15, 1958, twenty-five meetings on the Arrow program and air defence requirements were held, each one examining the need and costs of the Arrow. Each time a decision was taken, the program was approved.

CAPABILITY

The Arrow was acknowledged by numerous experts to be highly advanced for its time, incorporating such features as fly-by-wire, 4,000 psi hydraulics, transistorized electronics, an engine built with titanium in mind from the ground up — features that would not be seen in some instances until years later in other production aircraft. With the more powerful Iroquois engines, instead of the lower powered J75 engines installed in the first five aircraft, the Arrow was expected to break speed records.

COST

The flyaway cost of the Arrow was going to be $3.5 million, $1.5 million more than estimated when the project was conceived; not an appreciable difference if costs were truly out of control. The American single-engined F-106 cost was $2.8 million. With further orders, the flyaway cost per Arrow could have reduced to $2.6 million.

Over and above the $318 million in sunk costs of development, approximately $29.4 million was paid in termination charges for the Arrow and another $21.1 million for Sparrow missile development. At least $15.1 million had been spent on the Astra fire control system with an estimate of $28 million in termination charges. The overall total that is known is $412.2 million wasted.

Surveys at the time indicated that for projects the size of the Arrow, approximately 25 percent of monies spent would find their way back in terms of taxes. This would not occur for acquisitions from other countries.

After cancellation, the Department of National Defence returned $262 million to the government, of which only $41 million came from the Arrow program. This money, if invested in the Arrow, would have paid for the remaining development costs as well as for thirty-seven complete aircraft, given that all the parts and materials were on hand waiting to be assembled.

Foreign sales of the Arrow could have helped to boost production and, thus, lower the per-plane manufacturing cost. It has been argued that the Arrow had no buyers; that it could not be sold to foreign governments. Test pilot Jan Zurakowski explained to this author, however, that normal practice at the time the Arrow was being developed was for an aircraft to be put into service in its own country in order to demonstrate its capability. Demonstrated results from the successful operation of the aircraft would then be used to stimulate the interest of foreign buyers. This, of course, did not happen with the Arrow, because of its cancellation. Still, there were those in the USAF who saw its capabilities during testing and were impressed enough to want it in their inventory. If the Arrow had been completed and allowed to go into production, once it proved itself perhaps there would have been opportunities for foreign sales even in the face of acknowledged pressure from U.S. industry. This was the case in the sale of the CF-100 to Belgium, in the license-built version of the British English Electric Canberra to the U.S., which became the B-57, and the sale of the British Harrier jump jet to the United States.

One has only to look at the success of the French Mirage aircraft, which, after being accepted into service in France, was sold in quantity to other countries. Ironically, France was interested in purchasing the Iroquois engine for use in the Mirage series. The potential order was cancelled, though, when rumours began to suggest that the entire Arrow program might be terminated. Had this not occurred, the Iroquois could have had a long and storied history with the Mirage. As such, its fleeting existence was like a mirage.

The minister of finance, the person who should have known about the impact of continuing or cancelling the Arrow program, stated that he had supported the program in 1957, but by September 1958 he was in favour of cancellation. Was this change due to runaway costs? No! He said he would not let finances stand in the way of security and that it was the military that decided the fate of the Arrow.

It has been asserted by some that the cost of the Arrow program was going to have a disastrous impact on the Canadian economy. Government discussions noted it could have led to an increase in taxes, inflation, and possibly a recession, and yet none of these arguments were put forward by the minister of finance, Donald Fleming, in his remarks at the Cabinet Defence Committee meeting of September 7, 1958. In fact, he stated that he had supported the Arrow program — a clear indication that he did not feel it posed a threat to the Canadian economy — but that the military now no longer saw it as necessary. Indeed, it was *cancellation* that was subsequently described in Cabinet discussions as possibly initiating a recession or causing a psychological blow to the country in general.

Cost-plus contracting has been erroneously blamed for the rising costs. This contracting method is a necessary evil; without the flexible cost structure it provides, it could be difficult to attract private companies to develop and build expensive new weapons systems. That such contracts do not have guaranteed prices does not mean, however, that costs are bound to spin out of control. They can be dealt with through proper management and oversight. The RCAF exerted plenty of oversight on the project.

It does not appear to have been poor management at Avro or attempts by the company to abuse the cost-plus contracting method that caused the costs to increase. It was the continued changing of requirements brought forward by the RCAF themselves. Was A.V. Roe a perfect company? Probably not, but it should not be maligned for employing a standard of practice of the day, one that is still in use now for similar R&D type developments.

REPLACEMENT ALTERNATIVES

The value of the Arrow as a defensive weapon began coming into question only in concert with a belief that there was a diminishing threat from bombers, a belief that the Bomarc missile provided a superior method for handling that perceived diminished threat, and increased anxiety over the intercontinental ballistic missile (ICBM) threat. All of these perceptions were based on incorrect pieces of intelligence.

Bomarc missiles were purchased instead of the Arrow. Prime Minister Diefenbaker admitted in his memoirs that their purchase was a mistake. The Bomarc launch bases in the United States would be decommissioned two years after the Canadian bases became operational. The Bomarc was effectively obsolete before it arrived.

Charles Foulkes, the chairman of the Chiefs of Staff Committee, noted several reasons for abandoning the Arrow. At the top of the list was the diminishing threat from piloted bombers and the increasing threat from ICBMs, something the Arrow could not defend against. As for the bomber threat, he declared the Bomarc the weapon of choice, and that it was going to cost less than the Arrow. Finally, he noted that, with its high cost, the Arrow would not provide a defence capability commensurate with the expense (it's important to note that he did not say that the Arrow was unaffordable), and this was because it was believed the Arrow would essentially be obsolete as a weapon system.

The belief that there was a decreasing threat from bombers and an increasing threat from ICBMs was based on incorrect information, as was the belief in the potential of the Bomarc, and yet the technologically advanced Arrow was cancelled. Cabinet documents show that the number of ICBM missiles in the U.S. inventory, a number the Americans themselves provided to Diefenbaker, was actually incorrect — the Americans had considerably fewer ICBMs than they claimed. Likewise, the number of ICBMs the Soviets were believed to have was also inflated.

Minister of National Defence George Pearkes stated flatly in the House of Commons that continuation of the Arrow depended entirely on military factors. He did not mention cost. Later, he clarified his reasoning, stating that the threat to North America from the piloted bomber was diminishing. He went further, stating that it had been decided that Bomarc missiles, purchased from the United States, were the best weapon to handle the bomber threat, and that is why the Arrow was cancelled.

Pearkes stated that he had cut a deal with the United States to handle air defence between cancellation of the Arrow and operation of Bomarc. He is further on record stating that the expectation was that the United States would use Bomarcs to cover air defence for the western part of Canada, which the Bomarcs on Canadian bases would not be able to reach. Pearkes was such a supporter of the U.S. Bomarc program that, according to American records, he went so far as to say that he was in favour of abandoning piloted aircraft altogether unless the United States felt they were truly necessary.

Unfortunately, the Bomarc ran into serious difficulty. The Americans decided to reduce the program, and so Canada was left to defend its western regions alone. Pearkes felt that this was unfair.

In the end, the government was obliged to adopt the Bomarc missile, and its attendant SAGE ground control network, and gap-filler radar, in order to satisfy Canada's military obligations under the NORAD agreement.

The combined cost of the Bomarc/SAGE package plus the Arrow would have added significantly to the defence budget and there would, presumably, have been reduced or no funding for research into defence against the ICBM. It is interesting, though, that the cost of the alternative combined system being considered, of less-expensive American fighters and the Bomarc package, before cost-sharing and with sunk costs of the Arrow factored in, was actually going to be more than completion of the Arrow program.

Shortly after cancellation, the United States stated that Canada needed interceptors, that missile development was not progressing as fast as had originally been thought, and that Canada could purchase American aircraft.

On February 6, 1960, speaking to his Cabinet, the prime minister said that if security demanded the acquisition of American aircraft in place of the Arrow, then that would have to be the decision; but it would create great difficulties for him and for his minister of national defence. He also stated he had been against cancellation, but he had been persuaded otherwise! But why would cancellation create great difficulties if that was the right decision? Why did he require persuasion if cost was so clear cut? Given that the Arrow was supposedly going to destroy the Canadian economy with its uncontrolled costs, surely Canadians would have understood.

In his memoirs, Diefenbaker also states he was unaware the Americans were not going to be providing a conventional warhead for the Bomarc. Had he known this, he says, he would not have accepted it. Can the inference be made, that in that case the Arrow would have been put into production, given there were no other comparable aircraft then available?

Chief of the Air Staff Hugh Campbell maintained to the end that he needed at least one hundred aircraft, if not the Arrow then an aircraft with similar capability. But there were no aircraft of similar capability. Who better than he would know this, and yet his requirements and his advice were ignored.

The CF-100 was old and being phased out. Given this, and cancellation of the Arrow, and the failure of the Bomarc, the result was no surveillance of Canadian skies by Canadians, according to the documented records.

Canada had no aircraft to police against intrusion by aircraft like the U-2, according to the minister. But this had been part of the reason for developing the Arrow: to guard against intrusion from high-flying recon-naissance aircraft. The Bomarc was useless against this type of encroach-ment. CIA vulnerability tests against the U-2, performed with American aircraft, allowed the CIA to conclude the U-2 would not be vulnerable to existing aircraft from the Soviet Union. It would eventually be downed by a Soviet missile.

Canada procured sixty-six American F-101 Voodoos, even though Cabinet and the minister noted this number was inadequate to protect Canadian cities. Also, the minister at the time, Douglas Harkness, stated they were primarily for defending the U.S. Strategic Air Command bases, not Canada, and the number purchased, though meagre, should be ade-quate, given that they carried nuclear weapons.

The Liberals and others noted at the time that Canadian defence policy was being driven by the Americans for their own ends, as had been their push for certain equipment like the Bomarc/SAGE system. The leader of the Liberal party, Lester Pearson, was noncommittal on continuing or can-celling the Arrow. The Liberals, had they remained in power, were going to review the program.

Development of the single-engine and less-sophisticated F-106, the Delta Dart, from the original F-102 design, and touted as a potential re-placement aircraft for the Arrow, ran into all manner of difficulty. As a result, costs increased to the point where the project was nearly cancelled. Fewer aircraft than originally planned were ordered. The Cook-Craigie method, effective on the Arrow, did not favour the F-102/106 because of repeated modifications that meant redesign of tooling as well as of the air-craft itself. As a result, the first F-106 was delivered five years later than ex-pected. Yet, it was not abandoned, and became a good interceptor, serving well into the eighties.

On the other hand, the Arrow, a more sophisticated aircraft, also ran into delay, largely because requirements from the RCAF kept changing. Each major change was the result of external factors, related to problem-atic development programs elsewhere, most notably for foreign engines and the Astra fire control system. Each major change necessitated some redesign, but these all occurred prior to any flight testing. Many problems were also avoided because of the extensive testing programs, so when the first Arrows took to the air, they flew exceedingly well. There was no need to change the configuration, after the fact, and the result was thirty-one more Arrows awaiting assembly when termination occurred. Would further flight testing have uncovered other issues? No one can say. But, given the strategy of prior testing and the care taken in the design, they likely would have been minimal.

LONG-TERM IMPLICATIONS OF CANCELLATION

At cancellation, just when the economy was regaining steam after a mild recession, twenty-five thousand people in the industrial heartland of Canada and other parts lost their jobs. The third-largest company in Canada was destroyed and some 640 subcontractors were affected. According to the *Financial Post* at the time, if all the companies that were affected by the cancellation of the Arrow program were taken into account, as many as a hundred thousand people would be found to be affected in some way. Some smaller subcontractors may have gone bankrupt.

Not only was there a loss of jobs when the Arrow was cancelled, Canada also suffered a tremendous loss of scientific knowledge and talent. Cancellation initiated a brain drain. Twenty-five engineers from Avro were snapped up by NASA, to develop John Glenn's Mercury capsule. All were hired into prominent positions and went on to be leaders in such other NASA projects as Gemini and Apollo. Jim Floyd went on to consult on aspects related to the supersonic Concorde, while others went to other aircraft manufacturers abroad.

FINAL ASSESSMENT

It is submitted that the wrong decision was made at the wrong time by the wrong people and for all the wrong reasons. The piloted-bomber threat was not diminishing; the Soviets were not ahead in intercontinental ballistic missiles, even though they had launched Sputnik. Events had not made the Arrow obsolete as a weapon system and Hugh Campbell, Chief of the Air Staff, was ignored in his request for aircraft comparable to, if not the Arrow.

The Arrow was not some legendary super-aircraft whose myth has grown over the years. It was simply a highly advanced achievement at the leading edge of aircraft technology in a very complex environment that by all accounts had tremendous potential but was cut short.

It would have been a great airplane, as noted by the foreign aviation-related technical press and foreign engineers at the time. The fact that it was not allowed to go to completion is not a slight against it. If it had progressed, it would have been modified as new technologies came along.

It is possible that, over time, the company might have gone into an entirely different direction, perhaps into the multi-role fighter game, or back into the civilian aircraft market. It could also have merged with or been purchased by a foreign company, or closed down entirely. But these are not arguments for slighting its achievements or against its being established in the first place.

What A.V. Roe Canada did do was symbolize what Canadians were capable of but were not allowed to complete. But let there be no mistake. Canadians have done great things since and will continue to do so.

Postscript

IN 1988, IN AN ARTICLE on the Arrow in *Engineering Dimensions*, the journal of the professional engineers of Ontario, a comment was made regarding the recovery of Arrow test models that were known to have been launched into Lake Ontario. The article went on to say that perhaps in the future some enterprising enthusiasts would go searching for and find them.

———

A bit of background. As part of the Avro Arrow testing protocol, it was determined that wind tunnel testing and aeroballistics testing (firing small models from a canon under controlled conditions) would not provide the aerodynamic data required by the design team, because of the limitations of each method. Instead, it was decided to build eleven instrumented, free-flight, one-eighth scale test models and launch them atop Nike rocket boosters — nine over Lake Ontario from the Canadian Armament Research and Development Establishment (CARDE) test range at Point Petre, and two from the U.S. test range on Wallops Island, Virginia.

The first four models were designated "crude" models, the fuselage being a rectangular box-like structure with delta wings, approximating the look of the Arrow. The others were mini Arrows, accurate right down to the engine inlets and nacelles. Each of these was launched at an angle of 45 degrees and achieved altitudes of nineteen thousand feet before falling into Lake Ontario, some as far as nine miles down range, according to videos produced by Avro at the time. According to test reports, when the model and rocket combination reached a speed of Mach 1.7, the booster rocket would fall away, leaving the model to continue in free flight until splashdown into the lake. This was a fire-and-forget exercise — the models were never meant to be recovered.

Test reports and the videos of the flights indicate all separated from their boosters properly. Of particular note, though, is that after separation the trajectory was not a straightforward downward arc. Rather, the models and boosters tended to veer off in various directions. This might partly explain why finding them has proven so elusive.

―――――――

There has been a great deal of interest in finding the models. Among them, diver Mike Fletcher of the Sea Hunters group saw the article noted earlier, and on August 11, 2003, contacted this author for more information.

The Sea Hunters, a team of underwater archaeologists and divers, typically searched for shipwrecks, filming their activities in order to turn them into popular television documentaries. Now they were preparing to search for the models of the Arrow. Conducted in October 2003, the effort was chronicled in a television episode of *Sea Hunters* titled "The Search for the Avro Arrow Flight Models."

The dive was restricted to a narrow window of time and space. Searches were made just off of Point Petre, with another brief search conducted off Wallops Island. A number of targets were examined, including one promising one from a previous search effort. This one appeared to have nacelles protruding from the lake bed and was of approximately the correct length.

The Sea Hunters team were given permission to dive on that target and move some of the silt covering it. What they uncovered were additional exhaust nacelles, four in all, bundled together in a quadrant fashion. It was clear that this was neither an Arrow model nor a Nike booster. After conducting additional research at the archives, this author found documents indicating this was likely a booster rocket for the Velvet Glove missile, test prototypes of which had been launched atop a booster arrangement composed of four Demon rockets — each essentially a seven-and-a-half-inch-diameter tube containing rocket fuel — strapped together.

The latest and most serious and comprehensive effort to find the models has been undertaken by OEX Recovery Group. OEX is sponsored by Osisko Mining and Osisko Gold Royalties. They are working in collaboration with several institutions including the Bank of Montreal, National Bank, Comark Securities, and others, supported by the Canada Aviation and Space Museum, the Canadian Coast Guard, the Royal Canadian Air Force, the Royal Canadian Navy, Kraken Robotics, Scarlett Janusus Archaeology, Shark Marine Technologies, and the Canadian Conservation Institute, to name a few. A more complete listing is on the Osisko Mining website. The effort was initiated as part of the Canada 150 activities.

On July 14, 2017, John Burzynski, president of Osisko Mining, announced that a contract had been awarded to Kraken Sonar for this renewed search for the one-eighth scale models. Finding and recovering them would bring back a piece of Canadian aerospace history.

Kraken was the group whose equipment was used in 2014 in the successful search for the long-lost ships of the ill-fated Franklin expedition in the High Arctic. It has a state-of-the-art underwater robot called ThunderFish (its Autonomous Underwater Vehicle or AUV) and a state-of-the-art sonar, AquaPix Synthetic Aperture Sonar (SAS) system, both of which were used to comb the lake bed off Point Petre in a grid pattern.

The sonar was sent into the waters of Lake Ontario on July 28, 2017. On August 8, it was announced that the group had found a Velvet Glove missile, not just the booster as uncovered by the Sea Hunters. Judging by the imaging, the prospects that a Velvet Glove may have been found are quite promising, but as of this writing, a more definitive assessment of this particular object has yet to be made, as it is not one that has been further investigated. Later announcements indicated they also found both the Glove quad booster and one of the Arrow Nike rocket boosters.

On September 8, 2017, a press conference was held to reveal that what was perhaps an Arrow free-flight model had been found. The images that were shown at first glance resembled one of the nine models sent aloft by the Nike boosters, but upon further scrutiny it became obvious that the object pictured was not.

On October 10, 2017, an announcement was made that another model had been found. This one did look more promising, but as it was completely encrusted with zebra mussels, further work would be required before a definitive statement could be made.

At the end of the 2017 search, the team began its review of the accumulated data. Several hundred targets were identified, including Nike boosters, Velvet Glove missiles, and a host of other objects, perhaps including the actual models themselves.

In 2018 the search and recovery began anew with a slightly expanded search area. In addition, work was undertaken to retrieve the artifact first announced the previous September. On August 12, 2018, after carefully preparing the item underwater and moving it to a specially built enclosure, the artifact was brought to the surface, with divers following its progress, to ensure it remained stable on its journey. The entire process of recovery is well documented in the online article "'Raise the Arrow' Team Recovers First Artifact from Lake Ontario," by Joanna Calder, on the Government of Canada, Maple Leaf — Royal Canadian Air Force web page.[1]

The Canadian Conservation Institute is the agency responsible for restoring the recovered artifact. Restoration of this one has involved removal of zebra mussels and other contaminants, and further preparations so that it can eventually be placed on display, at the Canadian Aviation and Space Museum. Other artifacts, if and when recovered, are earmarked for the National Air Force Museum in Trenton, Ontario, and perhaps other museums in Canada.

The entire search effort and recovery has been documented by producer, director, and cinematographer Robert Barrett and will be included in a documentary on the Arrow called *Into the Wild Blue*. The latter will also include interviews that were made some years ago of some of the ex-Avro employees, including Jim Floyd and others who had or have been involved with the Arrow in some fashion over the years.

Even though this artifact is not one of the nine Arrow models, the work done to locate, recover, and restore it has been nothing short of amazing. The effort that has gone into it, and the knowledge gained, has set the stage for the eventual discovery, retrieval, and restoration of one or more of the nine models. This latter work will commence in the spring of 2019 as an expanded search area and analysis of already located targets will be undertaken. As it is, the search and recovery team has done a great job in bringing this piece of Canada's aerospace history back to life and will only add to it once the free-flight Arrow models are found.

What exactly is the artifact that has been found? The current thinking, according to Dr. Richard Mayne, director air force history and heritage, Department of National Defence, and this author, is that this artifact is likely related to both the Avro Arrow and the Velvet Glove programs as a crossover test item. This would increase its importance to Canada's aerospace heritage, since it would combine two significant Canadian technological achievements, the Arrow and the Velvet Glove.

In documents on the Velvet Glove, which this author initiated the process of declassification of, there is discussion of Delta test vehicles (DTVs). According to these documents, two Delta vehicles were successfully launched in April of 1954, with a third launched in October of that year, just prior to the first Arrow model launch in December. While information on the first Delta has not yet been found, information on the second indicates it was rail-launched, using an internally placed rocket motor. The third was boosted atop a single Demon rocket that delivered 8,000 pounds of thrust for 2.8 seconds, after which an internal motor of 4,500 pounds thrust kicked in for a further 1.55 seconds.[2] Avro personnel were present at the Delta #3 launch, and are listed in the test report.

The Delta test vehicles were cylindrical, like missiles, but with large delta wings, hence the resemblance to the Arrow. On the Delta 2 and 3 vehicles, the fuselage was ten inches in diameter with a back-end extension of eight inches in diameter. According to the documents, these models were of an experimental design used to examine structural adequacy, roll and yaw stability, and various other launch and flight parameters. On the back extension, each delta had two small winglets and a vertical fin. In the Delta #2 vehicle, the winglets were fixed, but in the Delta #3 they were movable. The Delta #3 also had explosive bolts where it attached to the Demon rocket, as this was the method of separation in flight. The Delta #3 also carried a telemetry package.

The size and shape of the artifact found in Lake Ontario resembles that of the Delta #3 schematic contained in the documents mentioned earlier and included in Appendix C; however, the winglets appear to be fixed, indicating it may in fact be the Delta #2 version. With exception of the mode of launch and mode of separation from its booster in the Delta #3 variant, the Deltas were physically the same. As mentioned, the configuration of Delta test vehicle 1 has not yet been ascertained.

One early Arrow report discussing the free-flight test program mentions the use of early models, which could be a reference to the initial "crude" models. However, there is one major difference. In that report, there is mention of the use of an internal sustainer motor, that would initiate after separation from the booster. This part is similar to the setup described for the Delta #3 test vehicle. The latter sat atop a Demon rocket but, upon separation via explosive bolts, was accelerated further by an internal sustainer motor. Could the Arrow report be referencing the Delta #3?

A second Avro report, the summary report of the first seven Arrow free-flight models, discusses use of a DTTV #2 for assistance in measuring the differences in accuracy between the various tracking devices at the Point Petre test range. According to a former CARDE employee familiar with the program, the "D" in the report stands for "Delta," and not "Doppler"; i.e., the "D" is not a reference to the Doppler-radar tracking equipment. In one of the figures of the test results in the report, the vehicle is simply listed as DTV #2, not DTTV #2, but they are one and the same. It was initially believed this was indeed a reference to the DTV #2 mentioned earlier as one of the three launched in 1954. But upon further examination of the report, this author concludes it might actually be a separate DTV.

In this same report, there is a listing of references in the back. References 42 and 43, which no longer seem to exist, are shown as pre-free-flight model reports "P/F.F.M./27, DTV #1 and DTV #2, fired at Picton (Data reduction (July 56) and evaluation of range with DTV #1 and #2 (July 56))" and report "P.F.F.M./28 Evaluation of range with DTV #1 and #2 (July 56)." These two references show up in the report itself as tests conducted April 30 and June 6, 1956. Within the report, these test vehicles are simply referred to as TTVs, not DTVs.

Typical TTVs are referenced earlier in the report as being five-inch-diameter HVARS or high-velocity aircraft rockets; essentially small rail-launched missiles. What makes the TTVs of April and June different, however, is that, according to the report, they simulated separation, as per the Arrow models. Hence, they may in fact have been DTVs, as per the references 42 and 43, mounted atop Demon rockets as per DTV #3 from 1954. The purpose, according to the Avro report, was to test the tracking equipment, including the Doppler, at Pt. Petre. And so there may be up to five DTVs in Lake Ontario: these two referenced in the Avro report, launched in 1956, and the first three, launched in 1954.

Apart from what is mentioned in the Avro reports, the other documents on the DTVs are from the Velvet Glove files. They were likely used by that program, for structural integrity and aerodynamic tests, as noted earlier, and also perhaps for test-tracking purposes.

Velvet Glove itself was being designed for carriage on subsonic aircraft. Maybe a purpose of the Delta was to investigate a potential upgrade to supersonic aircraft like the Arrow. Additional research into all these possibilities continues. And what of the Velvet Glove itself?

After the Second World War, the Defence Research Board of Canada (DRB) recognized the strides being made in missile development and technology in other countries and came to the conclusion that Canada had to get involved in order to keep up. A Guided Missile Advisory Committee was established in October of 1946, and by 1947 small groups of Canadian scientists were being sent to the United States to study developments in guided missile technology.

By 1949, with fears of potential attack from Soviet bombers increasing and with the subsequent development of the CF-100, the RCAF, in discussion with the DRB, concluded that a missile system for the CF-100 would be appropriate. In April 1950 the DRB engaged in discussions with its American and British allies as to a preferred course for Canada to follow so as not to duplicate missile research efforts in those countries. It was decided Canada should undertake a missile development program of its own.

A feasibility study was conducted and by June 1950 it was decided an air-to-air guided missile program was warranted. The primary aim was to train scientists, the military, and industry in the field of missile development, an aim that was achieved. But there was also a secondary aim: the development of a useful homegrown missile.[3]

On August 7, as the Korean conflict raged, the government gave approval for undertaking a technical study for the development of the air-to-air missile. On October 9, 1950, the Canadian Armament Research and Development Establishment (CARDE) was given the task of preparing a technical proposal for a missile development. By March 1951 approval was given to commence actual development. In August 1951, Canadair Limited was made a subcontractor to CARDE as supplier of airframes, hydraulic control equipment, and boost assemblies. It was also given contracts for the installation of pylons, launchers, and other equipment on the F-86 Sabre aircraft.

Canadian Westinghouse Company Limited would eventually be contracted to provide the missile electronics and test equipment. A.V. Roe Canada Limited was to provide pylons, launchers, and other equipment for installation on the CF-100 aircraft. Other players included the National Aeronautical Establishment (NAE), responsible for coordinating the design and installation of the pylons and launchers on both the Sabre and CF-100, and the Defence Research Telecommunications Establishment, responsible for designing the microwave fuse of the missile.

The Velvet Glove was a semi-active, X-band radar homing missile. In use, the target aircraft is illuminated by the fighter aircraft radar, the missile picks up the reflected signal from the target and homes in for the kill. The Glove was designed to target B-50–type subsonic bombers in formation at altitudes between 30,000 and 35,000 feet and from a distance of no less than 2,000 yards and up to 4,500 yards from the fighter aircraft. It was to have a velocity of Mach 2.3 when launched at Mach .85, using a rocket motor of 7,600 pounds thrust.

The Glove was 318 pounds loaded and 248 pounds with its fuel spent. It was about 6 feet long and eight inches in diameter and carried a sixty-pound fragmentation-type warhead. It could be launched individually or in a ripple fashion from rail-type launchers. CF-100s would carry a load of four missiles for a 75 percent kill probability off all four. Sabres would carry two for a 50 percent kill ratio; single-shot kill probability would be 30 percent.[4]

One of the key figures behind the Glove design was Gerald Bull. A student working on his Ph.D. at the University of Toronto, Bull became the aerodynamicist on the Glove, designing its body, wings, and fins. According to the test reports mentioned earlier, he was also the chief aerodynamicist for the Delta test vehicles.

Initial testing of the Glove was on small replicas fired from a gun at high velocity and monitored while in flight, in much the same way as small models of the Arrow would initially be tested. This technique led Bull to develop bigger and bigger guns, which he hoped could be used someday to launch satellites into orbit. This latter pursuit would lead him to try to develop such a gun for Saddam Hussein in Iraq. Once in Iraq he became involved in their missile weapons program. The result was that he was assassinated in 1990. The culprit(s) was (or were) never found, but it was thought that a foreign country was involved.[5]

In addition to the high-velocity-gun testing, the aerodynamics and structural stability of the Glove were tested via ground-to-air launches and air-to-air launches from modified CF-100s and Sabre aircraft. For the ground-to-air launches, the Velvet Glove was mounted atop booster rocket motors designed by Canadair.

Initially, a booster made of seven five-inch, light alloy plastic rockets from Britain was tried. This proved unreliable, and on December 12, 1951, exploded in the first test. In a second trial, a triplex booster was used, with three seven-and-one-half-inch Demon rockets, also from Britain. This rocket motor proved unstable. Eventually, a quad-booster arrangement was arrived at, with four Demon rockets for thrust. It is one of these that was probably uncovered by the Sea Hunters back in 2003.[6]

On March 11, 1952, Canadair was given the go-ahead for production of six quad-boosters, followed on June 17, 1952, for an additional 24. All were completed by March 1953 and by 1954, thirty-three ground-launched vehicles had been fired as part of a phased test program for design of the final Velvet Glove prototype.

Each phase would test certain design parameters, which, after analysis, would be incorporated into the final design. This meant each phase would have a test program, which resulted in the launching of several test vehicles of differing configurations, either from the quad boosters or self-launched from the ground, or from aircraft.

Each phase also had a specific name. For example, the boost test program was designed to test the booster, firing range facilities, ground operations, handling and firing procedures, and techniques for tracking the prototypes. This required design of boost test vehicles designated BTVs. BTV1 was the light alloy plastic rocket that exploded on launch and was immediately abandoned as a candidate. Nine BTVs would be launched in all, ensuring the quad booster arrangement would function properly.

The structural test program was to test the missile airframe in its final prototype form with investigation into the body joints, control section housing, and wing and fin structure. Designated structural test vehicles or STVs, four were fired. The first, on November 26, 1952, was a failure, but the remainder were successful, with results of the tests affecting the final missile design.

To test the stability of the missile, five vehicles were tested under what was termed the neutral-point test program. The name derives from the point on the missile at which, if the centre of gravity is located forward, stability of the missile increases, whereas if in back of this point, it decreases. These vehicles were designated stability test vehicles STV-1 through STV-5.

In addition to the booster test, and structural and neutral-point test programs, there were many others. These included the stowage program (for missile installation on an F-86) and the propulsion program, for testing the ground-launch system and propulsion unit. They were designated propulsion-test vehicles, PTV(G).

There was also the roll stability program for both ground-launched and air-launched vehicles, designated roll-test vehicles, ground and air, or RTV(G) and RTV(A), respectively. These were followed by an aerodynamics test program, controls test program, guidance test program, fuse test program, and then the prototype test program. Each had its own designated vehicles.[7] In the launch-test analysis reports, vehicles with a (G) were launched atop the boosters; those with an (A) were air-launched, and those with no designator were self-launched. Air launchings took place over Point Petre and Cold Lake Alberta, from modified CF-100 and F-86 Sabre aircraft.[8] Special test vehicles included environmental test and motor test vehicles. And then there were the Delta test vehicles described earlier.

By 1955, Velvet Glove development was nearly completed. Some four hundred scientists, specialists, and military personnel had been involved, along with several companies including Canadair, Avro, and Canadian Westinghouse. The aim of educating Canadian scientists, researchers, and industry on missiles and missile design had been achieved. Approximately $25 million had been expended and over one hundred airframes were eventually produced. There had been mention of developing the Glove further, for use on the supersonic Arrow, but this never materialized. The Glove program, perhaps not surprisingly, was instead terminated, like the Jetliner and the Arrow, this one in favour of the American Sparrow II missile, a missile which itself would be abandoned by the RCAF for use on the Arrow, in favour of the Falcon missile.[9]

There is an actual Velvet Glove on display at the National Air Force Museum in Trenton. This missile was transferred there from Concordia University. It had been sitting in the test lab of a professor of electromagnetics when seen by this author, who suggested it be donated to the museum. There used to be a Velvet Glove missile at DND when the base in Rockliffe was operational. Efforts to locate this one have not yet been fruitful but photos of it can be found online. It had been presented to George R. Pearkes by Gerald Bull, according to a plaque that was attached to it.

Quite apart from the search for the Arrow models, in 2008–9, the Canadian government noted the need for replacing its aging CF-18 jet fighter fleet. Some called for a rebuilding of the Arrow. Over the years there had been some attempts to do that. A full-size replica was built and used for the movie *The Arrow*, with actor Dan Aykroyd. A second replica was built by volunteers and was originally on display in Toronto. There were also those who believed that, since parts from the original Arrows have been found, and numerous original drawings have been recouped, a new/old flying Arrow could be built.

Now, the passion of those calling for a renewed Arrow program is laudable. A few considerations, though, are in order. Firstly, regarding old parts, it would not matter if an entire aircraft was found, it might make for an excellent museum piece but that is about it. It could even be restored to fly, but it would be a one-of-a-kind novelty best suited for air shows, not combat.

With respect to old drawings, here again it would not matter if all the drawings and technical documents were recovered. The fact remains that today's aircraft are not manufactured with the same materials or processes as used in the 1950s. This would, of course, require a complete redesign, analysis, and test program, effectively starting from scratch — as in the original case.

When the Arrow flew, it embodied features that were ahead of its time. That does not mean, though, that it could be "time-tunneled" into the future, to go up against today's modern aircraft and missiles. It means that in 1959 Canada was on the leading edge of technology and that some features employed in the Arrow would not be seen in other aircraft until years later. Rather than continue with the lead that the Arrow had, the government of the day chose to throw it all away, as had been done with the Jetliner.

All other countries that have maintained their military aircraft industries have now had all the intervening years since 1959 to surpass those early developments and introduce technologies not even dreamed of back in the fifties. For one example, fly-by-light — whereby wires have been replaced by fibre-optic cables, which are lighter and can transmit huge quantities of data via lasers and specialized circuits. For another example, stealth.

Call the end product what you will, a renewed Arrow or something else, what is actually being requested by some is the resurrection of a military fighter aircraft industry in Canada for what would amount to be only a few aircraft. The difference back in the fifties was that the military aircraft industry was still wide open for new players. Today it has collapsed somewhat, as large companies have merged, leaving little if any room for a new player.

Is there even a need for a high-altitude interceptor, or is the Canadian requirement now for a multi-role fighter? One must realize that in today's scenarios, a hostile bomber might be well within its own country's boundaries when it launches an attack using cruise missiles. Recently, the Russians announced that they have developed an air-launched hypersonic cruise missile. Neither an interceptor nor a multi-role fighter would be of much use against that threat, although a fighter could be employed in other scenarios.

When the Arrow was conceived, the RCAF had examined the threat that might materialize in the years to come. That threat was originally expected to come from advanced piloted bombers from the Soviet Union, attacking from the north, across the pole. The RCAF, together with Great Britain and the United States, conducted a review of available and anticipated aircraft of the day. The results showed that no aircraft would be good enough to counter the perceived threat and so the Arrow was commissioned.

Today the situation is vastly different in terms of aircraft, capabilities, missile developments, and the like.

Moving forward, in 1997–98, Canada entered into an arrangement with the United States and seven other countries to develop and produce a multi-role fighter, the F-35, as a follow-on to the CF-18. The F-35 would be unlike anything else. It would replace aircraft in use by the USAF, the U.S. Navy and the Marines. It would be the next-generation fighter well into the 2030s. With its stealth capability, it would be set apart from all other fighters, as the Arrow had been before. Like the Arrow, it would carry its weapons in an internal weapons bay, but for reasons of stealth, not of aerodynamics for speed. (Missiles hanging off the wings would destroy its stealth characteristics, as they would present large targets to radar detection systems.)

By 2010, the Conservative government approved the acquisition of the aircraft as a sole-source procurement because it was the only aircraft that had stealth and met all the other essential military requirements. By 2011, though, not only was the issue of sole-source coming into question but so was the projected cost. By 2012, after publication of a negative auditor general's report on the subject, the program was halted as a review was undertaken. The problems with the acquisition are well documented in Kim Nossal's book *Charlie Foxtrot*.

When the election was held in 2015 and the Liberals came to power, the latter declared the F-35 would not be purchased. This time the Liberals wished to conduct an open competition for the CF-18 replacement. In a truly open competition, though, the F-35 would have to be allowed to compete. It could not be excluded simply on political grounds. And what of that capability for stealth? If it was a hard requirement, would it not result once again in a sole-source acquisition?

Stealth, or, more accurately, low observability, can provide a great advantage. Both Russia and China are developing low-observable fighters. While it is true that certain radar can be tuned to detect these aircraft, stealth capability, at least for now, delays detection, thus offering an advantage that could mean the difference between survival and destruction.[10] As well, any detecting radar might first be neutralized through the use of a targeted initial attack, allowing the stealth aircraft to penetrate defences more readily. In addition, even if a stealth aircraft is "seen" by certain radar, its exact position, for a missile counter-strike, is not easily determined.[11]

Non-stealth aircraft tend to be beacons detectable at far greater distances with little effort. Would a Canadian Arrow design incorporate stealth? That might be wise, but would add complexity and cost to an already challenging development for this Canadian alternative.

Also, perhaps more important than stealth is the software that makes the F-35 fly and launch weapons. It also provides the pilot with the capability of knowing what is going on all around. This 360-degree situational awareness is achieved by fusing data from all onboard and external sensors and presenting the result to the pilot. The F-22 Raptor is a classic example of this. It also has stealth, speed, and manoeuvrability beyond that of the F-35. The problem is that it is not for sale.[12] Any Arrow design would be wise to incorporate this data-fusion capability; but, again, at what cost and complexity?

The F-35 was supposed to be a more affordable alternative to the F-22 but problems have plagued its development and consequently costs have increased. Many of the problems in this aircraft lie with the aforementioned software. Concerning some software issues with the F-35, in 2015 the Pentagon reported the following:

> The Pentagon discovered deficiencies in the plane's Block 2B software system. Block 2B oversees the plane's initial warfare capabilities, like its various data links and live-weapon firing system. The worst deficiencies were found in the Block 2B's navigation and accuracy software aspects ... encountered issues with weapon delivery accuracy. The software still had trouble in the use of radar, passive sensors, friend-or-foe identification, and electro-optical targeting. The 2BS5 software package, which deals with sensors, also continues to run into difficulties. According to the report, "fusion of information from own-ship sensors, as well as fusion of information from off-board sensors is still deficient ..."[13]

These issues with the F-35 are being introduced here to demonstrate that such sophisticated software represents a whole new area of development when considering rebuilding a military airplane in Canada. Whether multi-role or not, this type of software capability will likely be required for going up against modern and future warplanes and their highly sophisticated weapons, or against sophisticated ground-launched weapons.

The next question, of course, is what would be the cost of rebuilding a military aircraft capability — or, to put it another way, what would the government and Canadians tolerate as a reasonable cost for such an undertaking? Whom would Canada sell to, given that the F-35, with all its problems, remains on the books and has commenced deliveries — not to mention the competition that would come from all the other foreign aircraft that are still in production.

Would it be possible to convince the government that such a development could be undertaken in Canada, for the dollar amounts that had been originally tabled for the F-35? Could it be done within a reasonable time frame, given that one would have to attract various types of engineers and technical specialists while re-establishing an entire research, manufacturing, and production facility where none exists today?

In order to participate in the development of the F-35, Canada has paid a recurring sum to the United States. It was reported in May 2017 that, in April, Canada had paid $30 million to remain a joint partner in the development. CBC News indicated Canada has paid $373 million U.S. since 1997, but, in return, Canadian companies have obtained on the order of $926 million in F-35–related contracts. The longer Canada remains a partner, the more Canadian aerospace companies can get.[14] One can only hope, though, that the contracts being secured include those involving the development of advanced technologies.

If the F-35 gets its problems solved, it will offer that 360-degree situational awareness along with low observability, and may be more effective than other aircraft as a result, even if its speed and manoeuvrability are not on par with some other aircraft. It will also offer interoperability with Canada's largest partner — the United States — and with all other recipient countries, and, as a result there will be an abundant supply of spares for maintenance. If the bugs are solved and the price is right, it should be carefully considered; especially if a threat assessment produces a requirement that deems low observability or stealth and 360-degree situational awareness to be essential.

The F-35 was originally sole-sourced on the basis of the requirement. Clamoring for a competitive process rather than a sole-source procurement is fine. But who among those demanding competition is in a position to question the requirement or the threat assessment? And who would be in the best position to identify the required capability, if not the military — the politicians? This was in some respects the issue with the Arrow. While the chief of the air staff identified the need for the aircraft, others including the minister believed that, since the threat from aircraft had allegedly diminished in favour of the missile threat, the Arrow was no longer required.

In correspondence received from C. Fred Matthews, former supervisor of experimental flight test engineering at Avro, he writes of his discussions with the late John Bracken, former head of the Conservative Party. The latter was his wife's uncle. In December of 1958, Matthews states that Bracken confided in him that "there were few if any politicians then in Ottawa who had any understanding of technology in general or whether the Arrow was an important or viable system for the defence of Canada and North America."[15]

Matthews amplifies this statement by noting that in the mid-sixties two generals in the USAF at Hanscom Field effectively made similar comments to an ex-Avro employee. Both had been involved in evaluating the Arrow when they were lieutenant colonels and majors, and both deemed the aircraft to be outstanding. One of them, though, was on the team that eventually briefed Ottawa on the need for missiles. He said the prime minister and his staff were so technically naive that a standing joke was that they should try to sell them the Brooklyn Bridge.

The issue here is not to attack those from the past but to ask how one fixes this problem, this disparity in knowledge between the so-called professionals and the decision-makers. Perhaps a committee of technically knowledgeable, non-partisan individuals might be in a position to act as a go-between, helping both sides to understand each other's requirements and constraints, without adding yet another bureaucratic layer to an already complex process.

Indeed, in shaping defence policy itself, Kim Nossal, in *Charlie Foxtrot*, proposes the creation of a Standing Joint Committee on Defence Policy of parliament that would seek to "review defence policy, to develop an institutional memory, and to provide ongoing feedback to the government on changes that might, in the committee's view, be needed in light of changes in the geostrategic environment."[16] At the project or program level, perhaps an arm's-length technical committee would also be useful in bridging the gap between the military and the government. Such a committee could also assist in keeping tabs on some of the issues that can affect programs negatively, such as "Canadianization" — the modification of existing platforms to suit Canada's specific needs, rather than simply purchasing a product outright.

An example of the effects of "Canadianization" rests with the submarine acquisition program of 2011. According to media reports some $1 billion was spent over and above the initial cost, on "Canadianization."[17] On the other hand, the CC-177 Globemaster transport aircraft, a billion-dollar-plus expense, was purchased in record time from the United States complete and ready for operational use as Canada's main military transport aircraft. No modifications were made. The aircraft was essentially accepted as is, save for the paint scheme. This was effectively an off-the-shelf (OTS) or military-off-the-shelf (MOTS) successful acquisition.

Even off-the-shelf purchases, though, have run into difficulty where the term off-the-shelf was not well understood, and therefore where an external technical committee might have assisted. An example is the Cormorant search-and-rescue helicopter. This helicopter was sold to the government as an off-the-shelf procurement, that is, readily available with few if any modifications required. Problems, however, were encountered and introduction into service was subsequently delayed. For the reasons, one has only to look at an internal report from the Department of National Defence available online.

In the *Review of the Canadian Search and Rescue Helicopter*, dated July 2007, from the Chief Review Services of DND, the following is noted: "The single most significant issue affecting this acquisition project was the early and unchallenged assumption that the procurement was essentially *off-the-shelf*, contradicting views that the aircraft now has less than 30 percent commonality with the *off-the-shelf* version ..." Elsewhere in the report the following is stated: "The lack of a common understanding of what constitutes *off-the-shelf* contributed to this situation and acted to the detriment of the project."[18] The Cormorant was not really off-the-shelf, requiring numerous modifications. Might an arms-length technical committee have assisted before rather than after the fact?

In considering non-American aircraft for Canadian defence, "Canadianization" may be of concern as well as interoperability with the United States. Also, though, obtaining spare parts in a timely fashion and at reasonable cost could be problematic, given the proprietary nature of some foreign equipment. The upfront capital cost might be attractive, but the cost of spares could be enormous, assuming such spares were even available when needed.

Should Canada purchase the rights to produce and manufacture an existing foreign aircraft, and that plane is taken out of service by the originating country, would Canada be left catering to its small numbers alone? Would this eventually require yet another purchase of new aircraft at a later date?

Assuming that fighter aircraft will not be replaced by new tactics — for example, by fleets of less expensive but highly advanced smart drones capable of swarming attacking aircraft or missiles like bees, or controlled chaff — the F-35, with all its attendant flaws and acknowledged problems, should remain in contention. This said, a Government of Canada announcement in December 2017 indicated the F-35 had, in fact, been put back in the running.

As for a homegrown product, it is not impossible to restart, but it is doubtful whether the government or the Canadian taxpayer would entertain such a massive undertaking as developing a military aircraft industry, for only a few aircraft, and especially doubtful in view of the latest defence initiative already underway, the shipbuilding program.

Why even try regenerating a military aircraft industry when a brighter future could be had in other areas, such as in advanced drone development, artificial intelligence, medical and environmental technological development, advanced security software development, quantum information processing development, and so on.

What is required is the political will to adequately fund advanced research and development projects in the appropriate areas; a country that believes in itself; and a country that will see such developments to fruition, not termination.

Appendix A

Some Notes on the Flight Controls and Stability
Augmentation System in the Avro Canada CF-105 Arrow

C. Fred Matthews (former Avro supervisor of experimental flight
test engineering and acting deputy chief flight test engineer, and
one of the three original flight directors of Project Mercury)

Aircraft control in the roll, pitch, and yaw axes is typically provided by ailerons for roll control, elevators for pitch control, and rudder for yaw control. The pilot controls the aileron and elevator surface movements by means of a control column (or wheel), and the rudder surface movements by means of rudder pedals.

In early and simple aircraft, the interconnections between the pilot's controls and the control surfaces are solid mechanical connections (wires and rods). As aircraft speed and size increased, pilot loads became excessive. To solve this problem, hydraulic systems were added to drive the surfaces. In such fully powered control systems, the pilot's controls mechanically moved servovalves that fed hydraulic fluid to actuator jacks. Because such powered systems provide little or no feedback feel to the pilot, numerous mechanical schemes (e.g., bob weights, springs, etc.) were often added to give some artificial feel in response to the inputs.

With further increases in aircraft speed and size, the power needed at the control surfaces also increased. To avoid ever-increasing sizes and weights of jacks, hydraulic pressures were often increased. Because of the Arrow's supersonic speed capability and the size of its control surfaces, the aerodynamic loads on the control surfaces were significant (e.g., equivalent to lifting six elephants standing on the elevators). However, the space available for control jacks was severely limited because of the thin shapes of the delta wing and the vertical tail. Therefore, to minimize the size of the jacks in order to fit them into the available space, Avro developed a unique 4,000 psi hydraulic system — the world's first for aircraft. This increased pressure not only minimized jack size, it also saved weight, although it created design headaches because the hydraulic components (e.g., jacks) were not available off-the-shelf and therefore required special development.

All aircraft designs are a compromise between providing inherent stability and providing manoeuvrability — e.g., air liners are more stable and less manoeuvrable than fighters. The Arrow was no exception to compromise in that its design was the first (another first) to intentionally include some flight envelope areas where dynamic stability was marginally negative (e.g., it was directionally unstable in some areas of the flight envelope above 40,000 feet). Instead of adding fin area to eliminate these cases (which would have added drag and penalized performance), Avro developed a revolutionary, sophisticated, computer-controlled, electronic flight control system — fly-by-wire (another world first).[1] Over the aircraft's wide speed and altitude ranges, the system provided automatic adjustment to the amount of control surface movement required to generate a change in attitude. That is, at a given altitude, increased speed decreased the amount of control movement required to produce a given attitude change.

CONTROL MODES

The Arrow's control system included three modes of operation:

- Normal — pilot in control
- Automatic — ground control and fire control system in control
- Emergency — pilot in control

Normal Mode

In the normal mode, the pilot controlled the aircraft by the fly-by-wire control system. His pressure on the controls was sensed by force transducers in the control column hand grip, which fed amplifiers and electronics in a computerized command servo. The servo altered the position of hydraulic control valves. Valve movement directed pressure to the appropriate side of the hydraulic jacks that provided the mechanical deflection of the control surfaces. Increased pilot pressure resulted in increased control surface deflection.

Calibration of control sensitivities in all three axes was a major part of the Mark I flight test program. Pitch sensitivities throughout the flight envelope were of particular concern (see "Flight Test" paragraph later on).

At medium speeds in roll, the system produced a roll rate in proportion to the force applied to the stick. At high or low speeds, the forces for a given roll rate were increased slightly. In yaw, the amount of rudder movement for a given force on the rudder bar was decreased as the loading on the rudder increased.

As this fully powered control system was irreversible with no direct mechanical linkage from the pilot to the control surfaces, it provided no inherent feedback. Therefore, artificial feedback from the servos to the control column was added to provide resistance pressure on the control column so that, although it was the pilot's pressure against the feedback that generated the control signals, the movement against the instantaneous feedback gave him the feeling of a conventional control column where motion was the control generator. Electronic portions of the control system were digital and transistorized (in 1958).

Elevator and aileron trim could be selected by a four-way switch on the control column. Rudder trim could be selected by a toggle switch on the pilot's right-hand console. A control surface response indicator on the left-hand console showed the amount of control surface deflection relative to the main surface. In later Marks, at approximately 45,000 feet, the ailerons were to be automatically deflected downward by a pressure switch in order to reduce elevator trim drag. On descent to about 42,000 feet, they returned to their normal position.

For reliability, the hydraulic portion of the control system featured two independent hydraulic circuits — "A" and "B." Each engine had two engine-driven hydraulic pumps. One pump on each engine pressurized circuit "A." The other pump on each engine pressurized circuit "B." Both circuits fed the dual-sided control jacks. To prevent pressure fluctuations, an accumulator was part of each circuit.

Failure effects:

- Failed engine — rates of control movement would be slower
- Either hydraulic circuit failed — available G at high speeds would be restricted
- Both circuits failed — emergency flying mode
- Both engines failed — on later Marks, a ram-air-driven turbine, on the left side of the fuselage, could be selected by the pilot. When selected (at not more than 350 knots) it would extend into the airstream and provide sufficient pressure to the "A" circuit for operation from 350 knots down to 140 knots (landing speed).

A major contributor to the design of the fly-by-wire system was Richard R. Carley under the direction of the Chief, Aerodynamics, Jim Chamberlin. After the cancellation of the Arrow, they both joined NASA's newly formed Project Mercury (as did I), where they were instrumental in applying the fly-by-wire concept to the Mercury capsule controls and later to the Gemini capsule controls.

Automatic Mode — Automatic Ground-Controlled Intercept (AGCI) and Fire Control

Eventually, the Arrow was to incorporate a fire control system integrated with a ground-controlled intercept capability and interfaced to the fly-by-wire control system. This integrated concept was a major revolution in systems design. The concept was that a system of ground radars and computers would guide the aircraft to the point of radar contact with the target, at which time the fire control system would take over. Both phases were automatic with the pilot out of the control loop, except in emergencies. This integrated ground control/fire control/flight control and stabilization concept was facilitated by the electronic nature and design of the fly-by-wire system.

In Automatic Mode, elevator and aileron positions were controlled by an Automatic Flight Control Subsystem (AFCS), which allowed ground control to manoeuvre the aircraft for Automatic Ground Control Interception (AGCI) or for Automatic Ground Control Approach (AGCA).

Other functions to assist the pilot were to be included: holding set course, altitude, or Mach number; and automatic navigation from a dead-reckoning computer utilizing data fed into it by the navigator.

RCA was to provide the ground control interface and fire control system with its proposed Astra system.[2]

Emergency Mode

If certain flight conditions exceeded their limits, the control system automatically reverted to an emergency mode with the pilot in control. In this mode, the hydraulic components of the elevators and ailerons were controlled mechanically with pilot's feel on the controls provided by bob weights and springs attached to the control column. Rudder coordination and yaw stabilization were provided by an emergency yaw damper system.

STABILITY AUGMENTATION (DAMPING)

The Arrow's fly-by-wire control system facilitated implementation of stability augmentation, which was superimposed on the basic control system. The augmentation was active in the normal control and automatic control modes and provided automatic stabilization in three axes. Its purpose was not only to counteract aerodynamic instabilities but also to damp aircraft responses to other non-pilot inputs (e.g., gusts, engine cut). For example, in the case of a single-engine landing, afterburning was normally not required unless to correct any approach errors, in which case some 5,000 pounds. of asymmetrical thrust would suddenly be added. Most aircraft would swing sharply with this amount of asymmetric power, but the Arrow's stability augmentation system would immediately damp it out. Test pilot Spud Potocki said that when he cut an engine while climbing in full afterburner, the sideslip indicator stayed perfectly steady because the damping system had taken over.[3]

The Arrow's damping system was designed and produced by Minneapolis-Honeywell.[4] It used sensors mounted on the long pitot tube that protruded from the nose of the aircraft ahead of any aircraft shock wave. These sensors measured aircraft motions in three axes and provided control signals to a differential servo superimposed on the basic control servo. The damping signals moved the controls completely independent of the pilot's control column and coordinated rudder movement with movement of the ailerons and elevators. Unlike the pilot's control signals to the basic control servo, the damping signals were not fed back to the pilot's controls.

The damping system provided stability augmentation in three channels:

- Pitch — elevators
- Roll — ailerons
- Yaw — rudder

Because yaw stability was of major importance in the higher speed ranges, the electrical and hydraulic supplies for rudder control were duplicated. In the emergency mode, only rudder damping was provided.

With the gear down in normal and AFCS modes:

- Roll — enough damping to help counteract any Dutch roll (yaw due to roll)
- Yaw — intentional sideslipping permitted but any transient yaw disturbance would be damped
- Pitch — enough limited damping to support the pilot's control

On the second flight of the first aircraft, 25201, I was in the radio control truck at the start of the runway. As we watched the aircraft accelerate down the runway and lift into the air, the starboard wing suddenly took a sickening drop but immediately righted itself. To avoid a crash as the wing dropped, Zura had immediately disconnected the damping system by means of a switch on the control column. Later, it was determined that the damping sensors had been hooked up backwards by Honeywell technicians and were amplifying attitude disturbances instead of damping them.

SOME STEPS IN DEVELOPMENT OF THE CONTROL SYSTEM

Control System Simulator

During development of the aircraft configuration, extensive wind-tunnel testing and free-flight model testing were conducted to derive performance and stability-control parameters. These tests were used to verify or modify computer analyses and simulations. A major tool in developing the control system was a flight simulator incorporating all of the elements of the control system. These were coupled to an analog computer (the largest in Canada), which incorporated the aerodynamic parameters for stability, control, and performance that had been derived from the various analyses and development tests.

Before the first flight of the first Arrow, the pilots regularly "crashed" the simulator. After the flight tests began, flight test results were fed into the computer to adjust the control parameters. From that point on, the simulator worked well and became an effective element of the aircraft development program.

Flight Test

A major task in the flight test program was to fine-tune the sensitivities of the fly-by-wire and damping system. Therefore, a number of the Arrow flights in the test program for the five Mark I aircraft were devoted to fine-tuning the control system. These flights included handling tests by RCAF test pilot Jack Woodman. This emphasis on tuning the control system started immediately after the very first flight when alterations to the elevator controls were made that eliminated some longitudinal pitching at medium speeds that had been experienced by Jan Zurakowski.

On Jack Woodman's first flight, the pitch controls were calibrated with linear sensitivity. He found this to be too sensitive — a 5 G turn would take only two inches of stick movement. The sensitivity was modified to include a gradient so that the stick was less effective near the centre, but preserved total pitch authority at the extremes of its movement. His comment after his second flight — excellent. This is one example of how the flexibility of a fly-by-wire system facilitates modifications.

To facilitate control system testing, the Mark I Arrows included a dial in the cockpit to let the test pilot vary the control sensitivity. Telemetered and recorded data of settings and responses would then be combined with the pilot's report and analyzed.

As a result of these refinement tests, the aircraft handling became more manageable, so that landing speed were reduced to 145 knots from 185 knots, which reduced the length of runway required. In one test, the aircraft used less than 3,000 feet.

Fine-tuning development of the fly-by-wire and damping systems continued until the Arrow contract was cancelled. Shortly before cancellation, one of my flight test engineers, Red Darrah, rode in the back seat of 25203 to tune the control system for pilot Spud Potocki. This was the only flight of an Arrow with someone in the rear seat.

Appendix B

Avro to NASA

Much has been written about the group of ex-Avro engineers who went to NASA, so a brief recap will suffice. When a disagreement arose between the National Aeronautical Establishment (NAE) in Canada and Avro regarding the performance of the aircraft, the NAE and RCAF solicited the advice of the National Advisory Committee for Aeronautics (NACA), precursor to NASA. The latter initially agreed with the NAE's conclusions. Then a second meeting was arranged, this time with Avro engineers in attendance. Countering the points raised by the NAE, the Avro engineers demonstrated that their own numbers were in fact correct, explaining the reasons why and how the data had perhaps been misinterpreted. NACA ended up agreeing with Avro. From the recollections of an ex-Avro engineer, this encounter may have set the stage for NASA's later interest in Avro employees when the cancellation of the Arrow program occurred.

When the program was cancelled, as stated previously, Jim Floyd hoped his staff could be maintained somehow. It soon became clear, however, that this was not going to happen, and, as a result, there would be no significant work for this highly talented team in Canada. At the time, the NACA

Space Task Group (STG) had won the right to develop Project Mercury and was looking for experienced personnel.

While the team under Wernher von Braun were developing the rocket, the STG was responsible for the capsule. According to Avro engineer and NASA recruit Bryan Erb, the STG had fewer than a hundred people. Brilliant researchers all, most, however, had only ever worked on small-scale vehicles. Complicating things further, the STG had little success recruiting talent from U.S. industry. This was partly because Mercury was only a two-year project and not many were prepared to leave their established careers for this short-term work, work that might be a one-time effort. Also, these people would be needed in the industry, to fulfill the contract work that would be forthcoming.

In contrast, the cancellation of the Arrow program in Canada had created a tremendous pool of available talent. The Avro team brought much-needed industrial experience; they had worked on large complex systems with the groundbreaking Jetliner, the CF-100, and finally the Arrow, while also liaising with other industrial players and government. They were the right people at the right time. Their skill sets, which included experience in flight control, flight operations, structures and materials science, communications and instrumentation, flight mechanics and guidance, navigation control, and management and leadership, to name only a few, made the ex-Arrow team the perfect complement to the personnel already in place at the STG.

As already noted, the Avro group also brought with them transferable knowledge. Bryan Erb, who had worked on the thermal aspects on the Arrow, worked in the development of the Mercury capsule's heat shield and went on to Project Apollo. The fly-by-wire control concepts for the capsule came courtesy of the Arrow's Jim Chamberlin and Richard Carley. Jim Chamberlin also borrowed from the Arrow's clamshell cockpit for the dual-door arrangement used in Project Gemini for quick ingress and egress.

Owen Maynard, who became chief of the Systems Engineering Division for the Apollo spacecraft, was instrumental in the development of the lunar landing module. John Hodge became flight director on the Mercury, Gemini, and Apollo programs.

As noted, C. Fred Matthews was one of the three original directors on Mercury, but was also responsible for flight monitoring and the flight controllers stationed at the various tracking stations worldwide. Tecwyn Roberts would go on to have a major role in the design of the Mission Control Center in Houston. Not from the original twenty-five but also involved in the space program were Robert Lindley, Mario Pesando, and Carl Lindow.

Robert Lindley, chief engineer at Avro when the cancellation occurred, took a position at McDonnell Aviation and would go on to be in charge of work on the Gemini program. Pesando, chief of project research at Avro, worked on the Saturn V rocket for RCA. Lindow, former project manager on the Arrow, became project engineer on the Saturn S-1 and Saturn S-1B rocket proposals for Boeing. The list goes on. Without a doubt, NASA would still have found the ways and means to achieve their goals without the Avro team; but with the team, the time frame for achieving those goals was perhaps considerably shortened.

The following citation given to Jim Chamberlin by NASA is indicative of the esteem and respect given to all the Canadians, for their outstanding contributions to the manned space program. It reads:

> National Aeronautics and Space Administration (NASA) Manned Spacecraft Center presents this certificate of commendation to James A. Chamberlin for his out-standing contribution to this nation's space flight programs, for the technical direction and leadership of Project Mercury, for his creation and promotion of the Gemini concept and for his guidance in the design of all manned spacecraft used in the United States' exploration of space to date.
>
> — Robert R. Gilruth
> Director, Manned Spacecraft Center, Houston, Texas

The Original Twenty-Five Avro Employees Who Went to NASA

Name	Place of Birth
Aikenhead, Bruce A.	Canada
Armitage, Peter J.	England
Carley, Richard R.	Canada
Chalmers, Frank	Scotland
Chamberlin, James A.	Canada
Chambers, Thomas V.	England
Cohen, Jack	England
Cohn, Stanley	Canada
Duret, Eugene L.	Canada
Erb, Richard B.	Canada
Ewart, David D.	England
Farbridge, Joseph	England
Farmer, Norman B.	England
Fielder, Denis E.	England
Galezowski, Stanley	Canada
Hodge, John	England
Hughes, John K.	England
Jenkins, Morris V.	England
Matthews C. Frederick	Canada
Maynard, Owen	Canada
Packham, Leonard	Canada
Roberts, Tecwyn	England
Rose, Rodney G.	England
Shoosmith, John N.	England
Watts, George A.	Canada

The author thanks Jim Floyd, Bryan Erb, the late Owen Maynard, and C. Fred Matthews for the information they shared regarding the NASA Canadians. Some of the material from Jim also appears in his vignette submission to *Wayfarers: Canadian Achievers* by Charles J. Humber.

Appendix C

Selected Figures

This list of figures and captions corresponds with the selected images that follow.

196   The first artifact recovered in the latest search for the Arrow test models is likely the delta test vehicle similar to the one in this diagram sitting atop a demon rocket booster. Current thinking is the delta was related to both the Arrow model test program and the Velvet Glove missile development program.

Source: Library and Archives Canada

197   The Sparrow II missile, chosen over the Velvet Glove for use on the CF-100 and the Avro Arrow, was itself abandoned for use on the Arrow in favour of the Falcon missile.

Source: Library and Archives Canada

198   This diagram of the Arrow was one actually passed on to Brik, the Soviet double agent, by his spy within Avro, a man named Lind.

Source: From the personal collection of Donald G. Mahar

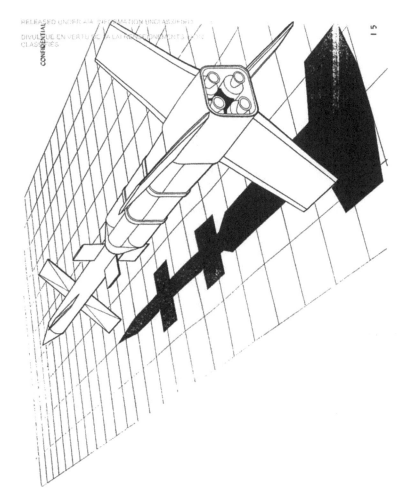

15

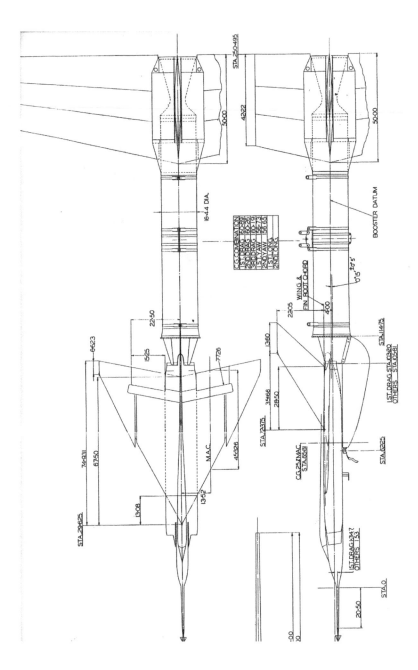

Appendix C.

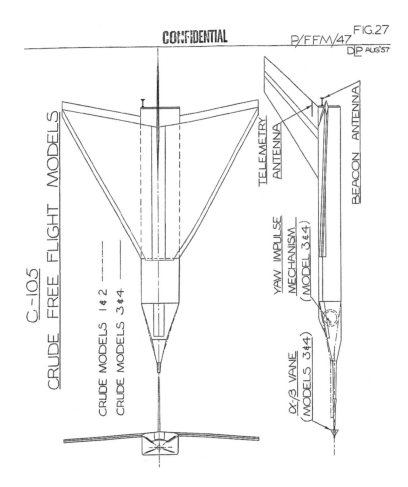

P/FFM/47 FIG.27
DP AUG'57

C-105
CRUDE FREE FLIGHT MODELS

CRUDE MODELS 1 & 2 --------
CRUDE MODELS 3 & 4 ————

TELEMETRY ANTENNA

BEACON ANTENNA

YAW IMPULSE MECHANISM (MODEL 3 & 4)

α/β VANE (MODELS 3 & 4)

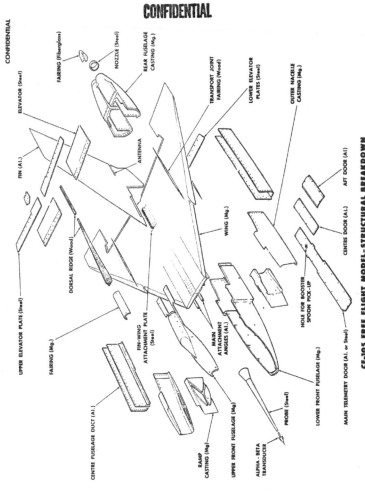

CONFIDENTIAL

CF-105 FREE FLIGHT MODEL—STRUCTURAL BREAKDOWN

FIG. 34

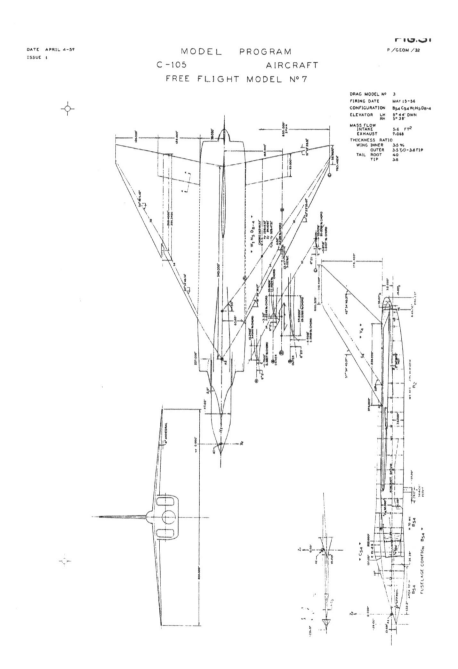

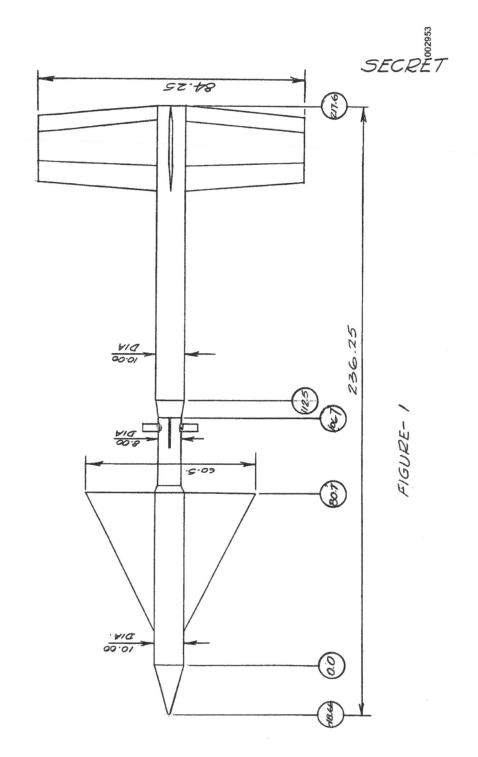

002953

FIGURE-1

Appendix C

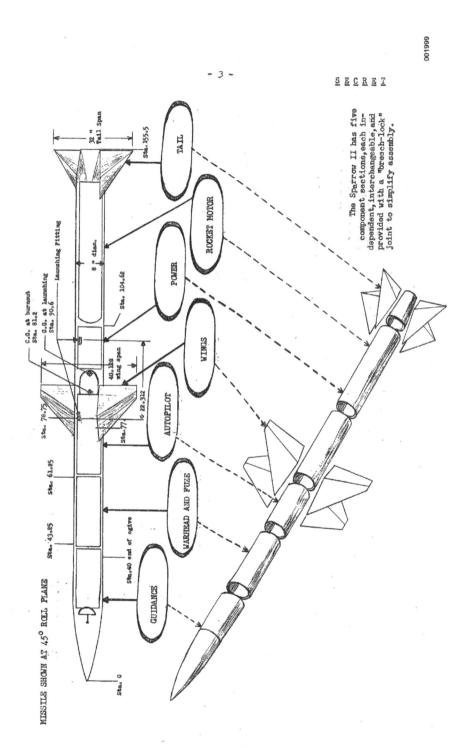

- 3 -

SECRET

The Sparrow II has five component sections, each independent, interchangeable, and provided with a "breech-lock" joint to simplify assembly.

MISSILE SHOWN AT 45° ROLL PLANE

TAIL

ROCKET MOTOR

POWER

WINGS

AUTOPILOT

WARHEAD AND FUZE

GUIDANCE

32 " Tail Span

Sta. 155.5

8 " diam.

Sta. 104.62

Launching Fitting

C.g. at launching Sta. 90.6

C.g. at burnout Sta. 81.2

Sta. 78.75

40.128 wing span

22.312

Sta. 77

Sta. 61.25

Sta. 43.25

Sta.40 end of ogive

Sta. 0

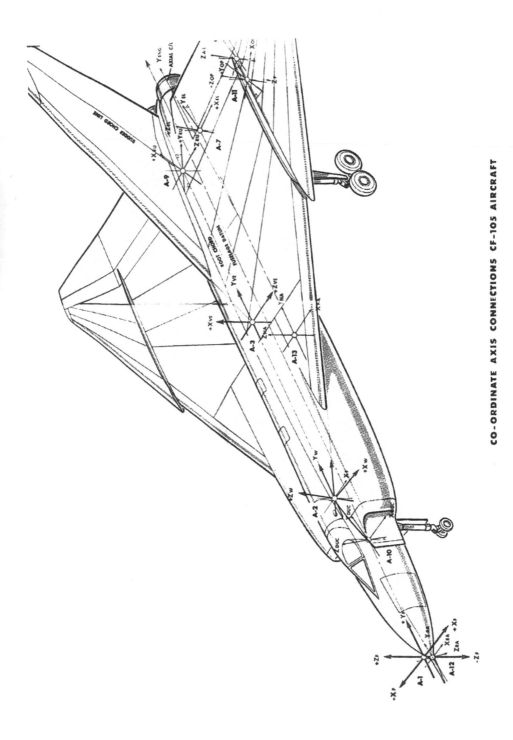

CO-ORDINATE AXIS CONNECTIONS CF-105 AIRCRAFT

Appendix D

Selected Documents

The following captions correspond with the selected documents that follow. They chronicle the various events and statements leading to the termination and destruction of the aircraft and related technical records.

Page

205   In the absence of documentation to the contrary, it was said the Jetliner could not be sold. Revealed in *Requiem*, this memo shows the USAF Aircraft and Weapons Board approved the purchase of twelve Jetliners.
Source: Library and Archives Canada

206   National Airlines President B.T. Baker praises the Jetliner and says he is ready to do business on a reasonable basis. Instead, A.V. Roe would be told to stop development of the Jetliner.
Source: Library and Archives Canada

207   This extract from a CIA document from 1957, declassified in 2011, reveals intelligence information regarding Soviet missile capabilities. A key reason for the cancellation was the belief that missiles were supplanting bombers as the new threat.
Source: CIA website

208– In these recommendations of the Cabinet Defence Committee, the Chiefs
210   of Staff express doubt that the extremely high cost of the Arrow will pro-
      vide defence returns "commensurate with the expenditures in view of the
      changing threat and the possibility that an aircraft of comparable perfor-
      mance can be obtained from the United States production at a much less
      cost." Note the cost is linked to the return on investment given the change
      in threat, not that the aircraft is unaffordable. There were no comparable
      aircraft, and by 1959 cost had significantly decreased, as shown by Hugh
      Campbell in his own letter to the minister.
      Source: Library and Archives Canada

211   In this memo it is noted that costs of the Arrow compare favourably with
      those of less complex aircraft in the United States.
      Source: Library and Archives Canada

212– At the September 3 meeting of Cabinet, Defence Minister Pearkes
215   tables figures from Avro, showing a dramatic drop in price by moving
      from the Astra/Sparrow development, to the Hughes/Falcon combina-
      tion. Paragraph 4a is most prophetic. Paragraph 4f highlights the division
      among the Chiefs of Staff on the need for aircraft in light of the changing
      threat. Likewise, paragraph 4h questions why one might spend large sums
      on a program that might turn out to be "obsolete."
      Source: Library and Archives Canada

216– In this meeting of Cabinet on September 7, 1958, the minister of finance,
218   Donald Fleming, states that he would not put finance ahead of safety in
      regards defence. He supported the program a year previously, but now
      "more important, the military authorities had now decided that the air-
      craft was not necessary."
      Source: Library and Archives Canada

219– In this memo of October 21, 1958, Avro states in writing they will provide
220   a complete, operational aircraft for $3.5 million in a fixed-price contract.
      Source: Library and Archives Canada

221 At the time, some had argued that the Arrow had in fact been cancelled back in September when the announcement had been made to cancel the Sparrow and Astra development. This memo from November 1958 from Pearkes, requesting new contracts for the Hughes/Falcon system, demonstrates the opposite.
Source: Library and Archives Canada

222 On the engine front, American manufacturer North American Aviation requests detailed data on the Iroquois.
Source: Library and Archives Canada

223 At the January 13, 1959, meeting, Minister Pearkes acknowledges the memo from the Chief of the Air Staff in which he notes the cost is decreasing appreciably, availability time is shortened, and the radius of action has increased. Rather than support the program he states the Canadian contribution of aircraft would be small in comparison to that of the United States. Then he mistakenly gives the range of the Arrow, not the radius of action, as three hundred to five hundred miles.
Source: Library and Archives Canada

224– Contrary to the idea that, had the Liberals remained in power, they too
226 would have terminated the Arrow program, this letter from C.D. Howe to then Liberal leader Mike Pearson indicates although he had advised cancelling at the last meeting they had on the subject, the decision taken was to review the program, not cancel. He also acknowledges that Pearson was non-committal.
Source: Library and Archives Canada

227 February 6, 1959. The Cabinet Defence Committee reiterates comments from the Chiefs of Staff Committee regarding the changing threat; advances in technology, especially with missiles; and the reduction in numbers of interceptors required, and that these factors raise doubts that monies spent on continuing the program will provide returns commensurate with the expense.
Source: Library and Archives Canada

228–   February 17, 1959. The decision to cancel was made by Cabinet, and
229   the prime minister was reviewing the draft announcement to be made.
        The finance minister indicates it would be taken on the best military
        advice.

        Source: Library and Archives Canada

230   February 19, 1959. The day before Black Friday. The prime minister de-
        cides the time to make the announcement will be the next day, before the
        weekend, when the Canadian Broadcasting Corporation (CBC) is set to
        air a documentary on the development of the Arrow.

        Source: Library and Archives Canada

231   February 20, 1959, Black Friday. A terse telegram is sent to the company
        at 12:30 p.m. ordering all work to cease. This wording results in the im-
        mediate layoffs of some fourteen thousand employees at Avro and Orenda.

        Source: Library and Archives Canada

232   The infamous memo of March 26, 1959, in which Chief of the Air Staff
        Hugh Campbell recommends destroying the completed aircraft and en-
        gines. The minister asks for concurrence from his deputy minister (DM).

        Source: Directorate of History, Department of National Defence

233   This extract from a CIA document shows that there was some concern
        over the U-2s vulnerability. Tests were carried out to determine if the more
        capable of American aircraft could compromise the U-2. They could not,
        and so it was concluded the Soviets could not, either. Countering intru-
        sions by aircraft like the U-2 was what the Arrow was designed to do but
        was never given the opportunity.

        Source: CIA website

234   April 24, 1959. Hugh Campbell notes that the Minister of National
        Defence has stated the aircraft "will" be reduced to scrap. All signatories
        on this memo are aware of the sequence of events but choose to allow the
        prime minister to be the one tagged as being responsible for the destruc-
        tion. There is indication the U.K. might make a request for some Arrows,
        and so five are to remain intact.

        Source: Directorate of History, Department of National Defence

235 April 27, 1959. Deputy Minister of National Defence Frank Miller writes to the Deputy Minister of the DDP requesting confirmation on the method of disposal. He notes the method may change depending on inquiries from the U.K.
Source: Directorate of History, Department of National Defence

236 On May 15, 1959, the go-ahead to destroy the remaining aircraft and engines is finally given.
Source: Library and Archives Canada

237 June 2, 1959. Minster Pearkes responds to a Mrs. Bailey, who had asked about saving one or more aircraft. Pearkes states directly that the Arrow was cancelled because it would be inadequate by the time it entered service. Conspicuous by its absence is any mention of costs as a factor.
Source: Library and Archives Canada

238 On July 2, 1959, a draft response is prepared for the minister of the DDP, should he be asked about the abruptness of the cancellation. The draft response again addresses the utility of the aircraft and that no funds should continue to be spent on something deemed to have "no future military value."
Source: Library and Archives Canada

239 This memo from July 6, 1959, provides the status of the aircraft as they were being scrapped. The fourth and fifth aircraft were to be finished off by July 10, 1959.
Source: Library and Archives Canada

240 January 21, 1960. Final instructions are given to destroy the remaining documentation on the Arrow.
Source: Library and Archives Canada

241 At the Cabinet committee meeting of February 6, 1960, the prime minister realizes that he has made a mistake. He states he was against cancelling the Arrow but was persuaded otherwise. He states he thought Canadians would accept the wisdom in the decision but to accept other aircraft now, in the face of all those statements about a decreasing threat and reduction in any need for interceptors, would be embarrassing.
Source: Library and Archives Canada

242–   June 3, 1960. President Eisenhower is briefed on what to expect from
243   Prime Minister Diefenbaker, in regards questions on the Bomarc and air
defence in general. Of particular note is page 2, in which it is stated that
the Canadian minister of national defence confided privately to Defense
Secretary Gates that Canada would abandon interceptors altogether unless
they, the United States, saw their retention as "really important."
Source: Eisenhower Library

244–   Cabinet meeting of July 15, 1960. It is stated that interceptors will be re-
245   quired for years to come. What a difference a year makes. It is also admitted that the prime minister had received incorrect information about the
numbers of ICBMs in the U.S. arsenal, that the CF-100 was inadequate,
and that there would therefore be no surveillance of Canadian airspace by
Canadians.
Source: Library and Archives Canada

246   November 30, 1960. The USAF had expressed interest in the Iroquois.
While problems had arisen during the test phase, it was the RCAF opinion
that the major mechanical difficulties had been overcome. The engine had
obtained its fifty-hour preliminary flight rating test (PFRT).
Source: Library and Archives Canada

247   February 3, 1961. The USAF replies; they did not require the Iroquois.
Source: Library and Archives Canada

Appendix D

IN REPLY PLEAS

No......S.1038-C

Department of National Defence

CANADIAN JOINT STAFF
1700 MASSACHUSETTS AVE., N.W.
WASHINGTON 6, D.C.

14 August, 1951.

Referred to..

AUG 1

File No.S.6

Cnp'd to ...

Chief of the Air Staff,
Department of National Defence,
Ottawa, Ontario, Canada.

__Avro Jetliner C.102__

1.   Recently the Avro Jetliner was flown from Toronto to Washington for demonstration. The USAF and the USN are both interested in this aircraft but the only concrete proposal for purchase had come through the US AMC at Wright Field.

2.   It is now confirmed that the USAF wish to purchase 12 Jetliners. A recommendation was made to this effect by a specially appointed committee representing all USAF Commands, to the Aircraft and Weapons Board. This Board approved the purchase of 12 aircraft.

3.   The USAF intend to use the C.102 as a high-speed bombing trainer.

4.   There is another application for the C.102 which is of exciting interest, this being high-speed jet fighter refuelling. It is not known, at present, whether an order has been placed but the Flight Refuelling experimental section at USAF HQ are anxious to get 4 C102s for test in this type of work.

(H.G. Richards)
Group Captain
for Air Member
Canadian Joint Staff

205

THE AVRO ARROW

NATIONAL AIRLINES
3240 N.W. 27th Ave.
Miami 42, Florida.

February 26th, 1951.

Mr. R. Dixon Speas,
U.S. Representative,
A. V. Roe Canada Limited,
P. O. Box 111 - La Guardia Field,
New York Airport Station, New York.

Dear Dix:

It will be most appreciated if you will keep in communication with
J.D., regarding the developments of the Jetliner. As you know, we
are interested and ready to do business if a reasonable basis for so
doing can be reached.

It was a real pleasure to ride and fly the Jetliner when it was in
Miami a few weeks ago. It will undoubtedly have tremendous passenger
appeal after the average passenger's first fears have been reduced
or eliminated by knowing it is in scheduled operation. A great many
people are anxious to fly in it but are naturally a little shy of
such a new development, as they were 30 years ago in flying the old
Jenny's.

I haven't been in the plane when it was fully loaded, but I think its
performance at the time I flew it was excellent. It handled well
with one or two engines out and didn't seem to be in the least bit
tricky.

Ramp handling was no more difficult than a conventional type aircraft.
The heat from the jets was not noticeable.

While the noise level in the rear of the plane was a little higher than
it was in the front, it certainly was less than in a plane powered with
reciprocating engines.

I think you have a grand airplane and it can do a fine job on the
airlines if your Company can build and sell them on a basis acceptable
to the airlines.

Best regards,

"B. T. Baker" - President.

GTB:mst:A:M

CONCLUSIONS

GENERAL CONCLUSIONS

1. We estimate that the Soviet guided missile program is extensive and enjoys a very high priority. *(Paras. 17, 27, 29–30, 50)*

2. We believe that the USSR has the native scientific resources and capabilities to develop during this period advanced types of guided missile systems, in all categories for which it has military requirements. *(Paras. 29–38)*

3. We estimate that the USSR has the industrial base and related industrial experience to series produce the missile systems it will develop during this period. However, in view of competing demands, the limited availabliity of electronic equipment will seriously restrict the extent and variety of Soviet guided missile production until about 1958. Thereafter, expanding electronics production will probably make this restriction much less severe. *(Paras. 45–48)*

4. We estimate that the USSR has requirements for various sizes of nuclear, high explosive (HE), and chemical (CW) warheads, and has the capability to develop them on time scales consistent with the missiles in which they would be employed. In view of competing demands, the availability of fissionable materials will impose limitations on the extent of Soviet nuclear warhead production during the period of this estimate. *(Paras. 39–42, 54, Annex A)*

SPECIFIC SOVIET CAPABILITIES AND PROGRAMS

Surface-to-Air Missiles

5. We estimate that surface-to-air missile systems have one of the highest priorities among current Soviet military programs. At Moscow, an extensive system of surface-to-air missile sites has been constructed, and all sites are probably now operational. This system can probably direct a very high rate of fire against multiple targets at maximum altitudes of about 60,000 feet and maximum horizontal ranges of about 25 n.m. *(Paras. 27–28, 32, 56–60)*

6. During the period 1958–1961, surface-to-air systems with increased range and altitude capabilities for static defense of critical areas, and with low and high altitude capabilities for defense of static targets, field forces, and naval vessels, could probably become available for operational employment. Sometime between 1963 and 1966, the USSR could probably have in operation a surface-to-air system of some capability against the ICBM. *(Paras. 61–67)*

7. We estimate that series production of surface-to-air guided missiles is now under way in the USSR, and that it will probably produce such missiles in large quantities. Nuclear warheads could now be incorporated into a limited number of surface-to-air missiles. We estimate that some percentage of surface-to-air mis-

- 3 -

7.   The RCAF now has nine all-weather squadrons which are
located on five bases across Canada. The present programme calls for
the re-equipping of all nine squadrons with the Arrow, which will require
a production order of 169 Arrow aircraft. This number, along with the
aircraft recovered from the 37 development and preproduction order,
will provide sufficient aircraft for nine squadrons, with training and
logistic backup, at a total cost of two billion dollars extended over the
period 1959/60 to 1963/64.

8.   A study of the financial implications of continuing this programme
and its impact on the overall defence programme, and the necessity of giving
consideration to future requirements such as defence against intercontinental
ballistic missiles have necessitated a review of the air defence programme.

9.   The Chiefs of Staff have reviewed the air defence programme
and the following are the main points considered during this review:

   (a)   The Changing Threat

         The advent of Sputnik and the advances being made in the USSR in
         developing missiles have considerably changed the assessment of
         the threat to North America. It is now considered that the major
         threat in the 1960's will be from ballistic missiles, and the
         manned bomber will be a subordinate threat which is expected to
         decrease in importance after 1962-63. But a combination of
         ballistic missiles and the manned bomber may produce the threat
         until the present Soviet stockpile of manned bombers is depleted
         or evidence is given that they have re-opened production on
         manned bombers.

   (b)   The Rapid Advances in Technology

         The speeds and operating heights of jet bombers are now almost
         comparable to those of the manned fighter, and therefore to provide
         the manned fighter with the necessary advantage of height and speed
         requires very expensive and further intricate development which
         tends to increase the cost of the end product. Along with this, the
         rapid strides being made in the development of ground-to-air
         missiles, particularly in the last two years, by the United States,
         provides an additional accurate defensive weapon which perhaps is
         cheaper and is expected to provide greater attrition. The missiles
         of the Bomarc type which have been fully developed by the United
         States have a further attraction in that the U.S. has paid for the
         development of these missiles and is prepared to release them to
         Canada.

   (c)   The Diminishing Requirement for the Manned Interceptor

         It will be recalled that the early requirement in 1953 was for nine-
         teen squadrons, a total of between 500 and 600 aircraft. This has
         now been reduced to nine squadrons and consideration has been
         given in the last few months to reducing the requirement to five
         squadrons of about 100 aircraft now that the Bomarc missile is
         to be introduced into the Canadian air defence system.

- 4 -

(d)   Costs

The heavy costs of finishing the development and production
of a limited number of manned aircraft are shown as follows:

The present estimated cost of completing the development and
preproduction of the weapons system is $862 million, of which
$476 million has been committed so far. This expenditure is
to provide a proven design and facilities which can turn out
production. If the plan for equipment of nine squadrons (169)
is pursued, the unit production costs will be of the order of eight
million dollars per weapons system, giving a total production
cost of approximately $1400 million.

As mentioned earlier, consideration has been given to reducing
the requirement to five squadrons, requiring an overall number
of 100 aircraft. This number could be provided by a production
order for 80 aircraft and recovering 20 from the development
and preproduction order. However if only 80 aircraft are
produced, the unit cost rises to the order of $10 million per
copy. Details of costs are shown in Appendix "B". The
Chiefs of Staff have grave doubts as to whether a limited
number of aircraft at this extremely high cost would provide
defence returns commensurate with the expenditures in view
of the changing threat and the possibility that an aircraft of
comparable performance can be obtained from United States
production at a much less cost and in the same time period,
1961 - 1962. Comparative costs of similar numbers of
CF105 and US F106C are shown in Appendix "A". Therefore
the Chiefs of Staff consider that to meet this modest requirement for interceptor aircraft it would be more economical to
procure a fully developed interceptor of comparable performance
from United States sources.

Recommendations

10.   It is recommended that Cabinet approve the recommendations
of Cabinet Defence Committee as follows:

   (a)   Approval in principle be given to:

          (i) the installation of 2 Bomarc bases in the Ottawa -
              North Bay area; and

          (ii) the installation of two additional heavy radars in
               Northern Ontario and Quebec and the installation
               of the associated gap filler radars.

SECRET

- 5 -

(b)   Authority be granted to commence negotiations with the
       United States for cost-sharing and production on the
       following items:

       (i) the installation of 2 Bomarc bases in the Ottawa -
            North Bay area; and

       (ii) the installation of 2 heavy radars in Northern
            Ontario and Quebec and the installation of gap
            filler radars.

(c)   Consideration be given to:

       (i) abandoning the CF105 Arrow programme and
            associated fire control and weapons systems projects;
            and

       (ii) authorizing the Chiefs of Staff to investigate and
            submit proposals for:

            (1) any additional missile installations required;
                 and/or

            (2) any additional interceptor aircraft of a proven,
                 developed type that may be required in lieu of
                 the CF105.

MINISTER OF NATIONAL DEFENCE

Department of National Defence,
22 August, 1958.

APPENDIX "A" - Comparative Costs of 100 CF105's and US F106C's.

           "B" - Cost of air defence programme, including 80 CF105's
                 from production and 20 from preproduction order.

           "C" - Air defence programme, including additional
                 Bomarc sites.

OR
PA

S1038CN-180 (CAE)

M E M O R A N D U M

28 Mar 58

AMTS

Arrow Cost Versus Cost of Comparable Aircraft

1 Previous attempts have been made to assemble, design and development costs for the USAF F106 in order that they might be compared with our Arrow programme. While the costs directly attributable to the various USAF orders for the F106 have been obtained it has been impossible to assemble true costs of the F106 design and development phase. This situation results from the manner in which the F106 has developed, i.e. it is first of all a development of the F102 and a portion of the costs of design and development of this aircraft should be borne by the F106. In addition the MA-1 electronics system of the F106 is developed from the $360.0M MG-10 and 14 programmes and an unknown portion of this cost should be borne by the F106 in any true comparison. There are other major areas of this nature which preclude the desired comparison, the most important of which are the fact that USA contractors enjoy the use of certain Government facilities without cost and that the J75 has several applications whereas the more advanced Iroquois is still in the development stage.

2 Notwithstanding the foregoing, costs attributed by the USAF to their many orders for Century series aircraft have been assembled and are summarized as Appendix "A". If these are viewed in the light of the qualifications in para 1 it is apparent that Arrow costs compare favourably with the somewhat less sophisticated aircraft in the USA. Production costs included for 200 Arrow aircraft were obtained from BDP and are of course only an estimate which is subject to change as more information becomes available during the development phase.

3 It has been interesting to learn that RCAF fly-away costs for the CF-10, from production were less than for the comparable F89 Scorpion. Similarly, quantity production of the F86 and T33 was undertaken in Canada at a lower per aircraft cost than from USA production.

4 It may, therefore, be concluded that quantity production of an aircraft as complex as the Arrow can be undertaken in Canada at a cost comparable to that for production of a like aircraft in the U.S.A.

(Signed) G. G. Truscott

(G.G. Truscott) A/C
CAE
6-6273

Attach.
JCSmith/MC S/L
MP2/A WS
2-0282
Circ
MP2
CAE

- 2 -

Visit of the Queen and Prince Philip in 1959

1. **The Prime Minister** said he had asked to have this brief meeting to inform the Cabinet of the announcement he intended to make, when the House of Commons met, that the Queen and the Prince Philip would visit Canada from approximately mid-June to the end of July next year. It had been thought advisable to make this announcement at once to prevent leaks that were otherwise bound to occur.

2. **The Cabinet** noted with approval the Prime Minister's intention to announce that the Queen and the Prince Philip would visit Canada from mid-June to the end of July of next year.

Air defence requirements; recommendations of Cabinet Defence Committee
(Previous reference Aug. 28)

3. **The Minister of National Defence** said that, since this subject had last been discussed, Mr. John Tory, one of the directors of A.V. Roe, and Mr. F.T. Smye, Vice-President of Avro Aircraft Ltd., had discussed the future of the CF-105 with the Prime Minister, the Minister of Finance, and himself. These men recommended that the airframe and Iroquois engine elements of the programme be continued but that the fire control system (ASTRA) and the weapon (SPARROW) projects be dropped and substitutes obtained in the United States. Instead of ASTRA and SPARROW they had suggested the U.S. Hughes MA-1 system and the FALCON, respectively. He had had cost estimates prepared on this suggestion and comparisons made with other alternatives. These were as follows:

Expenditures for 100 aircraft, from September 1st, 1958:

105/Astra-Sparrow	$1,261.5 million	or $12.61 million each
105/Hughes MA-1-Falcon	$ 896 million	or $ 8.91 million each
U.S. 106	$ 559 million	or $ 5.59 million each
BOMARC (to provide roughly equivalent defensive strength)	$ 520.3 million	4 batteries of 60 missiles each (no cost-sharing with the U.S.)

4. **During the discussion** the following further points emerged:

(a) If it turned out in a year's time that the U.S.S.R. was going to equip its air force with newer, more modern bombers, then Canada would have to buy BOMARC or an interceptor from the U.S., or both, assuming the CF-105 was abandoned.

(b) If, on the other hand, it was clear at that time that the U.S.S.R. was not producing bombers, arrangements would have to be made with the U.S. for defence against missiles.

(c) There would be no chance of resuming the CF-105 programme once it was cancelled. It would be better to cancel it now than to be confronted with no more work for Avro, and the other companies involved, after production of 100 aircraft was drawing to an end in 1961 and 1962. It was unwise to encourage the aircraft industry to continue to produce equipment that could quite well be obsolete by the time it - was available.

(d) BOMARC might possibly be manufactured in Canada, under licence, by Canadair, which had the closest connections with the company in the U.S. doing this work. Avro and the other companies in the CF-105 programme would probably not be involved in such a project.

(e) It had been said by some that not only were manned interceptors becoming obsolete but so also were naval surface vessels. The latter eventuality, however, was further in the future than the first. Nuclear-powered anti-submarine submarines would be the most useful defence against enemy submarines equipped to launch atomic weapons. But they were very expensive. Failing that, the surface ships and the anti-submarine aircraft, with which Canadian forces were being equipped, provided a reasonable defence against possible assaults from the sea.

(f) The Chiefs of Staff were divided on the question of the CF-105. The Chief of the Air Staff felt there was a useful role for the manned interceptor, but the specific type of equipment and armament he preferred would depend upon the amount of money that was available. The heads of the other two services felt the nature of the threat was changing so quickly that the situation should be kept under review for a year. They did feel that the CF-105 programme, as it presently stood, was not the best way to spend so much money. The Chairman was of the view that BOMARC would give the best defence for the money likely to be available.

- 4 -

(g) The truth was that no one could forecast with reasonable precision what the requirement might be a year hence. Each of the military services had their own special reasons for the views they held. The Navy and the Army were particularly concerned that going ahead with the CF-105 might mean less money for them in the future. However, it would be unwise to look for reductions in these two services, even with the CF-105, unless some very drastic steps were taken.

(h) The Conservative Party, right from Confederation, had always been a vigorous protagonist of the theory that Canada's needs should be met from within Canada. To abandon the CF-105 even though it was so expensive and might be obsolete would be hard to explain. On the other hand, it would be equally hard to explain, in three or four years, why the government had spent vast sums of money on a relatively small number of aircraft which might by then be virtually useless.

5. The Minister of Finance reported on the representations made to him by Mr. Tory and Mr. Smye of Avro. The CF-105 programme supported 25,000 persons in employment. If it were abandoned, the highly skilled pool of talent drawn together for the project would be dispersed and many of the people concerned would go to the United States, never to return. No portion of Avro's profits had been invested in other sectors of the group of which Avro was now a part except in the aircraft industry. Although controlled by the Hawker-Siddley group, Avro was in large part owned by Canadians. They had stated that the R.C.A.F. made a major mistake three years ago by recommending the adoption of SPARROW and ASTRA. A great deal of money could be saved by using the FALCON and the Hughes fire control system. Finally, they said that, if the programme with their proposed modification were continued, their company would have a reasonable opportunity before the end of 1962 to look for other business. If they found little or none, then Avro would be in real difficulties.

Mr. Fleming said he had pointed out to Messrs. Tory and Smye that their arguments, that the Falcon missile and Hughes fire control system developed by the United States should be good enough for Canada, could also be used against them in regard to the airframe and engines which they wanted produced in Canada by their own firm. Mr. Smye, in particular, had been very critical of some R.C.A.F. decisions and officers.

Appendix D

6. <u>The Minister of National Defence</u> felt bound to say that the R.C.A.F. had conscientiously made the recommendations they thought would be the best in the interests of the defence of Canada. The government of the day was responsible for the decisions reached and the present government would be responsible for any decision on the future of the CF-105. He also said that the figures on savings mentioned by Mr. Smye should be treated with reserve. The latter had not been aware, for example, that there were a number of types of FALCON.

7. <u>The Cabinet</u> deferred decision on the recommendations of the Cabinet Defence Committee regarding air defence requirements, including the future of the CF-105 programme.

R. B. Bryce,
Secretary to the Cabinet.

Sept 7/1958

- 16 -

(b)   an effort being made to
interest others at the conference in the
possibility of establishing a Commonwealth
financial institution to assist in
financing the development of the new
and emerging members of the Commonwealth;
and,

(c)   the understanding that there
would be reasonable consultation with
Commonwealth governments affected before
concessional sales of agricultural surpluses
were made.

Air defence requirements; recommendations of Cabinet Defence Committee
(Previous reference Sept. 3)

42.   The Prime Minister opened the
further discussion of the proposal of the Minister of
National Defence to cancel the CF-105 programme by stating
that although ministers were relatively well agreed on the
purely defence aspects, the serious problem still requiring
consideration was the effect on employment and the general
economic situation.

43.   The Minister of Finance said that in
considering matters of defence he naturally put the
safety of the country ahead of finance. When it had been
recommended a year ago that the CF-105 programme be continued,
he supported the recommendation. Now, however, the military
view was that the programme should be cancelled. In these
circumstances, he did not see how the government could
decide not to discontinue it. The arguments for continuing
were that Canadian military requirements should be found
in Canada, that cancelling the programme would throw
upwards of 25,000 men out of work with serious effects
on the economy, and that national prestige should be
taken into account.

As regards the first, other things
being equal or nearly so, military equipment should be
produced in Canada. But in this case the cost per aircraft
was twice as much as the cost of a comparable unit which
could be obtained in the U.S., and, more important, the
military authorities had now decided that the aircraft
was not necessary. On the employment aspect, while a
decision to discontinue would undoubtedly be painful,
nevertheless, the workers involved would in time be
absorbed in the national economy. There would still
be an important aircraft industry in Canada without the
CF-105. Finally, one had to agree that not going ahead
would be a blow to national prestige. But no one even
knew now what the price for maintaining this aspect
of our prestige might be.

44. Mr. Fleming said he had asked himself
if there was a middle course between cancelling the
programme and going into production. Unfortunately, there
was not. Once production was ordered the government
would be committed. There was no time that was the
right time for a decision like this one. He was sure,
however, that it would be better to cancel now than be
faced with a final shut down of the plants three or
four years hence. Another factor to be kept in mind
was that, by deferring cancellation, the programme, in
effect, become the present government's programme, whereas
in cancelling now it could be said that the government
had considered all aspects of a project started by the
previous administration and had come to the conclusion
that the best course was to abandon it. Finally, one
had to keep in mind that by going ahead, and thereby
adding approximately $400 million a year for four years
to the defence appropriation, air defence would assume
a disproportionate share in the defence budget. This was
nearly the value of a year's wheat crop. An increase in
railway freight rates, which was being considered, was
a trifle by comparison. A good deal of northern development
could be undertaken for much less. In short, cancelling
the programme would be of much greater help to the economy
as a whole than continuing it.

45. During the discussion the following
further points emerged:

(a) In the forthcoming winter,
unemployment would be higher than it was
last year. Cancelling now, apart from
the effect on the employees concerned, might
well be the one psychological factor which
would result in a break in the economy
and lead to a drastic down-turn from which
recovery would be extremely difficult. The
programme should be allowed to continue over
the winter and a decision taken then as to
its future. During that period, management
could consider what their plants might do
in the future.

(b) On the other hand, continuing
the programme, even for only six months,
meant that orders had to be placed now
for materials for production. Did this
proposal mean that the pre-production order
of 37 should be completed? If this were the
case, only a few planes for identification
purposes would be available and the
individual costs would be astronomical.

(c) The U.S.S.R. had always said
that western economies would ultimately
collapse. Carrying on a project like this
involving so much of the taxpayers' money
and whose returns were questionable was
surely only playing into Russian hands. The
money could be put to better use elsewhere.

- 18 -

(d) On the other hand, while
cancellation might be sound in theory,
it might result in a recession. If employment
prospects were better, the project could
be dropped quickly. Continuing, even for only
a few months, involved insignificant amounts
compared with what would have to be spent
during a real depression.

(e) If the project were abandoned,
arrangements could quite probably be made
with the U.S. to purchase 106Cs and also to
secure atomic heads for the weapon with
which they would be equipped. The U.S.
authorities had also indicated in the last
few days that they would be prepared to
consider seriously cost-sharing and production
sharing of defence equipment. They had
also said they would be prepared to relocate
northwards some of their proposed Bomarc
installations. These Bomarc bases hardly
seemed to cover Canada at all. They were
most concerned at the moment over improvements
to the warning system.

(f) Surely the Canadian public
would give credit to the government in the
long run for good housekeeping and it appeared
that on defence and on sound economic grounds
it was good housekeeping to discontinue
the programme now.

46. The Cabinet deferred decision on the
recommendations of the Cabinet Defence Committee regarding
air defence requirements, including the future of the
CF-105 programme.

R.B. Bryce,
Secretary to the Cabinet.

A. V. ROE CANADA LIMITED

170 UNIVERSITY AVE. TORONTO, ONTARIO.

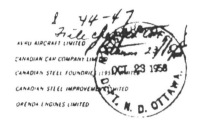

October 21, 1958

The Hon. George R. Pearkes, V.C.,
Minister,
Department of National Defence,
Ottawa, Ontario.

Dear Mr. Pearkes:

        The purpose of this letter is to confirm
some of the remarks I made during our meeting in your
office on Thursday, October 16th, to the following effect:-

        That, on the basis of installing the
Hughes MA1 fire control system, and the adoption of the
Falcon and/or Genie missiles, and as the result of other
substantial economies and savings proposed by the Company,
it is now estimated that we can produce and deliver 100
operational Arrow aircraft, complete in all respects
including the Iroquois engine and the MA1 fire control
system, for approximately $3,500,000. each. This excludes
the development and tooling costs, which it is assumed
would continue in accordance with existing contracts, and
the small amount of GFE presently proposed. However, the
originally estimated cost of development, that is, on the
basis of the 37 aircraft programme, would also be substant-
ially reduced, inasmuch as the last 17 of these aeroplanes
have been calculated as part of the aforementioned 100
operational aircraft.

        In order to substantiate the validity of
this estimate, and on the basis that it would make a substantial contribution to the Government's deliberations
concerning the Arrow programme, it was stated that the
Company would be prepared to enter into a fixed-price type
of contract on the basis of $3,750,000. for a complete,
operational aircraft, including the Iroquois engine and the
MA1 fire control system, excluding only GFE.

        ...2

-2-

It is realized that, in essence, this is
a statement of intention in principle, and that a definitive
proposal would have to be submitted, outlining the terms
of contract, and clarifying and defining the specification
in detail in accordance with our normal practice.

Should you wish it, Avro Aircraft and Orenda
Engines would be happy to prepare proposals in conjunction
with the Officers of your Department and the Department of
Defence Production in line with the principles outlined in
this letter.

Yours sincerely,

FRED T. SMYE.

fts-dc

SECRET 44-47 E.A

Ottawa, Ontario.
5 November, 1958

The Minister,
Department of Defence Production,
Number 4 Temporary Building,
Ottawa, Ontario.

My dear Colleague:

        Arising out of the Cabinet agreement of September 23, 1958, to cancel the contracts for the Astra integrated electronic system and the Sparrow guided missile and to continue the development of the Arrow aircraft and Iroquois engine utilizing an electronic system and missile combination which is in production in the United States, this Department has investigated the ways and means of implementing this decision. All alternatives have been discussed with the USAF, and as a consequence the RCAF recommend, and I concur, that the Hughes Aircraft Company MA-1/Falcon/Genie system be selected.

        To implement the revisions to the Arrow programme in line with this decision, it is intended to proceed immediately to re-engineer and prototype the new system into one Arrow aircraft and simultaneously design and fabricate the armament pack for the Falcon and Genie missiles. The re-engineering and prototyping will be done in Canada at Avro, Malton.

        I have attached Contract Demand 462043, Amendment number 10, for the re-engineering and prototyping phase and Contract Demand 862021 for the procurement of two Hughes electronic systems, support spares and test equipment. There are sufficient funds in the 1958-59 Department of National Defence appropriation to cover these requirements. Would you, therefore, arrange the necessary contractual coverage to permit this work to proceed at an early date.

        Yours sincerely,

ORIGINAL SIGNED BY
GEORGE R. PEARKES

cc: Minister of National Defence,
    CAS
    file

~~S105CT 100~~ (NTS/MHS)

/035CT

Ottawa Ont
12 Sep 58

Detachment Commander
Technical Services Detachment RCAF
Avro Aircraft Limited
PO Box 4004 Terminal "A"
Toronto Ontario

Iroquois Engine
Request for Engine Data

1   North American Aviation Inc., has requested,
through #1 RU, Wright Patterson AFB, data on the Iroquois
engine including performance, availability, installation
procedures and configurations. The request specified
Series 2 and 3 engines for use at M - 3.0.

2   Please arrange to have this information dispatched
to North American via the regular channel. For your information
the #1 Requirements Unit reference is: 51-01-T(TLO) dated
19 Aug 58.

(W R Cole) S/L
for CAS

S/L WR Cole/JM
20282

Orig
Circ
Local
File

Appendix D

19-1   SECRET   JAN. 13, 1959

- 8 -

Report on Arrow (CF-105) aircraft programme
(Previous reference Dec. 31, 1958)

28. The Prime Minister asked that the statements which had appeared in the Globe and Mail of that day on the Arrow (CF-105) programme be analysed so that he could answer them in detail.

29. The Minister of National Defence said that, as far as the Chiefs of Staff were concerned, there were, as at December 31st, 1958, no new military factors, either in regard to the manned bomber threat or new developments to meet this threat, which they considered would have any bearing on the Arrow aircraft programme. He read from a report submitted to him the day before by the Chief of the Air Staff. It indicated that the MA1/Falcom/MB1 could be worked satisfactorily into the Arrow aircraft and would provide a suitable interceptor weapon capability. There were at present five Mark I Arrow aircraft, and their handling and performance characteristics were extremely reassuring. The adoption of the Falcon and Hughes systems had given additional fuel storage space so that, in a supersonic mission, the radius of action of the aircraft had been increased from 238 to 354 nautical miles, and in a subsonic mission from 347 to 506 nautical miles. Another effect of the adoption of the U.S. fire control system and weapon to the Arrow programme was that development could be speeded up. The Avro Company had now advised that the first operational aircraft could be delivered for squadron use by September 1960 and that after January 1st, 1961, aircraft would be delivered at the rate of four per month. If 100 aircraft were required, the last aircraft could be delivered some time in 1963.

As far as the costs were concerned, the original price for 100 aircraft, as from September 1st, 1958, was $12.86 million per aircraft. The revised figures under the new programme, as from April 1st, 1959, would be $7.02 million per aircraft. The price had, therefore, dropped from $12.86 million to $7.02 million per aircraft. (This did not include cancellation charges of the Astra/Sparrow systems).

He then referred to the relative contributions of the United States and Canada towards the deterrent forces in North America. Figures from the U.S. indicated 800 supersonic interceptors in service and sufficient funds to procure another 650. The United States had recently decided to cancel the F-106C and F-106D programme and to use the funds so saved to develop the long range reconnaissance aircraft, F-108, which was not dependent on SAGE and was now on the inventory of NORAD. An additional 100 interceptors from Canada would make a small contribution. Furthermore, the CF-105 could not cover all of Canada. Its range was limited from 300 to 500 miles.

C. D. HOWE
ROOM 72 – 759 VICTORIA SQUARE
MONTREAL 1, CANADA

January 22nd
1959

Personal

Dear Mike

I am glad to give you my views on the

CF-105. I am planning to attend your luncheon at the

Reform Club this Saturday, and if you have a few minutes

either in the morning or afternoon, I will be glad to see

you. I may be able to have a word with you then. I

will give you a ring on Saturday morning with that in mind.

There is no doubt in my mind that the

CF-105 should be terminated - costs are completely out

of hand. The electronics equipment, which is an essential

part of the project, has never been ordered. This by

Government decision taken several months ago.

It seems to me that the proper line of attack

should be directed to the Government's temporizing and

fumbling with this decision. You will recall that when the

matter was last discussed by our Defence Committee in

1957, it was decided to continue the project for the time

being, and have a complete review of the matter in September

1957. I had then recommended that the project be terminated

due to runaway costs, but there were obvious reasons then
why the decision should be deferred until autumn.   Since
then, costs have continued to mount, and results of test
flights have been far from conclusive, both as to the aircraft and its jet engine, which is also a development project.

I think you have been right in being completely
non-committal as to the decision to continue or terminate,
which is obviously one for the Government of the day, but
you have a wide open field for showing the cost to the country
of the delay in the decision, should the decision be to terminate.

I would suggest the question on the order paper
asking the expenditures on the Arrow project and its jet engine
from the beginning of this Government's first Session of
Parliament to the date of termination, including estimated
termination costs.   The reply to such a question will give
you a basis for your criticism about delay in the decision.
You can also point out that it is a very expensive way to
prevent unemployment of the staff involved in the threatened
layoff.

You can also point out that when the Government decided not to proceed with the fire control missile
and electrical equipment for this aeroplane, the Government
had then decided not to proceed with the aircraft and engine.

- 3 -

Subsequent expenditures on both aircraft and engine were
definitely an unemployment relief measure, and an expensive
one.

I would also like to talk to you about the
decision regarding admitting CPA to TCA's transcontinental
route.   I would urge that you do not follow Chevrier's line
that the Government is not carrying out its announced intention of allowing competition on this route.   Rather, I would
argue that the Government is breaking down its own successful transportation service, one that has furnished the best
of transport by air to the Canadian people, at practically
cost of the service.

Keeping in mind the high cost of ground
service for one round trip per day, the result will be loss
of revenue to both CPA and TCA, with no improvement in
service to the public.

I look forward to discussing this, and one or
two other matters with you on Saturday, February 7th.

With best regards.

Yours sincerely,

C. D. Howe

Honourable Lester B. Pearson,
Leader of the Opposition,
House of Commons,
Ottawa, Ontario.

19-10

THIS DOCUMENT IS THE PROPERTY OF THE GOVERNMENT OF CANADA

TOP SECRET

46/.59

Cro: : o.

MEMORANDUM TO THE CABINET:

CF-105 Avro Arrow Programme; report of the Cabinet Defence Committee

1.　　　At a meeting on February 5th, the Cabinet Defence Committee had before it recommendations of the Minister of National Defence that further development of the CF-105 aircraft be discontinued now and that the Chiefs of Staff be asked to present at an early date their recommendations on what requirements, if any there were, for additional air defence missile installations in Canada and for interceptor aircraft of the nature of the CF-105 or alternate types.

2.　　　During the consideration of these matters, the Chairman of the Chiefs of Staff Committee reported that the Chiefs of Staff had reviewed the position concerning the production of the CF-105 and that "they are still of the opinion that the changing threat and the rapid advances in technology, particularly in the missile field, along with the diminishing requirements for manned interceptors in Canada, create grave doubts as to whether a limited number of aircraft of such extremely high cost would provide defence returns commensurate with the expenditures."

3.　　　The Committee concurred in the recommendations of the Minister of National Defence and agreed that they be submitted to the Cabinet for consideration at an early meeting.

W.R.Martin,
Secretary,
Cabinet Defence Committee.

Privy Council Office,
February 6th, 1959.

Arrow(CF-105) aircraft; report of Cabinet Defence
   Committee; decision to terminate development
            (Previous reference Feb. 14)

12.   The Prime Minister said a draft
announcement on the termination of the development
contract for the Arrow had been prepared. It included
a section on arrangements with the United States for
production sharing and a section on the acquisition by
Canada of nuclear weapons for defence. He had gone over
the draft in great detail but it was not yet in the
right form to be made that day.

13.   The Minister without Portofolio (Mr.
Macdonnell) reported that, the previous day in Toronto,
the Premier of Ontario had spoken to him in strong
terms about the effects of terminating the Arrow contract
upon the municipalities in the vicinity of Malton.

14.   The Minister of Finance said Mr. Frost
had also spoken to him in pungent language about work
on the Arrow being stopped. Mr. Frost had complained
about so little notice being given to Avro, and had
asked why other contracts could not be given to the
company. He had replied that the matter had been
exhaustively considered, that all possible alternatives
had been reviewed, and that the decision would be taken
in the light of the best military advice available. He
had also told Mr. Frost that, right from the outset, it
had never been said that actual production would proceed
and that everyone understood that the matter was to be
reviewed year by year.

15.   During the discussion the following
points emerged:

(a) The sooner the announcement
could be made the better, because the
decision to terminate was bound to
leak out and the longer the announcement
was delayed the more would be the cost.

(b) The most appropriate time for
the announcement appeared to be the
following Friday. This, as proposed,
should refer not only to the Arrow
termination but also to production
sharing and to the acquisition of
nuclear weapons. The Prime Minister's
statement should be followed by one
by the Minister of Defence Production,
which would deal in greater detail with
production sharing. In considering this
question of timing, the possibility of a
motion to adjourn the house to discuss a
matter of urgent public importance should
not be overlooked.

(c) It would be desirable that notes
be exchanged with the U.S. to implement
the agreed arrangements on sharing the
costs of the new radars, gap fillers,
S.A.G.E. and the two Bomarc stations in
Ontario and Quebec.

- 5 -

16. <u>The Cabinet</u>,-

(a) agreed that the development
of the Arrow aircraft and Iroquois
engine be discontinued, effective as
of the time of announcement;

(b) that an announcement
concerning this decision, the production
sharing with the United States, and the
acquisition of atomic weapons be made
in the House of Commons, probably on
Friday;

(c) that the contractors be
notified of the termination of their
contracts at the same time; and,

(d) that an agreement be made
with the United States, in the form
of an exchange of notes, for the
implementation of the agreed arrangements on the sharing of the costs of
Bomarc and S.A.G.E. installations in
Canada and the associated extension
of radar coverage.

- 2 -

Statement on the Arrow
(Previous reference Feb. 17)

1. **The Prime Minister** said that he would make a statement announcing the termination of the Arrow contracts in the house the following day. The C.B.C. Television Service would present a programme on the following Sunday or Monday on the development of the Arrow. It would be well to make the statement before the broadcast.

He had gone over the **draft statement** several times but thought that it should be redrafted by a committee of ministers. The redraft could be considered by Cabinet before the statement was made in the house.

2. **The Cabinet** approved the suggestion of the Prime Minister that Messrs. Fleming, Pearkes, Fulton, Smith, and O'Hurley meet that afternoon to revise the draft statement on the Arrow aircraft and related matters.

CONFIRMATION

TOR 2151

TO AVRO ATTN J L PLANT MALTON (TCO VIA CN TELEGRAM) *A.l.*

FROM D L THOMPSON D D P OTTAWA

TAKE NOTICE THAT YOUR CONTRACTS BEARING THE REFERENCE NUMBERS SET
OUT BELOW INCLUDING ALL AMENDMENTS THERETO ARE HEREBY TERMINATED AS
REGARDS ALL SUPPLIES AND SERVICES WHICH HAVE NOT BEEN COMPLETED AND
SHIPPED OR PERFORMED THEREUNDER PRIOR TO THE RECEIPT BY YOU OF THIS
NOTICE STOP YOU SHALL CEASE ALL WORK IMMEDIATELY, TERMINATE SUB-
CONTRACTS AND ORDERS, PLACE NO FURTHER SUBCONTRACTS OR ORDERS AND
INSTRUCT ALL YOUR SUBCONTRACTORS AND SUPPLIERS TO TAKE SIMILAR ACTION
STOP YOU ARE REQUESTED TO SUBMIT TO THE DEPARTMENT OF DEFENCE
PRODUCTION, OTTAWA, ONTARIO FOR CONSIDERATION, ANY CLAIM WHICH YOU MAY
HAVE AS A RESULT OF THIS TERMINATION STOP SUCH CLAIM AND THOSE OF YOUR
SUBCONTRACTORS AND SUPPLIERS, IF ANY, ARE TO BE SUBMITTED ON
THE PRESCRIBED DEPARTMENTAL TERMINATION CLAIM FORMS STOP ON RECEIPT
OF THIS NOTICE, YOU SHOULD MAKE APPLICATION IN WRITING TO THE CHIEF
SETTLEMENT OFFICER, DEPARTMENT OF DEFENCE PRODUCTION OTTAWA, FOR THE
REQUISITE SET OF FORMS STOP YOUR CLAIM AND ALL CORRESPONDENCE
CONCERNING IT SHOULD BE ADDRESSED TO MR. D. B. WALLACE, CHIEF
SETTLEMENT OFFICER, DEPARTMENT OF DEFENCE PRODUCTION STOP
REFERENCE NUMBERS OF TERMINATED CONTRACTS: BX69-12-44; SERIAL 2-B-5-309;
BX18-26-97; SERIALS 2-B-4-715; 2-B-4-593; 2-B-7-1455; 2-B-8-27;
BX18-772778 SERIAL 2-BX-8-14; BR18-872803 SERIAL 2-BR-8-149

FEB 20/59   12.30 PM   DC

231

CANCELLED

1038CN-80 (CCAS)

APR 2 1959

<u>MEMORANDUM</u>

26 Mar 59

The Minister (Through Deputy Minister)

<u>Arrow Cancellation - Disposal of Material</u>

1   In your approval to my recommendation of
13 March 1959 on courses of action to be taken in respect
to disposal of material arising out of the cancellation of
the Arrow, you desired to be informed before final action
was taken on the method of disposal being considered for
the disposition of the airframes and the Iroquois engines.

2   Two methods may be followed:

    (a) Declaring as surplus material to Crown Assets
        Disposal agency. This course is not recom-
        mended for the reason that this agency has
        the prerogative of selling this material in
        its original state. This course could lead
        to subsequent embarrassment, that is, air-
        frame and engine could conceivably be placed
        on public view or even, in fact, used as a
        roadside stand. This, I am sure, you will
        agree is most undesirable.

    (b) Relinquishing any DND interest in the air-
        frames and engines to DDP for ultimate
        disposal by that agency. In this case DDP
        can reduce it to scrap. This course is
        recommended.

3   I would appreciate being advised whether you
concur in the method recommended.

(Hugh Campbell)
Air Marshal
Chief of the Air Staff.

cc: Deputy Minister

D.M. May I have your comments
please Group Leader

TOP SECRET

U-2 Vulnerability Tests

Vulnerability of the U-2 was tested against the F-102 and F-104 fighters at Eglin AFB in December 1958. The tests were conducted under optimum controlled ground and air environment for the attacking pilot (i. e., outstanding pilots, isolated air space, ideal weather, pre-selected intercept point, etc.). The F-104 cannot cruise at altitudes over 60,000 feet, but it possesses a capability to convert speed to altitude and attain co-altitude of the U-2 for a period of less than 30 seconds. The F-104 was equipped with air-to-air missiles of the infra-red seeking variety and airborne radar that locates the aircraft and allows the pilot to visually acquire the target to complete the attack. The F-104 radar malfunctioned at high altitudes. The pilot of this fighter could not visually acquire the target in sufficient time to solve the fire control problem. The F-102 all weather fighter consistently acquired the target and was able to solve the fire control problem for launching air-to-air missiles. To be successful, the missiles require outstanding high altitude performance and a slant range in excess of five miles.

The performance of both aircraft exceeded the present capability of operational Soviet fighters. The standard operational Soviet fighters cannot attain co-altitude of the U-2. A new fighter, the Fitter, of which an estimated 120 have been produced, is considered capable of co-altitude for a period of several seconds. It is not, however, presently considered operational. The standard Soviet all weather fighter, YAK-25/Flashlight, is considered capable of acquiring the U-2 on airborne radar. However, to complete a successful intercept would require an air-to-air missile with a slant range in excess of seven miles. The USSR is considered to have air-to-air missiles, however, there is no intelligence source that indicates that the missiles are operational.

Conclusions

1. The F-104 can attain co-altitude, but the difficulty in visually acquiring the target makes any single attack a low probability of successful intercept.

2. The F-102 with its radar can acquire the U-2 and possesses the performance to solve the fire control problem, however, air-to-air missiles of outstanding performance and long range are required to accomplish airborne intercept. There is no known operational deployment of air-to-air missiles by the Soviets.

3. Successful intercept of the U-2 by the Soviet defensive fighters for the next few months is unlikely.

TOP SECRET

233

24 Apr.59.

The Minister (Through Deputy Minister)

Arrow Cancellation - Disposal of Materiel

1   In my memorandum of 26 Mar, same subject, dealing
with the recommended method for the disposition of the Arrow
airframes and Iroquois engines, I recommended in para 2 (b)
disposal by DDP in which case "DDP can reduce it to scrap."

2   Your approval by memorandum of 8 April is predicated
on the understanding that the aircraft "<u>will</u> be reduced to scrap."

3   I wish to advise that the intent of your direction
has been communicated to DDP and agreement obtained. However, we
are informed that such action is being withheld in respect to 5
aircraft pending the outcome of the enquiries being made on
behalf of the Royal Aeronautical Establishment, Farnborough, of
which I understand you are aware.

(Hugh Campbell)
Air Marshal
Chief of the Air Staff

cc: Deputy Minister

The suggestion in para 3
is presumably the one of
which the UK He spoke

The five in question should
not be reduced to scrap until
a decision has been reached
to offer of R.A.E.

APR 28 1959

APR 2 7 1959

Deputy Minister,
Department of Defence Production,
No. 2 Temporary Building,
Ottawa, Ontario.

Dear Sir:

Arrow Cancellation
Disposal of Airframes and Iroquois Engines

While there is an agreed understanding at the
termination team levels of our respective departments as to the
method of disposal to be adopted in respect to the Arrow airframes
and Iroquois engines, I think that it would be well to confirm this
understanding by stating the position of this department.

It would be our understanding that in relinquishing
DND interest to your department in the existing Arrow airframes and
Iroquois engines now in their whole state, that:

      (a) there is no intention of allowing the
           completed aircraft to be flown, maintained
           in service or left in the whole state;

      (b) every effort will be made to salvage engines,
           instruments and parts that can be used or
           returned to the original supplier or such uses
           as may be stated by this department;

      (c) the aircraft, as a whole aircraft, or airframe
           or engine will not be put up for disposal as
           such but will be reduced to scrap after all
           useful and creditable materiel has been removed.

I would appreciate confirmation of your understanding
and agreement to this expression of our views. However, may I add,
we would be willing to review our position if the present enquiries
from the U.K. are found to warrant such consideration.

Yours sincerely,

(Signed) F. R. MILLER

A/C MB MacKinnon/pk
C/Mat
2-3417

(JA Easton) A/V/M
AMTS
2-2743

Mgr. Jones.

207-6-3.
207-2-253.

X

MR. C. A. HOME
DDP MALTON

J. L. BUSH
DDP (O)

IT HAS BEEN CONFIRMED THAT THERE IS NO REQUIREMENT FOR ANY ARROW AIRCRAFT OR IROQUOIS
ENGINES(.) IT IS THEREFORE IN ORDER TO PROCEED WITH REDUCTION OF THE MARK ONE
AIRFRAMES AND IROQUOIS ENGINES TO SCRAP AS PREVIOUSLY DISCUSSED.

J. L. Bush   306   4   6-6600
                                         May 15, 1959

Appendix D

Departmental file

Mr. Jones.

```
FILE BX
REC'D                JUN 3 1959
ACTION
BF DATE
DISCUSS
NOTE & F/A
```

Dear Mrs. Bailey:

Thank you for your letter of May 13th, 1959 and your offer of assistance in storing Arrow aircraft.

Although I appreciate your offer, I am afraid that no useful purpose would be served by retaining these aircraft, and, it has been decided that they will be scrapped.

The programme was cancelled because the Arrow would be inadequate for the defence of Canada by the time it would be ready for operational service. Military developments are advancing at a rapid pace and the aircraft would be progressively less useful as time went on. In addition to this, only five aircraft were completed and this is far too small a number to equip even one RCAF Squadron.

In my opinion, any expenditure for storage of these aircraft would be a waste of public funds and I trust that, now that you are aware of the facts, you will agree that our decision is in the best interests of Canadian citizens.

Yours sincerely,

Mrs. W. H. Bailey,
2005 Eglinton Avenue West,
TORONTO 10, Ontario.

DLT/e

Original Signed by
THE MINISTER

207-6-3

Mr. ~~Speaker~~ _Chairman_, since the inception of the CF-105 project,
successive governments have approached this programme cautiously
because the rapid changes in air defence had rendered major projects
in other countries obsolete before the equipment could be made
available to the armed services. In keeping with this approach, the
principal contractors were authorized to do only such manufacturing
as was necessary to ensure that delays would not occur in the event
that military considerations would warrant full production after
completion of the basic development stage. Authorization to proceed
was usually limited to a year at a time.

This situation continued for over five years and at no
time were the principal contractors given to understand that the
development of the Arrow weapon system would lead inevitably to
full production. In fact they knew that a decision on the future
of the project would be made towards the end of 1958 or the beginning
of 1959 as a result of a thorough appraisal of the Arrow's usefulness
as an air defence weapon.

With this information, with the knowledge that defence
requirements change rapidly, and with past experience on this project,
they should have been ~~adequate~~ prepared for any decision. ~~The prompt
closing of the plants indicates the extent of their preparedness.~~

The decision against placing the CF-105 into full production
was announced by the Prime Minister on February 20th. The efficiency
which gave effect to this decision should not be confused with abruptness. There could be no justification for a further expenditure of
defence funds on a project with no future military value.

The government has extended help to those affected by the
termination in several forms. Each employee was granted ~~generous~~
severance pay, the companies are being reimbursed the cost of _certain_ special
capital equipment as well as overhead costs which would otherwise
have been absorbed by CF-105 work. In addition, the government has

Department of Defence Production   July 6, 1959.

207-6-3

CF-105 Termination Status

1. ### Status of completed Aircraft and Iroquois Engines

   Three of the five completed Mark I aircraft have been completely dismantled. The fourth and fifth will be finished about July 10th and 17th respectively. The partially completed Mark II aircraft has already been dismantled.

   All completed Iroquois engines together with spare parts and tooling will be retained for the time being and are being moved to the test cells at Malton for storage.

2. ### Reclaimed Equipment

   During the dismantling operation all reuseable equipment is being salvaged either for use by the Department of National Defence or for disposal by Crown Assets Disposal Corporation at the best current prices.

   The J-75 engines which had been purchased from the United States government will be resold to that government at the original price less a discount for the use they received during the CF-105 programme and consideration for packing, handling and transportation costs. These prices are now being negotiated.

   The United States government has also agreed to repurchase the MA-1 Electronic system at the original cost less packing, handling and transportation costs.

THE AVRO ARROW

Aircraft Branch

60-57

c/o Avro Aircraft Limited,
Box 4004, Terminal "A",
Toronto, Ontario.

January 21st, 1960

Mr. J. C. Wilson,
Arrow Termination Co-ordinator,
Avro Aircraft Limited,
Malton, Ontario.

Dear Mr. Wilson:

Termination Instruction No. 81"A"
Records, Drawings, etc.

Instruction No. 77"A" dated December 9th, 1959,
required you to retain certain records and publications.

As the R.C.A.F. have now advised that there
appears to be no purpose in retaining the engineering data
on the Arrow aircraft, you are instructed to dispose of it
in the same manner as you have disposed of other records,
drawings, etc.

Yours very truly,

Original Signed by
C. A. Hore
C. Allen Hore
Senior Representative.

CAH/hs
cc Mr. J. L. Bush

JAN 2 5 1960

240

Appendix D

Improvements in air defence;
replacement aircraft for CF-100's in Canada
(Previous reference Feb. 4)

1. **The Minister of National Defence**, using
a map, informed the Cabinet on the location of interceptor and BOMARC squadrons in Canada and indicated the
depth of the defences these weapons provided. The
coverage of this form of defence was governed by the
location of the Pinetree stations and the warning lines.
If, several years ago, it had been physically and
financially possible to have situated the Pinetree radars
further north, this would probably have been done and the
BOMARC and interceptor bases consequently would have been
further north too. The expected range of the BOMARC "B"
was between 400 and 500 miles, that of the "A", about
150 to 200 miles.

2. **Mr. Pearkes** also read a copy of a letter
sent to the U.S. defence authorities, when the Pinetree
stations were first being installed in August, 1951,
recording the understanding of the Canadian Government
that the conclusion of the agreement for a one-third:
two-thirds cost-sharing arrangement in no way implied
that Canada was to be regarded as a recipient of aid.
Perhaps a cost-sharing arrangement for the F-101B's could
be regarded in a similar light.

3. **The Prime Minister** said that a committee of
the Ministers who were members of the Cabinet Defence
Committee plus Messrs. Churchill, Harkness, Nowlan and
MacLean should meet to consider the proposal and make
recommendations. If the Committee reported that security
demanded the acquisition of these aircraft, then that
would have to be the decision. To purchase them, however,
would cause great difficulties. It would place him and
the Minister of National Defence in impossible positions.
On the other hand, failure to re-equip would be bad for
the morale of the R.C.A.F. He thought the public had been
convinced of the wisdom of the government's decision to
cancel the Arrow. To obtain other aircraft now in the
face of statements that the threat of the manned bomber
was diminishing and that the day of the interceptor would
soon be over would be most embarrassing unless a reasonable
explanation could be given. Additional BOMARC's in Canada
might be an alternative. The Committee should first
examine carefully what had been said publicly by himself
and other Ministers about cancelling the Arrow and, in the
light of that, consider what was possible. In any event,
the safety of the nation should be the paramount consideration no matter what the consequences. He had been against
cancelling the Arrow but had been persuaded otherwise.

4. **During the brief discussion** it was said that,
even though a logical, reasoned case might be made for
obtaining the F-101B's, such a decision could not be
explained to the public. The repercussions of telling
CINCNORAD that Canada was not prepared to re-equip the
CF-100 squadrons would not be too great.

5. **The Cabinet** agreed that a Committee consisting
of the members of the Cabinet Defence Committee, other than
the Prime Minister, together with Messrs. Churchill, Harkness, Nowlan and MacLean, review and report on the proposals
of the Minister of National Defence for authority to discuss
with the United States various possible arrangements for
re-equipping on a smaller scale, the air defence force of
the R.C.A.F. in Canada.

SECRET

MEMORANDUM FOR MEETING WITH PRIME MINISTER DIEFENBAKER

Canadian Attitudes Toward Recent International Situation

The Prime Minister's comments will take place against a background attitude of intense interest in an East-West settlement, especially disarmament. His government's attitude toward the East-West struggle has shown some excessive caution in the past year or so, but the record of action in support of the United States on specific vital matters has continued to be generally good.

The Diefenbaker administration has tended to believe that a nuclear war would be so disastrous that the West must operate from the premise that genuinely peaceful East-West agreements can be achieved and that the West should avoid acts which appear threatening to the Soviets lest any chance of fruitful negotiations be jeopardized. In general the Canadian Government has tended to attach less weight than we have to the need for ostensible military strength, has given greater credence to Communist threats, has more readily accepted as sincere Communist protestations of good faith, and has been more inclined to worry over suggestions involving risks.

Therefore, it was not surprising that on May 10 the Canadians privately expressed great anxiety over the U-2 incident and any continuation of over-flights. They urged consultations in NATO and advised restraint. Publicly, however, the Government refrained from criticism.

Since the Paris meeting, Canadian support has been much in evidence. In a special statement on May 18 before the House of Commons, Prime Minister Diefenbaker blamed Khrushchev and defended the West, which he urged to remain united. He also suggested that disarmament talks continue.

Continental Air Defense

Prime Minister Diefenbaker would be interested in learning what the ultimate decision of the United States may be regarding the BOMARC B missile program. In Canada the BOMARC problem originated from a decision in February 1959 not to go into production of the CF-105, a supersonic jet intercepter designed and developed in Canada at a cost of over $400 million. In lieu of the CF-105 Canada announced a decision developed by the military establishments of the two countries whereby the USAF would underwrite about two-thirds of the costs of an improved continental air defense system in Canada, which would include 2 BOMARC squadrons, 1 SAGE fire control center, and

improved

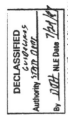

SECRET

for meeting on 6-3-60

SECRET
-2-

improved radar. A formal agreement is still pending but
Canada has already spent about $500,000 on the first BOMARC
site.

On March 24, USAF recommended to Congress a drastically
revised air defense plan which would retain BOMARC sites
only in the northeastern part of the continent, including
the two in Canada. On April 29, the House Appropriations
Committee eliminated funds for BOMARC production and the
House approved that action on May 6. Senate action is pending.

Downgrading of BOMARC has become a domestic political
football in Canada. The Opposition claims that a weapon is
being retained in Canada which the United States is abandoning and that decisions on defense matters involving Canada
are being made in Washington without sufficient consultation.

On May 18 the Defense Department appealed for Senate
amendments which would retain the modest BOMARC program proposed by USAF. A successful appeal would greatly mitigate,
but not end, the current controversy in Canada. Therefore,
the Prime Minister is likely to be interested in (1) our
assessment of the duration of the manned-bomber threat; (2)
whether the continental air defense system is regarded as a
part of the deterrent; and (3) whether the United States
contemplates a downgrading of the role of air defense. His
interest in such matters will be due largely to their political and financial implications for Canada. For example,
on April 1 his Defense Minister indicated privately to
Defense Secretary Gates that Canada would probably abandon
intercepters unless the United States regards their retention as really important and that Canada was strongly inclined further to reduce defense expenditures. However,
more recently the Canadian Minister of Defence Production
told Ambassador Wigglesworth that United States initiative
would be welcome in effecting an arrangement whereby Canada
would purchase 66 U.S. jet intercepters (101-B) and in return the United States would purchase 50 CL-44 cargo planes
from Canada. The Department of Defense has this idea under
active consideration and we have informally indicated to that
Department that we would support strongly such a proposition
if it is militarily sound.

North American Air Defense Exercise SKY SHIELD

It is suggested that you may wish to discuss Exercise
SKY SHIELD with the Prime Minister and seek to obtain his
assurances of Canadian cooperation and governmental agreement.

SKY SHIELD

SECRET

- 3 -

Convention between Canada and Norway for the avoidance of
double taxation and the prevention of fiscal evasion with
respect to taxes on income

     6. The Cabinet agreed that the Secretary of State
for External Affairs be authorized,-

     (a) to execute and issue an instrument
of full power authorizing the Minister of
Finance to sign, on behalf of the government
of Canada, subject to ratification, a
Convention between the government of Canada
and the government of the Kingdom of Norway
for the avoidance of double taxation and the
prevention of fiscal evasion with respect to
taxes on income; and,

     (b) to execute and issue the instrument
of ratification bringing the Convention into
force.

     (An order in council was passed accordingly;
P.C. 1960-978, July 16).

Air defence; proposals for reciprocal purchases of
aircraft
(Previous reference July 12)

     7. The Minister of Defence Production said that
at the meeting of the Canada-U.S. Committee on Joint Defence
the U.S. Secretaries had affirmed that interceptors would be
needed for the defence of North America for several years
ahead. They had also confirmed the outline of the transaction
which had been described when the Cabinet had last discussed
the matter. The two-thirds one-third share of the costs of
spares, ground handling equipment, etc., conformed with
similar cost-sharing formulae for installations in Canada
such as the BOMARC, heavy radars and gap fillers.

     8. During the discussion the following points.
emerged:

     (a) The $105 million would cover end
of production line units. It did not include
any development or pre-production costs.

     (b) The U.S. were now re-emphasizing
the bomber because in their own experience
missiles had not developed to the extent
expected and presumably the U.S.S.R. was
running into similar problems in its missile
programme. In fact, it was said in Montebello
that only 5 U.S. I.C.B.M.s were operational.
This was quite a different figure from that
which the Prime Minister had been given in
Washington in June.

Appendix D

SECRET

- 4 -

(c) If no interceptors were obtained,
was the defence of the north to be taken over
by the U.S.? The CF-100s were gradually being
phased out now as they became older and older.
By 1962 there would be none left in the system.

(d) The CF-100 was incapable of policing
Canadian skies against intrusions from aircraft
similar to the U-2. The F101B would fulfil this
policing role during the years when it would be
available. Without them there would be no
Canadian surveillance of Canadian air space.

(e) Again it was made clear that acquiring
F101Bs in the U.S. would require a great deal of
explanation in Canada. This would be most
difficult, if not impossible, to do successfully.

(f) The R.C.A.F. had been working for a
decision in favour of a replacement interceptor
for the CF-100 behind the government's back as
it were.

(g) The Minister of Defence Production
might see if the U.S. authorities could delay
making their plans for a little while to give
the Canadian government adequate time to reach
a decision on this important question. If the
exchange did not occur, the U.S. had to make
other plans for transport aircraft and the
disposition of the F101Bs which might otherwise come to Canada.

9. The Cabinet agreed to discuss the proposed
Canadian purchase of United States F101B aircraft and the
U.S. purchase of Canadian CL44 aircraft at a meeting the
following day.

Royal Commission on the automobile industry

10. The Prime Minister referred to his recent
interview with the United Automobile Workers during which
it had been noted that the plight of the small parts manufacturers was due to the high import of small parts into
Canada. The amount had increased by $40 million during
the last year. There had been total imports of $300 million
during that period. The small parts people had asked for a
Royal Commission on the automobile industry in Canada and
the question was whether such a commission would be desirable.

THE AVRO ARROW

Ottawa, Ontario
30 Nov 60

Air Member
Canadian Joint Staff
2450 Massachusetts Ave NW
Washington 8 DC

Iroquois – Engine History & Status

As requested by W/C AW Armstrong the history and status
of the Iroquois engine have been prepared. The status was taken
in Feb 59 but was recently checked and has not varied appreciably.
Engine XI16 has been shipped to the United Kingdom for inspection
by Bristol/Siddeley. All other engines and parts have been stored
and preserved. Engine X106 was, of course, removed from the B47
before the aircraft was returned to the USAF.

It is estimated the 50 hour PFRT engine could be prepared
in 2 months and the test completed to clear the mechanical configuration in 3 to 4 months. Should a slightly more advanced configuration
be required, such as an additional stage to the HP spool as Orenda
proposed to the USAF, the timing would be in the order of 8 months.

The six new test cells, with simultaneous data recording
instrumentation, could be employed for Iroquois development. The
altitude test tunnel could be completed in approximately 8 months.

The engine history as tabled is a frank and factual resume
and, although many problems and errors are mentioned, it is RCAF
technical opinion the engine had overcome the major mechnical
difficulties. The aerodynamic configuration, as stated in the
historical summary, was cleared by a 50 Hr PFRT before the program
terminated.

(WR Cole) W/C
AEng 5

W/C WR Cole/DB
6-6437

Orig
Circ
Local
File

Appendix D

CONFIDENTIAL
51-01-02(AM)
Our file ref.

DEPARTMENT OF NATIONAL DEFENCE

CANADIAN JOINT STAFF

CANADA

2450 Massachusetts Ave., N.W.
Washington 8 D.C.
U.S.A.

3 Feb 61

Ref Telecon A/C McKinnon - A/C Cameron
CJS Letter 51-01-02 8 Dec 60 to USAF - Copy to CMat   1040

Chief of the Air Staff
Air Force Headquarters
Department of National Defence
Ottawa 4 Ontario

Attention: CMat

Referred to... C MAT
FEB 8 1961
File No. 81055 CT-100
Chg'd to... CAE
8/2/61

Iroquois Engine – Possible USAF Application

1   This will confirm a negative reply from the USAF to our letter,
concerning possible use by the USAF of the Iroquois engine, has been
received.

2   The USAF indicated their studies covering the B58C have terminated as they do not intend to proceed with this version of the B58.
The STOL fighter is still being studied, however they believe existing
engines will be capable of satisfying this propulsion system requirement.
The projected USAF requirement for all jet engines indicates a steady
decline in the years ahead.

for (RA Cameron) A/C
Air Member
CJS(W)

c.c. AFHQ/CAE

CAFA 510

247

Acknowledgements

Through all of this process, I have benefited greatly from the help and advice of a number of extremely dedicated and knowledgeable archivists. To them I owe a huge debt of gratitude: individuals such as the late Carl Vincent, Paul Marsden, Glenn Wright, Carl Christie, Christopher Cook, and Isabelle Campbell, to name a few. In my research, I consulted the records of the Department of National Defence, the National Research Council, the Eisenhower Library in the United States, the Smithsonian, the National Archives in Washington, similar contacts in Great Britain, the CIA online database, the online NATO database, and various USAF bases.

Special thanks go to C. Fred Matthews, Brian Erb, and the late Owen Maynard, three of the twenty-five engineers who went to NASA. I would also like to thank former vice-president engineering at Avro, James C. Floyd; former vice-president and general manager, Orenda Engines. David J. Caple; the late Jan Zurakowski, and Spud Potocki; Major Bill March, the RCAF history and heritage historian at CFB Trenton; Dr. Richard Mayne, director, Air Force History and Heritage at CFB Trenton; author Donald G. Mahar for information on the Soviet spies at Avro; Karine Gélinas of the digilab at Library and Archives Canada, for assistance with the digitization of photos; Frank Harvey, former Avro employee and president of the Aerospace Heritage Foundation of Canada; David Waechter for information on his father's work at Avro in relation to the Arrow's speed; Ian H. Mitchell, former Avro employee; John Burzynski, president and chief executive officer of Osisko Mining, who led the latest search effort for the models; diver Mike Fletcher, now engaged in the search for the Arrow models with John Burzynski; Scarlett Janusas, president of Scarlett Janusas Archaeology; and Nancy Binnie, senior conservation scientist (chemist), Heritage Interiors Conservation Services; the Canadian Conservation Institute; and the Department of Canadian Heritage.

Finally, I would like to thank the team at Dundurn, in particular Beth Bruder, for support in this effort, and my editors, Dominic Farrell and Laurie Miller.

Notes

PREFACE

1. Briefly, in a cost-plus contract, the company is paid for allowable expenses and receives a percentage profit margin on top of this. Such contracts put all the risk on the government. Critics of such contracts allege that they make it easy for companies to artificially inflate and extend the work required, to increase the amount of profit. In a fixed-price contract, there is a set price for work done, often with incentives, but risk is more on the contractor.

CHAPTER 1: A FUTURE LOST

1. Shaw, E.K., *There Never Was an Arrow*, Ottawa: Steel Rail Educational Publishing, 1979. Shaw was an aviation engineering technologist on the Avro Arrow. She had worked on most of Avro's projects including the Jetliner and CF-100. After cancellation, she went to the University of Toronto to study economics and political science and went on to become an economic consultant. In her book she quotes the *Financial Post* article and quotes from the internal memorandum, which had been distributed by the International Association of Machinists.

2. "The Road to Serfdom," *Globe and Mail*, December 17, 1958, and quoted in E.K. Shaw's *There Never Was an Arrow*, Ottawa: Steel Rail Educational Publishing, 1979.

3. Brown, J.J., *Ideas in Exile*, Toronto: McClelland and Stewart, 1967, and quoted in E.K. Shaw's *There Never Was an Arrow*, Ottawa: Steel Rail Educational Publishing, 1979.

4. Floyd, J.C., "Arrow Flight Development, Report No. 70/ENG Pub 7," May, 1, 1958, from Department of National Defence.

5. Campagna, Palmiro, *Requiem for a Giant: A.V. Roe Canada and the Avro Arrow*, Toronto: Dundurn, 2003.

6. Letter, May 2, 1949, RG 70, Vol. 406, File 14008.

7. While researching information on the Arrow, I inquired about the Jetliner as well and the papers of C.D. Howe on the subject. I was told then by one of the archivists that back in the early 1960s representatives of Howe went to the archives, removed a number of files, and never returned them. I have not been able to corroborate this, but neither have I found any files related to the Jetliner under his name. The records I did find were copies in other sources as referenced herein.

8. Smye, Fred, *Canadian Aviation and The Avro Arrow*, Oakville, ON: Randy Smye, 1985.

CHAPTER 2: WAS THE ARROW THAT GOOD?

1. Sweetman, Bill, Broken Arrow, aviationweek.com/blog/1957-broken-arrow, accessed July 19, 2017.

2. Ibid.

3. Ibid.

4. Gunston, Bill, *Early Supersonic Fighters of the West*, London: Scribner, 1976. Note that the YF-12A was the predecessor to the Blackbird reconnaissance spy plane with better than Mach 3 performance.

5. Robin, Sebastien, "America's F-4 Phantom: Taking on the World's Best Fighters (At Almost 60 Years Old)," *National Interest*, June 27, 2016, nationalinterest.org/blog/the-buzz/americas-f-4-phantom-taking-the-world-best-fighters-almost-16738.

6. Woodman, Jack, "Flying the Avro Arrow," Canadian Aeronautics and Space Institute Symposium, Winnipeg, Manitoba, May 16, 1978.

7. "Evaluation of the Canadian CF-105 as an All-Weather Fighter for the RAF, Report by the Joint Air Ministry/Ministry of Supply Evaluation Team," Aeronautical Library, National Research Council, Ottawa, circa 1956.

8. Baldwin H. John, "Automatic Flight Control in the Arrow," *Aircraft* magazine, June 1958.

9. Brannan, Peter, "Arrow System Leads the Way," *Canadian Aviation*, March 1958.

10. Details on the engine and blades were provided by the late Ian Farrar, from Orenda engines.

11. Smye, Fred, *Canadian Aviation and The Avro Arrow*, Oakville, ON: Randy Smye, 1985.

12. "A Power Plant for the CF105 Supersonic Fighter Aircraft," February 25, 1955, RG24 acc/83/84/167, Box 6426, Vol. 5 S1038CN180.

13. "RG 24 Iroquois — Iroquois — General Status," memo dated 21 Oct 1958, 83/84/167, Box 6432, File S1038CN-180A-Vol. 25.

14. "RG 24, Iroquois Engine History and Status," Vol. 6255, File 1035-CT, pt. 3.

15. "CF 105 (Arrow) Programme," January 12, 1959, 73/1223, Series 1 File 12, Directorate of History, Department of National Defence.

16. Woodman, Jack, "Flying the Avro Arrow," Canadian Aeronautics and Space Institute Symposium, Winnipeg, Manitoba, May 16, 1978.

17. "RG 24, Arrow 2 — Aircraft Performance," January 17, 1958, 83-84/167, Vol.16, file S1038-180A.

18. Zurakowski, Jan, "Test Flying the Arrow and Other High Speed Jet Aircraft, *Canadian Aviation Historical Society Journal*, winter 1979.

19. "RG 24, Arrow 1 Flight Testing, Progress Report For Period 7 June 58 – 3 Nov 58," Box 6431, File S1038 CN 180A, Vol 13.

20. Ibid.

21. Zurackowski, Jan, "Test Flying the Arrow and Other High Speed Jet Aircraft," *Canadian Aviation Historical Society Journal*, winter 1979.

22. Dow, James, *The Arrow*, Toronto: Lorimer, Toronto, 1979.

23. "Memorandum, Minister, CF105 (Arrow) Programme," 12 Jan 1959, National Defence 73/1223 Series 1 File 12.

24. Zurakowski, Jan, "Test Flying the Arrow and Other High Speed Jet Aircraft," *Canadian Aviation Historical Society Journal*, winter 1979.
25. "Model Specification for Arrow 2 Airframe and Government Supplied Material Installations, January 1959," Avro Aircraft Limited, Department of National Defence — Report declassified by the Avro Arrow declassification board July 28, 1987.
26. Statement by Crawford Gordon, President, A.V. Roe Canada Ltd., to Annual Meeting of Shareholders, October 27, 1958, RG 49 Vol. 5, File 159-P-A-1 Vol. 2, Library and Archives Canada.

CHAPTER 3: WHY WAS THE ARROW PROGRAM TERMINATED?

1. "Government Policy in the Field of Canadian Air Defence and Defence Policy," MG 26, Series N2, Vol. 110.
2. Letter to Pearson, January 22, 1959, from C.D. Howe, MG 26, Series N2, Vol. 111, File Arrow(3) National Defence, Library and Archives Canada.
3. 574th Meeting Chiefs of Staff Committee, February 11, 1955, 73/1223 Series V File 2500D, Directorate of History, DND.
4. 273rd Air Council meeting, October 19, 1957, RG 24, Vol. 6433, File 1038 CN 181 Vol. 1.
5. Ibid.
6. AMTS Minute Sheet, RG 24, Vol. 1556, File 1913-103, Library and Archives Canada.
7. 273rd Air Council meeting, October 19, 1957, RG 24, Vol. 6433, File 1038 CN 181 Vol 1.
8. Ibid.
9. *Hansard*, January 23 1958 Debates, House of Commons, Canada, parl.canadiana.ca/view/oop.debates_HOC2301_04/490.
10. "Air Defence Concept — Bomarc," April 25, 1958, RG 24 Vol. 83-84-099, File 1933-103-2 Vol. 3, Library and Archives Canada.
11. "Brief for Minister of National Defence for Discussion with the United States Secretary of State," RG 49, Vol. 427, File 159-44-B pt. 1, Library and Archives Canada.
12. Ibid.

13. Department of Defence Production, Memo to File, January, 30, 1958, Annex I to Appendix G, RG 24, 83-84/167, Vol. 14, File S1038CN-180A.
14. Priority Message from Canairwash to Canairhed, RG 24, acc 83-84/167.20, Library and Archives Canada.
15. Cabinet Paper-Privileged, "Cooperation with Canada in Defense," CI-59-59-3-5-59, Eisenhower Library.
16. "Report on the Development of the CF 105 Aircraft and Associated Weapon System 1952–1958," Directorate of History, Department of National Defence.
17. Ibid.
18. "What Was the Missile Gap," CIA website, cia.gov/library/reading-room/collection/what-was-missile-gap, accessed November 7, 2017.
19. "Soviet Capabilities and Probable Programs in the Guided Missile Field," March 12, 1957, Top Secret, CIA online archives, cia.gov/library/readingroom/collection/what-was-missile-gap, accessed November 7, 2017.
20. Zurakowski, Jan, "Test Flying the Arrow." The cited quotation from Simonds in the *Telegram* is taken from this article. Simonds, it is further stated, argued against spending large sums on obsolete aircraft.
21. The memo was inserted in RG 2 Cabinet Conclusions, August 1958, Library and Archives Canada.
22. RG 2 Cabinet Conclusions, 28 August 1958, Library and Archives Canada.
23. RG 2 Cabinet Conclusions, 7 September 1958, Library and Archives Canada.
24. Ibid.
25. North Atlantic Council. Title. C-M(58) 141-Part2-CA, Council Memorandum. NATO Archives, Brussels, Belgium.
26. MG 32, Letter from Pearks to DDP, Series B19, Vol. 29, File 44-47, CF 105 Arrow Vol. 2 1958–1959.
27. Ibid.
28. Butz, J.S., Jr., Canada Seeks U.S. Defense Contracts, *Aviation Week*, March 2, 1959.
29. "Cooperation with Canada In Defense," Eisenhower Library.
30. Campagna, Palmiro, *Requiem*.

31. "Memorandum for Meeting with the Prime Minister," June 3, 1960, Eisenhower Library.

32. Top Secret minutes of the Canada–United States Ministerial Committee on Joint Defence, File 79/469, Folder 19 DHist.

33. Campagna, Palmiro, *Requiem for a Giant.*

34. Cabinet Conclusions, "United States Air Espionage over U.S.S.R.: Soviet Broadcast," RG 2 1960, May 8, 1960, Library and Archives Canada.

35. Ibid.

36. Cabinet Defence Committee, February 5, 1959, appended to the notes of February 6, 1959, RG 2, Library and Archives Canada.

37. "Manned Interceptor Requirements 1959-63," RG 24, acc/83-84/167, Vol. 19, Library and Archives Canada.

38. "Improvements in Air Defence; replacement of aircraft for CF-100s in Canada, Cabinet Conclusions, February 6 1960," RG 2, Library and Archives Canada.

39. Diefenbaker, John, G., *One Canada*, Toronto: Macmillan of Canada, 1977.

40. "Improvements in Air Defence; Report of Cabinet Committee (Previous Reference Feb. 6), Cabinet Conclusions, May 14, 1960," RG 2, Library and Archives Canada.

41. Letter Harkness to Secretary of State for External Affairs, December, 19, 1961, quoted in "The Development of the Introduction of the Bomarc Ground to Air Missile and the MB-1 Air to Air Guided Missile on Canadian Manned Interceptors for the RCAF for the Defence of Canada," Directorate of History, 73/1223 Series 1, File 628, Department of National Defence.

42. Cabinet Paper — Privileged, "Cooperation with Canada in Defense," CI-59-59-3-5-59, Eisenhower Library.

43. Foreign Report, "Canada's Defence Dilemma," February 5, 1959, *Economist*, MG 30 –E163 Vol. 17, File Canada defence policy-1959, Library and Archives Canada. This article was found in the files of Norman Robertson, the Undersecretary for External Affairs for Canada. It is possible that Mr. Robertson wrote it himself. It is marked confidential. I could not find the article in back issues of the magazine but found a similarly related one. Both are discussed in *Storms*.

44. Department of Defense Appropriations for 1961, Hearings Before the Subcommittee on Appropriations House of Representatives, Eighty-sixth Congress Second Session Re Appraisal of Air Defense Program Revisions in 1960 and 1961 Air Force Programs.

CHAPTER 4: WHAT DID THE ARROW PROGRAM COST?

1. Garthoff, Raymond L., "Estimating Soviet Military Intentions and Capabilities," cia.gov/library/center-for-the-study-of-intelligence/csi-publications/books-and-monographs/atching-the-bear-essays-on-cias-analysis-of-the-soviet-union/article05.html, accessed November 2017.
2. Floyd, James, C., "The Canadian Approach to All-Weather Interceptor Development," *Journal of the Royal Aeronautical Society* 62, no. 576, December 1958.
3. "Report on the development of the CF 105 Aircraft and Associated Weapon System 1952–1958," Directorate of History, Department of National Defence.
4. Floyd, James, C., "The Canadian Approach."
5. Report on the Development of the CF 105 Aircraft and Associated Weapon System 1952–1958, Directorate of History, Department of National Defence.
6. Ibid.
7. RG 2, Cabinet Conclusions, 28 August 1958. The notes of the 121st meeting of the CDC appear as a memorandum to cabinet for this meeting.
8. "Shelving the Arrow is Bad Military, Economic Medicine," *Canadian Aviation*, November 1958.
9. Ibid.
10. RG 2, Cabinet Conclusions, August 28, 1958. The notes of the 121st meeting of the CDC appear as a memorandum to cabinet for this meeting.
11. "Brief For Minister of National Defence for Discussion with The United States Secretary of State," RG 49, Vol. 427, File 159-44-B pt. 1, Library and Archives Canada.
12. Letter from Smye to Pearkes, RG 24, Vol. 6433, File 1038 CN-181,

Vol. 2, Library and Archives Canada.

13. CF 105 (Arrow) Programme, Memo to the Minister, January 12,1959, 73/1223, Series 1, File 12, Directorate of History, Department of National Defence.

14. Green, William, "The Mighty Arrow," *Royal Air Force Flying Review* 14, no. 6, February 1959.

15. House of Commons, Special Committee on Defence Expenditures, Chairman Halpenny, Minutes of Proceedings and Evidence, No. 1, Tuesday, May 3, 1960, Wednesday, May 11, 1960, Expenditures for Fiscal Year 1958–1959, XC2-243/1, Library and Archives Canada.

16. Smye, Fred, *Canadian Aviation and the Avro Arrow.*

17. "Arrow Cost Versus Cost of Comparable Aircraft," March 28, 1958, RG 24 acc/83-84/167, File 21, Library and Archives Canada.

18. More on the Cooke-Craige plan and its employment on the Arrow can be found in the book by the Arrowheads, *Avro Arrow: The Story of the Avro Arrow from its Evolution to its Extinction.*

19. Baugher, J., "U.S. Military Aircraft, F-106 Delta Dart, Convair," fighter-planes.com/info/f106_delta_dart.htm, accessed October 22, 2017.

20. Diefenbaker, John, G., *One Canada,* Toronto: Macmillan of Canada, 1977.

21. RG 2, "Cabinet Conclusions," August 28, 1958. The notes of the 121st meeting of the CDC appear as a memorandum to cabinet for this meeting.

22. Diefenbaker, John, G., *One Canada.*

23. Canada seems to have a penchant for spending large sums of money and getting little to nothing in return. First it was the Jetliner. One is also reminded of the modern day ill-fated Sea King helicopter replacement, the EH101. The case is well documented in Kim Nossal's book, *Charlie Foxtrot.* Essentially, in October 1992, the Conservative government of Brian Mulroney signed a contract worth $4.4 billion to purchase the EH101 helicopter from the consortium of Westland/Augusta. But with the election of the Liberals in 1993, the acquisition was cancelled. Canadians paid an estimated $478.3 million in cancellation fees, not to mention the layoffs

that ensued and not counting the monies that had been spent in the years before in government preparatory work. The government would eventually purchase a variant of the EH101 dubbed the Cormorant for its search and rescue function. Some have wondered why the Cormorant was so much less expensive than the EH101. The answer lies partly in the sophisticated equipment on board the latter, for surveillance, submarine hunting, and so on, versus the less-sophisticated search and rescue gear of the former.

24. Notes on: Government Policy in the Field of Canadian Air Defence and Defence Production, February 26, 1959, MG 26 Series N2 Vol. 110 Dept. of National Defence, General, Library and Archives Canada.

25. Ibid.

26. "The First Presidential Debate," *New York Times*, September 26, 2008, nytimes.com/elections/2008/president/debates/transcripts/first-presidential-debate.html, accessed July 19, 2017.

27. Center for Strategic and International Studies, "Defense Industrial Initiatives Current Issues: Cost-Plus Contracts," csis-prod.s3.amazonaws.com/s3fs-public/legacy_files/files/media/csis/pubs/081016_diig_cost_plus.pdf, accessed July 19, 2017.

28. Ibid.

29. "Report of the Auditor General to the House of Commons for the Fiscal Year Ended March 31, 1987," Chapter 9, Department of National Defence Major Capital Projects, publications.gc.ca/collections/collection_2015/bvg-oag/FA1-1-1987-eng.pdf, accessed July 20, 2017.

30. Nossal, Kim Richard, *Charlie Foxtrot*.

CHAPTER 5: WHO ORDERED THE BLOWTORCHING AND WHY WAS EVERYONE FIRED?

1. McCaffery, Margaret, "'A Flawed Plane and an Inept Corporation?' The Historian's View," *Engineering Dimensions*, September/October 1988.

2. To Chief of the Air Staff from H.C. Oatway, Chairman Defence Resarch Board, RG 24, 83-84/167, Vol. 7319, File 0315-02 Vol. 3, Library and Archives Canada.

3. "Arrow Aircraft/Iroquois Engine — Engineering Data," RG 49, Vol. 781, File 207-6-3, Library and Archives Canada.

4. "Arrow Cancellation — Disposal of Materiel," RG 24/83/84/167, Box 6428, File 1038CN-180 pt-26, Library and Archives Canada.

5. "Arrow/Iroquois Termination, Direction A15 0-13," April 7, 1959, RG 49, Vol. 781, File 207-6-3, Library and Archives Canada.

6. "Arrow Cancellation — Disposal of Materiel," April 8, 1959, 79/333, Directorate of History, Department of National Defence.

7. "Arrow Cancellation — Disposal of Materiel," MG 32, Series B19, File 44-47, CF 105 (Arrow) Aircraft, Vol. 2, 1959–1961, Library and Archives Canada. Also found in 79/333, Directorate of History, Department of National Defence, with additional notes and signatures.

8. Ibid.

9. "Arrow Cancellation Disposal of Airframes and Iroquois Engines," 79/333, Directorate of History, Department of National Defence.

10. McCaffery, Margaret, "Setting the Record Straight: The Designer's View," *Engineering Dimensions*, September/October 1988.

11. RG 24, 83-84/049, Vol. 1556, File 1913-103.

12. Note from J.L. Bush to C.A. Hore, RG 49, Vol. 782, File 207-6-3, pt. 3, Library and Archives Canada.

13. "CF 105 Termination Status," RG 49, Vol. 782, File 207-6-3, pt. 3, Library and Archives Canada.

14. RG 24, "Iroquois Engine — Possible USAF Application," letter dated December 8, 1960, Vol. 6474, File 1035CT-100, pt. 7, Library and Archives Canada.

15. Ibid.

16. "Record of Cabinet Decision, Meeting of July 7, 1959, Authorization to photograph Arrow aircraft," RG 49, Vol. 782, File 207-6-3, pt. 3, Library and Archives Canada.

17. Campagna, *Storms*.

18. "Arrow Electronic System — Installation of MA-1 in Mk 1 Arrow," Dec 10, 1958, RG 24, Vol. 6435, File 1038CM-1832, Library and Archives Canada.

19. "Re: Arrow Technical Reports, 1st September, 1959," RG 24/83/84/167,

Vol. 7319, File 0315-02, Vol. 3, Library and Archives Canada.

20. "Termination Instruction No. S1 'A,' Records, Drawings, etc.," RG 49, Vol. 781, File 207-6-3, pt. 4, Library and Archives Canada.

21. Hardesty, Von, "Made in the U.S.S.R.," *Air and Space Magazine*, March 2001, airspacemag.com/military-aviation/made-in-the-ussr -3844243 7/, accessed August 2017. This article details the fascinating account of how the Soviets reverse engineered the B-29 in order to produce their own aircraft capable of carrying nuclear weapons.

22. U-2 Vulnerability Tests, Top Secret, Project Chalice, March 31, 1959, cia.gov/library/readingroom/collection/what-was-missile-gap, accessed November 2017.

23. McCaffery, Margaret, "Setting the Record Straight: The Designer's View," *Engineering Dimensions*, September/October 1988.

24. Smye, Fred, *Canadian Aviation and The Avro Arrow*, Oakville, ON: Randy Smye, 1985.

25. Ibid.

26. McCaffery, Margaret, "Setting The Record Straight: The Designer's View," *Engineering Dimensions*, September/October 1988.

27. CF 105 Program I Pre-Termination Activity, II Post Termination, RG 49, Vol. 781, File 207-6-3, pt. 4, Library and Archives Canada.

POSTSCRIPT

1. Calder, Joanna, "'Raise the Arrow' team recovers first artifact from Lake Ontario," Government of Canada, Maple Leaf – Royal Canadian Air Force, ml-fd.caf-fac.ca/en/2018/08/18277, accessed August 29, 2018.

2. RG 24, Series R112, Vol. 33134, File 1934-103, pt. 18, 22, 23.

3. Gelly, Alain, and H.P. Tardif, *Defence Research Establishment Valcartier, 1945–1995, 50 Years of History and Scientific Progress*, Minister of Public Works and Government Services Canada, 1995.

4. RG 49, "Velvet Glove Project, Air to Air Guided Missile," Vol. 264, File 151.8.1.

5. William K. Fawcett, Gerry Bull and the IRAQI Supergun, February 14, 2003, redlandsfortnightly.org/papers/fawcett03.htm, accessed August 2017.

6. "Velvet Glove, Progress Summary Report 1, August 13, 1951 to March 31, 1953," Canadair, Montreal, Department of National Defence.
7. Ibid.
8. Davis, W.A.L., and A.W. Duguid, "Velvet Glove Project Air to Air Guided Missile, Transfer Report on Progress and Achievements of the Project From Inception to 1st November 55," Department of National Defence.
9. Gelly and Tardif, "Defence Research Establishment Valcartier."
10. "Revealed: China's Radars Can Track America's Stealthy F-22 Raptor," *National Interest*, February 19, 2016, nationalinterest.org/blog/the-buzz/revealed-can-chinas-radars-track-americas-stealth-f-22-15261, accessed August 2, 2017.
11. "How to Detect Stealth Aircraft?" *Defence Aviation: Aerospace/Defence Analysis and Podcast*, defenceaviation.com/2016/05/how-to-detect-stealth-aircraft.html, accessed July 2017.
12. "Lockheed Martin F-22 Raptor Validates Quantum Leap in Capability of 5th Generation Fighters, Continues Unprecedented Operational Successes," Media, Lockheed Martin, accessed August 2, 2017.
13. Bender, Jeremy, "Pentagon: Here Are All the Problems with the F-35," *Business Insider*, Military and Defence, March 20, 2015, businessinsider.com/here-are-all-the-problems-with-the-f-35-that-the-pentagon-found-in-a-2014-report-2015-3, accessed July 21, 2017.
14. "Liberals Fork Over Another $30 Million to Keep Canada at F-35 Table," *CBC News*, May 25, 2017, cbc.ca/news/politics/f-35-fighter-jet-joint-strike-canada-fee-1.4131285, accessed August 1, 2017.
15. Personal correspondence between this author and C. Fred Matthews, 2017.
16. Nossal, Kim Richard, *Charlie Foxtrot, Fixing Defence Procurement in Canada*, Toronto: Dundurn, 2016.
17. Bandera, Steve, "W5 Investigates Canada's Floundering Fleet," *CTV News*, November 12, 2011, ctvnews.ca/w5-investigates-canada-s-floundering-submarine-fleet-1.724641.
18. "Review of the Canadian Search and Rescue Helicopter," Chief Review Services, forces.gc.ca/assets/FORCES_Internet/docs/en/about-reports-pubs-audit-eval/p0583.pdf, accessed September 2018.

APPENDIX A

1. The second fly-by-wire system was Project Mercury. The second terrestrial production aircraft design to use a fly-by-wire control system was the F-16s, some twenty years later. The fly-by-wire concept though was tested in an aircraft in the U.S. before the Arrow.

2. The Astra system was a Canadian government contract with RCA Aerospace Systems of New Jersey.

3. The Arrowheads, *Avro Arrow. The Story of the Avro Arrow from Its Evolution to Its Extinction*, Erin, ON: Boston Mills Press, 1980.

4. Earlier, at the beginning of the CF-100 program, Minneapolis-Honeywell had provided a yaw-damping system to improve the CF-100's gun-firing accuracy.

Bibliography

BOOKS

Campagna, Palmiro. *Requiem for a Giant: A.V. Roe Canada and the Avro Arrow*. Toronto: Dundurn, 2003.

———. *Storms of Controversy: The Secret Avro Arrow Files Revealed*. 4th ed. Toronto: Dundurn, 2010.

———. *The UFO Files: The Canadian Connection Exposed*. Toronto: Dundurn, 2010.

Diefenbaker, John G. *One Canada*. Toronto: Macmillan of Canada, 1977.

Dow, James. *The Arrow*. Toronto: Lorimer, 1979.

Floyd, Jim. *The Avro Canada C102 Jetliner*. Erin, ON: Boston Mills Press, 1986.

Gelly, Alain, and H.P. Tardif. *Defence Research Establishment Valcartier, 1945–1995, 50 Years of History and Scientific Progress*. Ottawa: Minister of Public Works and Government Services Canada, 1995.

Goodspeed, Captain D.J. *A History of the Defence Research Board of Canada*, Ottawa: Queen's Printer and Controller of Stationary, 1958.

Gunston, Bill. *Early Supersonic Fighters of the West*. London: Scribner, 1976.

Knaack, Marcelle S. "Convair F-106 Delta Dart," in *Post-World War II Fighters, 1945–1973*. Vol. 1 of *Encyclopedia of U.S. Air Force Aircraft and Missile Systems*. Washington: Office of Air Force History, 1978. archive.org/stream/EncyclopediaOfUS AirForceAircraftAndMissileSystemsVolumeOne#page/n225/ mode/2up/search/f106. Accessed November 2017.

Mahar, Donald G. *Shattered Illusions: KGB Cold War Espionage in Canada*. London: Rowman and Littlefield, 2017.

Nossal, Kim Richard. *Charlie Foxtrot, Fixing Defence Procurement in Canada*. Toronto: Dundurn, 2016.

Organ, Richard, Ron Page, Don Watson, and Les Wilkinson. *Avro Arrow: The Story of the Avro Arrow from Its Evolution to Its Extinction*. Erin, ON: Boston Mills Press, 1980.

Peden, Murray. *Fall of an Arrow*. Toronto: Dundurn, 1978.

Shaw, E.K. *There Never Was an Arrow*. Ottawa: Steel Rail Educational Publishing, 1979, with reference to the Toronto *Globe and Mail*, "The Road to Serfdom," December 17, 1958, and Brown, J.J., *Ideas in Exile*. Toronto: McClelland and Stewart, 1967.

Smye, Fred. *Canadian Aviation and The Avro Arrow*. Oakville, ON: Randy Smye, 1985.

Whitcomb, Randall. *Avro Aircraft and Cold War Aviation*. St. Catharines, ON: Vanwell, 2002.

Wilkinson, Les, et al., *Avro Arrow: The Story of the Avro Arrow from its Evolution to its Extinction*. Erin, ON: The Arrowheads and Boston Mills Press, 1980.

ARTICLES

Baugher, J. "US Military Aircraft, F-106 Delta Dart, Convair." fighter-planes.com/info/f106_delta_dart.htm. Accessed October 22, 2017.

Bandera, Steve. "W5 Investigates Canada's Floundering Fleet." CTV News, November 12, 2011. ctvnews.ca/w5-investigates-canada -s-floundering-submarine-fleet-1.724641. Accessed August 2017.

Bender, Jeremy. "Pentagon: Here are all the problems with the F-35." *Business Insider*, March 20, 2015. businessinsider.com/

here-are-all-the-problems-with-the-f-35-that-the-pentagon-found-in
-a-2014-report-2015-3. Accessed July 21, 2017.

"Being Ernest: The Untold Story of Ottawa's Korean War Ace." *Ottawa
Rewind.* ottawarewind.com/2015/11/09/being-ernest-the-untold-
story-of-ottawas-korean-war-ace. Accessed November 2017.

Brannan, Peter. "Arrow System Leads the Way." *Canadian Aviation,*
March 1958.

Butz, J.S., Jr. "Canada Seeks U.S. Defense Contracts," *Aviation Week,*
March 2, 1959.

Calder, Joanna. "'Raise the Arrow' Team Recovers First Artifact from Lake
Ontario." *The Maple Leaf — Royal Canadian Air Force.* ml-fd.caf-fac
.ca/en/2018/08/18277. Accessed August 29, 2018.

Campagna, Palmiro. "An Aviation Chapter in Canadian History."
Engineering Dimensions, September/October 1988.

Center for Strategic and International Studies. "Defense Industrial
Initiatives Current Issues: Cost-Plus Contracts." csis-prod.s3.
amazonaws.com/s3fs-public/legacy_files/files/media/csis/
pubs/081016_diig_cost_plus.pdf. Accessed July 19, 2017.

"CF-105 Displays Advanced Engineering in Rollout." *Aviation Week,*
October 21, 1957.

"Department of National Defence — Major Capital Projects," chapter 9
in *Report of the Auditor General to the House of Commons for the Fiscal
Year Ended 31 March 1987,* publications.gc.ca/collections/collection_
2015/bvg-oag/FA1-1-1987-eng.pdf. Accessed July 20, 2017.

Fawcett, William K. "Gerry Bull and the IRAQI Supergun." *Fortnightly
Club of Redlands, California,* February 14, 2003. redlandsfortnightly.
org/papers/fawcett03.htm. Accessed August 2017.

"The First Presidential Debate." *New York Times,* September 26,
2008. nytimes.com/elections/2008/president/debates/transcripts/
first-presidential-debate.html. Accessed July 19, 2017.

Floyd, James. "The Avro Story." *Canadian Aviation, 50th Anniversary Issue,*
June 1978.

Floyd, James, C. "The Canadian Approach to All-Weather Interceptor
Development." *Royal Air Force Flying Review* 62, no. 576
(December 1958).

Garthoff, Raymond L. "Estimating Soviet Military Intentions and Capabilities," cia.gov/library/center-for-the-study-of-intelligence/csi-publications/books-and-monographs/watching-the-bear-essays-on-cias-analysis-of-the-soviet-union/article05.html. Accessed November 2017.

"Glued to Ground: Sees RCAF Like Wingless Kiwi." *Toronto Daily Star*, November 11, 1958.

Green, William. "The Mighty Arrow." *Royal Air Force Flying Review* 14, no. 6 (February 1959).

Hardesty, Von. "Made in the U.S.S.R." *Air and Space Magazine*, March 2001. airspacemag.com/military-aviation/made-in-the-ussr-38442437. Accessed August 2017.

Imray, Malcolm, et al. "Review of the Statement of Operational Requirement for the Fixed Wing Search and Rescue Aircraft, Final Report, Number CR-FRL-2010-0025." March 12, 2010. forces.gc.ca/en/about-reports-pubs/fixed-wing-search-rescue-aircraft-2010.page. Accessed August 1, 2017.

"Liberals Fork Over Another $30 Million to Keep Canada at F-35 Table." CBC News, May 25, 2017, cbc.ca/news/politics/f-35-fighter-jet-joint-strike-canada-fee-1.4131285. Accessed August 1, 2017.

Lockheed Martin Aeronautics Company. "Lockheed Martin F-22 Raptor Validates Quantum Leap in Capability of 5th Generation Fighters, Continues Unprecedented Operational Successes." defense-aerospace.com/cgi-bin/client/modele.pl?prod=83487&session=dae.26826377.1182342809.oyPYwn8AAAEAAAFKl-MAAAAN&modele=release. Accessed September 2018.

McCaffery, Margaret. "'A Flawed Plane and an Inept Corporation?': The Historian's View." *Engineering Dimensions*, September/October 1988.

———. "Setting the Record Straight: The Designer's View." *Engineering Dimensions*, September/October 1988.

"Revealed: China's Radars Can Track America's Stealthy F-22 Raptor." *National Interest*, February 19, 2016. nationalinterest.org/blog/the-buzz/revealed-can-chinas-radars-track-americas-stealth-f-22-15261. Accessed August 2, 2017.

"Review of the Canadian Search and Rescue Helicopter." Chief Review Services, DND, July 2007. forces.gc.ca/assets/FORCES_Internet/

docs/en/about-reports-pubs-audit-eval/p0583.pdf. Accessed
September 2018.

Robin, Sebastien. "America's F-4 Phantom: Taking On the World's Best
Fighters (At Almost 60 Years Old)." *National Interest*, June 27, 2016.
nationalinterest.org/blog/the-buzz/americas-f-4-phantom-taking-the
-world-best-fighters-almost-16738. Accessed September 20, 2017.

Stamp, Philip. "The Rousing Lessons of the Avro Arrow," *Globe and Mail*.
theglobeandmail.com/news/national/what-the-avro-arrow-can-teach-
justintrudeau/article35690898. Accessed October 29, 2017.

Sweetman, Bill. "Broken Arrow." *Aviation Week*. aviationweek.com/
blog/1957-broken-arrow. Accessed July 19, 2017.

Young, Scott. "The Way Up." *Jet Age*, Avro booklet, 1955.

Wallace, Lane E. "The Whitcomb Area Rule." history.nasa.gov/SP-4219/
Chapter5.html. Accessed November 2017.

Woodman, Jack. "Flying the Avro Arrow." Canadian Aeronautics and
Space Institute Symposium, Winnipeg, Manitoba, May 16, 1978.

Zurakowski, Jan. "Test Flying the Arrow and Other High Speed Jet Aircraft."
Journal of the Canadian Aviation Historical Society (winter 1979).

ARCHIVAL SOURCES

Library and Archives Canada

MG 26, Series N2, Vol. 110 and 111, File Arrow (3), File National Defence.

MG 30-E163, Vol. 17, File Canada Defence Policy-1959.

MG 32, Series B19, File 44-47 CF 105 (Arrow) Aircraft, Vol. 2,
1959–1961.

RG 2, Cabinet Conclusions, August 28, 1958.

RG 2, Cabinet Conclusions, September 7, 1958.

RG 2, Cabinet Conclusions, February 6, 1960.

RG 2, Cabinet Conclusions, May 8, 1960.

RG 2, Cabinet Conclusions, May 14, 1960.

RG 24, 83-84/167, Vol. 14, File S1038CN-180A.

RG 24, 83-84/167, Vol. 16, File S1038-180A.

RG 24, 83-84/167, Vol. 7319, File 0315-02, Vol. 3.

RG 24, 83-84/167, Box 6426, File S1038CN-180, Vol. 5.

RG 24, 83-84/167, Box 6432, File S1038CN-180A, Vol. 25.

RG 24, 83-84/167, Box 6431, File S1038CN-180A, Vol. 13.

RG 24, 83-84/167, Box 6428, File 1038CN-180, pt. 26.

RG 24, vol 6474, File 1035CT-100, pt. 7.

RG 24, 83-84/049, Vol. 1556, File 1913-103.

RG 24, acc 83-84/167.20.

RG 24, acc 83-84/167, Vol. 19.

RG 24, acc 83-84/167, File 21.

RG 24, Vol. 6255, File 1035-CT, pt. 3.

RG 24, Vol. 6435, File 1038CM-1832.

RG 24, Vol. 6433, File 1038CN-181, Vol. 1.

RG 24, Vol. 1556, File 1913-103.

RG 24, Vol. 83-84-099, File 1933-103-2, Vol. 3.

RG 24, R112, Vol. 33134, File 1934-103, pt. 15–19.

RG 24, R112, Vol. 33135, File 1934-103, pt. 20–24.

RG 49, Vol. 5, File 159-P-A-1, Vol. 2.

RG 49, Vol. 781, File 207-6-3.

RG 49, Vol. 781, File 207-6-3.

RG 49 Vol. 782, File 207-6-3, pt. 3.

RG 49, Vol. 427, File 159-44-B, pt. 1.

RG 49, Vol. 264, File 151.8.1.

Department of National Defence, Directorate of History

73/1223, Series 1, File 628.

73/1223, Series 1, File 12.

73/1223, Series V, File 2500D.

79/333, 79/469, Folder 19.

Debates, House of Commons, Canada, *Hansard*, January 23, 1958, parl.canadiana.ca/view/oop.debates_HOC2301_04/490. Accessed November 2017.

Ewart, D., and Taylor, W., C-105 Summary of Free-Flight Model Tests and Results (FFM #1 to FFM #7), July 1957, Department of National Defence.

Model Specification for Arrow 2 Airframe and Government Supplied Material Installations, January 1959, Avro Aircraft Limited, DSIS Department of National Defence.

Velvet Glove Project, Air-to-Air Guided Missile, Delta Test Vehicle No. 2, Experimental Aerodynamic Configuration, Part I: Announcement of Firing, and Part III: Firing Report, March 30 and April 21, 1954, Library and Archives Canada, RG 24, R112 series noted above.

Velvet Glove Project, Air-to-Air Guide Missile, Delta Test Vehicle No. 3, Experimental Aerodynamic Configuration, Part 1: Announcement of Firing, and Part III: Firing Report, October 6, 1954, and October 26, 1954, Library and Archives Canada, RG 24, R112 series noted above.

Velvet Glove Project, Air-to-Air Guide Missile, Index, April 1, 1954, Library and Archives Canada, RG 24, R112 series noted above. Contains references to Delta test vehicles 1 and 2, Library and Archives Canada, RG 24, R112 series noted above.

Velvet Glove Project, Air-to-Air Guide Missile, Status Report, March 1, 1954, Library and Archives Canada, RG 24, R112 series noted above. This report describes the building of several scale models of a delta mono-wing and a full-scale vehicle for testing launch characteristics.

Velvet Glove Project, Air-to-Air Guided Missile, Transfer Report on Progress and Achievements of the Project from Inception to 1st November 1955, DSIS Department of National Defence, Velvet Glove, Progress Summary Report 1, Canadair, Montreal, Department of National Defence.

Videos Consulted at the Archives

CF 105, 1/8 Scale Free-Flight, #312629.

CF 105, 1/8 Scale Model Free-Flight Tests, #312635.

CF 105, Free-Flight Model Tests, #312582.

CF 105, Free-Flight Models, #312639.

Free-Flight Model Test Report 1, #312696.

NATO

North Atlantic Council. C-M(58), 141-Part2-CA, Council Memorandum. NATO Archives, Brussels, Belgium.

Other

Cabinet Paper — Privileged, Cooperation with Canada in Defence, CI-59-59-3-5-59. Eisenhower Library.

CIA, "Soviet Capabilities and Probable Programs in the Guided Missile Field, 12 March 1957, Top Secret," CIA online archives, cia.gov/library/readingroom/collection/what-was-missile-gap. Document Number: 5076dee2993247d4d82b5c97. Accessed September 2018.

CIA, "U-2 Vulnerability Tests, Top Secret, Project Chalice, 31 March 1959," CIA website, cia.gov/library/readingroom/collection/what-was-missile-gap. Document Number: 5076dee2993247d4d82b-5c6d. Accessed September 2018.

CIA, "What Was the Missile Gap?" CIA website, cia.gov/library/readingroom/collection/what-was-missile-gap.

Evaluation of the Canadian CF-105 as an All-Weather Fighter for the RAF. Report by the Joint Air Ministry/Ministry of Supply Evaluation Team, Aeronautical Library. Ottawa: National Research Council, circa 1956

Floyd, J.C. Arrow Flight Development, Report No. 70/ENG, Pub 7. Ottawa: Department of National Defence, May 1, 1958

"Memorandum for Meeting with the Prime Minister," June 3 1960.

Roy, Reginald. George Pearkes interview, April 1967. University of Victoria, British Columbia

Photo Credits

Index

Italic page numbers indicate photos.

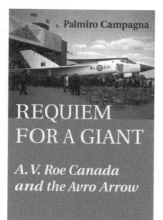

Requiem for a Giant:
A. V. Roe Canada and the Avro Arrow
Palmiro Campagna

No Canadian company has fuelled as much speculation about its demise as A.V. Roe Canada Limited. When its name was erased off the corporate map in 1962, A.V. Roe's most ambitious undertakings — the Jetliner, the Iroquois Engine, and the Arrow — were reduced to scrap.

In *Requiem for a Giant: A.V. Roe Canada and the Avro Arrow*, Palmiro Campagna supplies us with new information to help dispel the myths surrounding the company. With an array of recently declassified documents, Campagna investigates the star projects of A.V. Roe Canada.

Was the C-102 Jetliner technically flawed? Was the Avrocar a failure? Was the cost of the Arrow program spiralling out of control as historians have maintained? These questions and many others are put to rest in *Requiem for a Giant*.

Storms of Controversy:
The Secret Avro Arrow Files Revealed
Palmiro Campagna

The development of the Avro Arrow was a remarkable Canadian achievement. Its mysterious cancellation in February 1959 prompted questions that have long gone unanswered. What role did the Central Intelligence Agency play in the scrapping of the project? Who in Canada's government was involved in that decision? What, if anything, did Canada get in return? Who ordered the blowtorching of all the prototypes? And did Arrow technology find its way into the American Stealth fighter/bomber program?

When *Storms of Controversy* was first published in 1992, its answers to these questions sent a shock wave across the country. Using never-before-released documents, the book exploded the myth that design flaws, cost overruns, or obsolescence had triggered the demise of the Arrow.

Now, in this fully revised fourth edition, complete with two new appendices, the bestselling book brings readers up-to-date on the CF-105 Arrow, the most innovative, sophisticated aircraft the world had seen by the end of the 1950s.

Book Credits

Acquiring Editor: Beth Bruder

Developmental Editor: Dominic Farrell

Project Editor: Elena Radic

Copy Editor: Laurie Miller

Proofreader: Dawn Hunter

Designer: Laura Boyle

Publicist: Tabassum Siddiqui

Dundurn

Publisher: J. Kirk Howard

Vice-President: Carl A. Brand

Editorial Director: Kathryn Lane

Artistic Director: Laura Boyle

Production Manager: Rudi Garcia

Publicity Manager: Michelle Melski

Manager, Accounting and Technical Services: Livio Copetti

Editorial: Allison Hirst, Dominic Farrell, Jenny McWha,
Rachel Spence, Elena Radic, Melissa Kawaguchi

Marketing and Publicity: Kendra Martin, Elham Ali,
Tabassum Siddiqui, Heather McLeod

Design and Production: Sophie Paas-Lang

dundurn.com dundurnpress
@dundurnpress dundurnpress
dundurnpress info@dundurn.com

FIND US ON NETGALLEY & GOODREADS TOO!

DUNDURN